MARINE ECOLOGY AND POLLUTION

Marine Ecology and Pollution

Edited by
Prof. P.R. TRIVEDI
Chairman
Indian Institute of Ecology and Environment
New Delhi - 110 030
&
Prof. GURDEEP RAJ
Hony. Professor in Environment Science in
I.I.E.E., New Delhi
Reader in Chemistry
D.S. College, University of Delhi,
New Delhi - 110 003

AKASHDEEP PUBLISHING HOUSE
NEW DELHI - 110 002 (INDIA)

AKASHDEEP PUBLISHING HOUSE
4374/4B, Ansari Road, Daryaganj
New Delhi - 110 002
Ph.: 23261597, 23278000
Visit us at: www.anmolpublications.com

Reprint, 1995, 1997

Reprint, 2005

ISBN 81-7158-233-8

PRINTED IN INDIA

Published by Akashdeep Publishing House, New Delhi - 110 002 and
Printed at Mehra Offset Press, Delhi.

Preface

The present title aims at being the most complete work on "Marine Ecology and Pollution" hitherto published. In order to make the book more interesting, case studies have been selected from under-developed as well as developed countries. These case studies demonstrate the magnitude of existing problems.

The editing of the book is mainly based on the wide experience of editors who are engaged in teaching marine ecology and pollution at all levels. This book is expected to meet the requirements of a wide range of readers who are involved directly or indirectly with marine ecology and pollution, including environmental students, sanitary engineers, marine engineers, health physicists and technicians. This book is essentially for those who are developing concern and become actively involved in environmental matter.

A book such as this would never have been successfully completed without consulting the work of many authorities and seek the advice of colleagues to all of whom the editors are deeply indebted.

Finally editors express their sincere thanks to the publishers as well as the printers for bringing out this book promptly.

The Editors

Contents

1

Marine Ecology and Oceano-Graphic Environment

Introduction

The geographic distribution of organisms in the sea depends on their responses to currents, temperatures, and physical barriers; local distribution is affected by waves and tides type of bottom, salinity, and depth. Marine ecology is concerned with environmental factors and problems of organic adjustments quite different from those in fresh water. Animals are releatively more c nspicuous than plants. Succession is less evident, but such ecological processes represented by chemical cycles, co-operation, and disoperation, food chains, productivity, population, dynamicr niche segregation, speciation, and dispersal are fully as important as on land.

Distinct self-contained community units are more difficult to recognize in the sea than on land because of the apparently greater interrelation of benethic species and the free movement with circulating currents of plankton and nekton. Plankton is everywhere a basic link in food chains, but the general distribution and importance of plankton species in the sea is no more remarktable than that of soil organisms in terrestrial biomes. To consider the entire ocean community as a single biome, as has been suggested by some investigators, is stretching the concept beyond its usefulness. Since we identify biomes by differences in the life-forms, and functional adjustments of the conspicuous dominant or predominant organisms, we may properly recognize biomes that occur in the open ocean, on eroding rocky shores, on muddy and sandy beaches, and composing the coral reefs and atolls. Each of these biomes may be subdivided by the toxonomic composition of the predominant organisms into secondary communities equivalent to the biociations that we have recognized on land. Much of the early literature on marine communities has been reviewed by Gislen.

Habitat

The marine biocycle is considered to have benthic (bottom) and pelagic (open water) divisions, the littoral zone of the ocean shore extedds between the limits of high and low tides, the sublittoral zone covers the continental shelf to a depth of about 200 m. the approximate depth at which maximum wave action produces any effect. The average depth of the ocean is about 3800 m, but oceanic trenches (hadal zone) extend much deeper, the Marianas Trench in the Pacific Ocean to approximately 11.6000 m. The neritic biochare is above the continental shelf and is commonly 16-240 km (10-150 mi) wide. The oceanic biochore is subdivided vertically with the boundary between the epi-and mesopelagic zones, depending on the extent of effective light penetration.

Tides

The level of water in the acean rises and falls usually twice each day or at an interval of 12 hours and 26 minutes. In some parts of the world the tides are less regular or there may be but one daily. Flood-tide is the period in which the level is rising and covering more and more of the shoreline; ebb-tide is the period in which the water level is less than a meter, but the change may be much more than this on the shore, depending on its configuration, the Bay of Fundy opens broadly to the sea and tapers to a narrow head landward, and tides may be 6 to 10 or even 15 m. On the other hand, when bodies of water have only a relatively narrow connection with the sea, as does the Gulf of Mexico with the Atlantic, the range in water level is less than 30 cm. Even lakes have seiches, but they are hardly perceptible except in the larger lakes, where it may amount to a few centimeters.

Tides are caused by the attraction of the moon and, to a lesser, extent, the sun. Ween the sun's attraction is added to that of the moon, as occurs twice each month at the time of full moon and new moon, the fluctuations of the tides are unusually high and unusually low, these are called spring tides. When the tidal influences of sun and moon are opposed, as happens twice each month, the tides have the least amount of flow and ebb and are called neap tides.

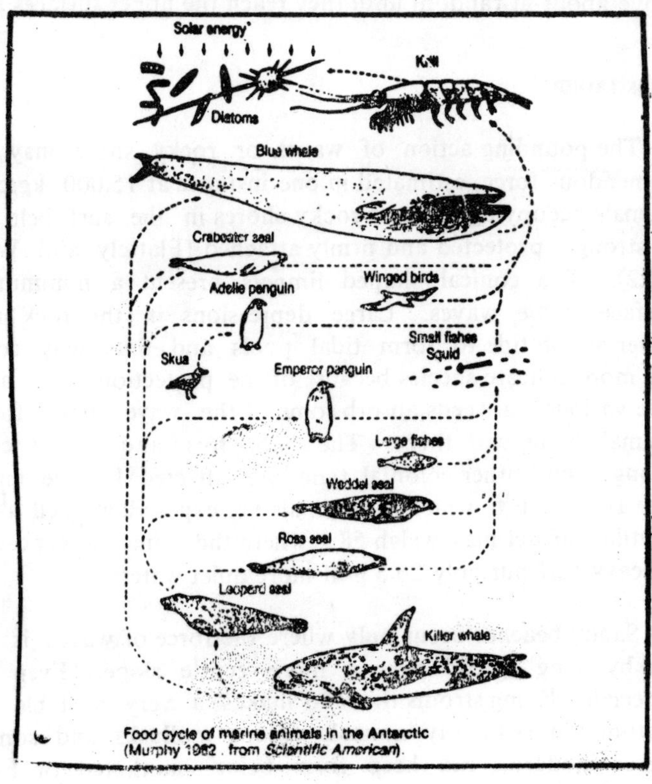

Food cycle of marine animals in the Antarctic (Murphy 1962 . from *Scientific American*).

Tides have their greatest effect on animals on the seashore, because of the associated pounding of waves and the alternative submergence in water and exposure to the air. However, the organisms appear well adjusted to this rhythmic submergence and exposure (Flattely and Watson 1922, Korringa 1947). For instance, as the stones on which the chiton occurs become exposed, the animals react positively to gravity and negatively to strong light, and move downward. They travel at maximum speed while the stone is still moist and become aggregated on the damp lower sides of the stones. When the stone again becomes immersed by the returning tide, the animals lose their geotactic orientation. and. since illumination becomes more or less equal on all sides of the stones, they move about at random until they reach the upper surfaces again.

Substratum

The pounding action of waves or rocky shore may have tremendous force, estimated in one instance at 15,000 kg/cm 2. animals occupying exposed rocky shores in the surf belt must be strongly protected and firmly attached (Flattely and Walton 1922). The conical shaped limpets present a minimum of surface to the waves. Large depressions in the rock retain water at ebb tide to form tidal pools and thus may contain the more delicate species because of the protection they afford. The various sea weeds absorb some of the wave shock for the animals living with them. The shape, form and size of corals, sponges, and other colonial type are affected by the amount of wave action to which the animals are exposed, a shell of the Mytilus mussel may weigh 58 g where the animal is exposed to a heavy surf but only 26.5 g in more quiet waters.

Sandy beaches occur only where the force of waves is reduced by being spread over a more gentle slope. Even here, especially during stroms the sand makes a very unstable substratum and not many animals except mollusks and some of the echinoderms can keep from being smothered or buried. Mud buttoms occur only in relatively quiet waters. Burrows made in mud hold their form better than in sand, so large population of animals can occur in mud.

Organic deposits are either calcareous or siliceous, the former being derived from the shells of foraminiferans, small pelagic mollusks, or flogellate coccolithophorids and the latter from skeletal material of diatoms and radiolarian protozoans.

Pressure

There is an enormous increase in the pressure of water upon the bodies of animals at great depths, and this may effect the vertical distribution of such species as crabs and mussels (Menzies and Wilson 1961). This is not. however, an important limiting factor in the vertical distribution of animals in general, as internal pressures closely counterbalance external pressures and life is known to exist at the greatest depths. Adjustments of internal pressures are not so rapid, however, to prevent injury in many species that are dredged at great depths and quickly hauled to the surface. Furthermore, individual species have diffrent limits of pressure tolerance.

Temperature and Currents

The temperatures of surface waters vary between the freezing point (– 1.9°C) in the tropics. Seasonal variations are small in polar and tropical waters but somewhat greater in the temperate zones.

Temperature varies with depth, more so in the tropics than elsewhere. At 60°N lattitude in the Atlantic Ocean, the mean temperature of the warmest and coldest months beneath the surface is about 10°C. On the equator the temperature beneath the surface is approximately 26°C, at 200 m 13°C, at 1000 m 4.51 C, and at 2000 m 3.3°C, (Ekman 1943). In temperate regions, seasonal thermocline develops near the surface in summer and is destroyed in autumn and winter when vertical mixing creates a layer of relatively uniform temperature in the upper 20 to 300 m.

Currents moving toward the poles from the equator consist of warm water, and currents moving in the opposite direction of cold water. Surface currents make wide circular movements in opposite directions in the northern and southern hemisphere.

Light

Much of the solar radiation is reflected from the surface of absorbed in the upper layers. Even in the clearest waters and at maximum radiation; the red, orange and ultraviolet are absorbed in the first 20 m. Green, yellow, and blue wavelengths penetrate further, depending on the water colour. When the sun is not at the zenith, light penetration is reduced, and the maximum penetration in the winter at higher latitudes is much less than during the summer.

Salinity

The salinity of sea water varies from place to place depending largely on the amount that it is diluted by the yellow of fresh water from rivers or melting glaciers or the amount that it is concentrated by evaporation. The Red Sea, for instance has a salinity of 40% (40 g of dry salts in 1000 g of seawater) while in some polar seas the salinity is less then 30%. The average salinity of the oceans as a whole is commonly given as 35% of which the chlorideion constitutes about 19% and the sodium ion little over 10%. The various major salts occur nearly everywhere in definite and constant proportions. As one would expect, the pH of seawater is high, averaging about 8, there is some similarity in relative proportions and concentrations of the variations in seawater and in the blood of body fluids of many invertebrate organisms. This may indicate that the sea is the habitat in which living forms first evolved.

The contrast in salinity between seawater (35,000 ppm) and fresh water (15 660 ppm) requires important difference in physiological adjustment of organisms to occupy these two habitats. The problem is one of osmotic regulation (Block 1951).

Most marine invertebrates are poikilosmotic in that they are nearily isotonic with seawater, they are highly permeable to water and gain or lose water according to concentration of the medium. A few marine segmented worms, flatworms, and crabs and all marine fish and mammals have at least some internat osmotic regulation and tend to be homoisomotic. All except the elasmobranch fishes maintain body fluids hypotonic to seawater in various ways. The skin has decreased its permeability to the free movement of water back and forth, the necessary water is obtained by swallowing surplus salts are secreted outside the body, especially through the gills, and there is a general decreased function or atrophy of water secreting organs such as the kidneys. The practical absence of insects and amphibians from the sea is largely due to their inability to secrete salts outwardly. The high osmotic concentration found in elasmobranchs is the result of huge quantities of urea retained in the body tissues and fluids.

These salts keep cycling through the ecosystem, but additions to the supply come continually from the land, being washed into the oceans by the rivers. Neritic waters are especially fertile and support a great mass and variety of animal life because of this land drainage and the pattern of water circulation on the continental shelf. Biological productivity decreases progressively from shallow waters over the continental shelf, to deeper waters, to the open ocean, but it also high over offshore banks and in areas of upwelling substantial amounts of nitrogen salts are also swept out of the air by precipitation and there is nitrogen-fixaztion by bacteria.

Oxygen

The oxygen supply of seawater comes by diffusion from the air at the surface and from photosynthesis of green plants down to the compensation point. It is continuously used at all depths in respiration of animals and plants and in the decomposition of organic matter.

The oxygen content of seawater (Hedgpeth 1957) is seldom limiting for the occurance of animals, except in the deeper waters of the brackish Black and Caspian Seas, where it is practically absent. Oxygen concentration is especially high on shores where there is splashing of waves. Surface waters of the Atlantic Ocean commonly have 4.5 to 7.5 cc/liter and abyssal regions may run 5 cc/litre. Oxygen is somewhat less abundant in the Pacific and Indian oceans. Oxygen may be reduced to lower concentrations between 100 and 1500 m, because of its use in animal respiration and in decomposition, than at lesser depths, where there is photosynthesis, or at greater depths, where the abundance of animals is greatly diminished.

Marine animals have a variety of mechanism and adaptations for respiration (Flattely and Walton 1922). Greatest difficulties occur in shore animals at low tide when they are exposed to the air, but the needs for oxygen at this time is decreased in many forms by curtailment of activity. Some crabs, barnacle, snails, and fish have become almost amphibious in being capable of respiring in air, although at reduced rates as well as in water. Pune mud bottoms may present anaerobic conditions a short distance below the surface, but mud bottoms mixed with sand contain an abundant and diversified found.

PLANKTON

Composition

The plankton of the sea includes a great variety of forms, even more than in fresh water (Biglow 1926, Hardy 1956). Rotifers, however, are uncommon in marine plankton and cladocerans are much less important.

The nannoplankton consists mostly of protozoans, algae, bacteria, fungi, and viruses. The bacteria are largely periphytic, in that they are attached to the surfaces of floating plants, animals, and to particles of detritus. Veny few occur freely suspended in the water (Harvey 1955). Bacteria, including nitrifying forms, occur at all depths but are especially abundant in or close to the bottom. They are generally more numerous in the winter than in the summer. Nitrogen-fixing organisms are chiefly blue-green algae and possibly yeasts (Oppenheimer 1962).

The green phytoplankton is composed primarily of diatoms, dinoflagellates, and small unarmored flagellates, but several other kinds of algae are present and occasionally important. The dinoflagellates Noctiluca and Ceratium are lumineseent and in some regions may give a glow at night to the entire sea. Bioluminescence is not limited to these organisms, however, but occurs also in various forms of bacteria radiolarians, sponges, coelenterates, ctenophores, nemertineans, worms crustaceans, brittlestars, brittlestars, mollusks, balanoglossids, tunicates, and fish (Harvey 1952).

The most important groups of protozoan zoo-plankton, other than the green flagellates which are usually considered with the phytoplankton, are the rhizopond Foraminifera, the actinopod Radiolaria, and the ciliate tintinnids. They may be enormously abundant at times.

Abundance

The actual abundance of plankton varies greatly from place to place and from one season to the next. Smaller species tend to be more numerous than larger ones. The mean annual abundance of diatoms is commonly in the tens of thousands per litre and for shorter periods the year algal blooms may increase the population to hundreds of thousands of cell per litre (Ricketts and Calvin 1948), zooplankton is, however, much less abundant. Large, populations of zooplankton generally follow large papulations of phytoplankton and by their grazing maintain the standing crop of phytoplankton at the size suited to prevailing conditions (Nielsen 1958).

The total net zooplankton (cc per unit volume of water) is some 50 times more numerous in the neritic coastal waters of the Atlantic coast of North America than in the sargasso Sea (Grice and Hart 1962). The abundance of plankton is generally higher in cold than in warm ocean waters correlated with the greater amount of phosphate present in colder water (Harvey 1955). Cold-water plankton tends to of be larger individuals size. There is generally in most taxonomic groups, however, a lower variety of species in cold than in warm waters. Annual productivity is also less in cold waters correlated with fewer generations per year. Productivity of zooplankton varies between 14 and 58 per cent of the net primary productivity.

Nektoa

Mollusks, fishes, birds, and mammals make up the nekton of the sea. Mollusks are represented by the squids; fish by the sharks, flying fish herrings, meackerels, as many others, including numerous varieties of small species; and mammals, by the seals, porpoises, and whales, The distribution of fish is irregular, but in general they occur more abundantly in neritic waters than in the open ocean. Likewise, they are much more numerous in the epipelagic than in lower strata. Most pelagic fish, except sharks, possess a swimbladder useful for maintaining hydrostatic equilibrium at the depth where there they occur; those fish that lack one are commonly bottom forms (Marshall 1954). in arctic waters fish are less abundant, and mammals relatively more important, than is the causé farther south,

Birds, like many other marine animals, are more numerous in the neritic blochore than in the opean ocean. In the ocean far from land occur only penguins, albatrosses, hearwaters, and petrels, and even these speaies become more common shoreward. Other marine species in neritic water are tropic-birds, pelicans, gannets, boobies,, cormorants, frigate-birds ducks, gulls terns skimmeers auks and murres. These marine birds may spend many days of weeks feeding and travelling over the water, but all must search out some shore cliff, or isolated islands on which to nest. Here they sometimes coneentrate in enormous numbers during the nesting season because of the limiting number or suitable nesting locations available.

Benthos

Benthos is of much greater variety in marine than in freshwatet habitats. These animals are very abundant in the littoral zone and decrease in numbers with depth until only scatterred individuals are found in the deep ocean frenches (Saunders ef al 1965). Benthos consists of sessile forms, the sponges barnacles, mussles, oysters, crinolds, corals, hydroids, bryozoans and some worms; creeping forms, such as crabs, lobsters, certain copepods, amphipods, other crustacoans, many protozoans, snails, echinoderms, some bivalves, and some fishes; and burrowing forms, including must clams, worms, and some crustaceans. Sessile and creeping forms are often grouped as epifauna are burrowing forms as infauna. Epifauna in the littoral zone decreases in variety towards the poles since it is subjected composition of infauna remains about the same.

In food habits, different species may be grouped as seston eaters, mostly sessile or semi-sessile forms that capture suspended food particles; sluggish motile forms collecting detritus or food particles from the bottom surface; sluggish forms that extract food particles from bottom material that they swalloos; carnivores, and scavengers.

Oceanic Plankton and Nekton Biome

This biome is characterized by the predominance of organisms possessing life-forms adopted to keep them afloat. Plankton and nekton predominate, although the deep-sea benthos may be considered as belonging to this biome. Seasonal aspection may bring drastic changes in species composition, especiallp in plankton. Dominance, in the sense used for terrestrial communities, probably does not exist, except possibly in the Sargasso Sea, where the floating vegetation establishes the habitat. The ecosystem is self-contained, however, since energy is derived from the sun and nutrient material continues to recirculate with little or no dependence on terrestrial resources.

The sargassum community of the Atlantic Ocean is of special interest, the floating Sargassum alga accumulates and is held within a limited area by circular ocean currents. This plant belongs to the intertidal zone of the Caribean islands but in turn lose in large amounts along with attached animals during the hurricane season. It continues to grow thereafter, but does not reproduce. The fauna that it contains to a truly littoral one rather than pelagic, but because the algae to cold and ice erosion, but the species accumulates in fresh amounts as fast as old plants die, the animals reproduce and maintain a continued existence far from any shore.

Food Chains

As in fresh-water and terrestrial communities, bacteria in the sea are largely responsible for the final decomposition of excreta and dead bodies to make their essential nutrients available for reabsorption by the green phytoplankton.

Nitrogen and phosphorus are least concentrated near the surface of the ocean, since this is the stratum in which they are most rapidly absorbed by the photoplankton. Excreta and dead organisms sink during the process of decomposition, so nitrogen regeneration is most evident at depths of 500 to 1500 m. The total non-living organic matter, either dissolved or in the form of particulate matter, is generally much larger than the biomass of living organisms at any one time. Organic matter makes up less than one-third of the total particulate matter, and all of it sinks slowly through the water, requiring months or even years to reach the bottom. Much of the particulate organic matter is still undissolved and accumulates on the ocean bottom. Numerous species of invertebrates depend on it for food, especially on the bacteria that it contains. The deep-sea fishes feed on these invertebrates or are carnivorous on other fish. Many of them have very wide mouths, distensible stomachs, and formidable teeth. In addition to these food coactions. it is also likely that many deep-sea fish and larger invertebrates undergo vertical migrations, so that they obtain food by preying on living organisms at more moderate depths. Much that is known about the life histories of these deep benthic species has been summarized by Marshall.

Especially fertile regions of the open ocean occur when there is deep mixing of waters by turbulence and upwelling. Vertical water currents bring nutrients up to the surface from intermediate depths where they had accumulated. Prominent regions of more or less permanent upwelling occur aronnd the Antarctic continent, off the coasts of California, Peru, and Somali, and Off the west coasts of both north and south Africa. In many areas, very small phytoplankton and bacteria form the first link in the food chain, which goes next to the microzooplankton before reaching the carnivorous net zooplankton of copepods, euphasiids, and other crustacean forms. Most animals depending on small organisms and organic detritus for food have various filter-feeding mechanisms for straining the material out of the water. They do not actively search and catch individual items through directed actions. Invertebrate animals may also be able to absorb some essential salts and dissolved organic compounds to build their skeletal structures and for general metabolism, but there is considerable controversy on this point.

The balcen or whalebone whales (Mysticeti) are toothless but possess large plates in their mouths that strain out the plankton (especially copepods, euphausiaceans, mysidaceans) that they use as food. Only occasionally are small fish as food. Only occasionally are small fish or other invertebrates ingested. Some whales reach tremendous proportions, and the differential in size between these animals and their food is one of the most remarkable in the animal kingdom. Much more common is the feeding on plankton by squids, the young stages of most fishes, and such adult fishes as sardine, anchovy, menhaden, herring, and mackerel. The menhaden is unique in having such fine-mesh gill-rakers that it can feed extensively on diatoms, which because of their smaller size cannot be readily secured by other large mariue animals.

Balanoid-Gastropod-Thallophyte Biome

This community extends from high-to below low tide levels on rocky shores (Lewis 1964). Benthic animals and attached algal plants are conspicuous and important, the benthos is mostly epifauna, as too hard to permit development of extensive infauna. When the tide is out the organisms are subjected to drying, the occasional inflow of fresh water, higher temperatures, and greater light intensities Organisms to avoid desiccation when the tide is out by variously crawling under stones or thick algal growths, closing thick shells or operculae, retreating into crevices, or secreting a mucous seal. Most organisms are also faced with the pounding action of waves, various holdfast or anchoring devices have developed, and many species protect their more delicate structures with a hard shell. The adaptations for life on the seashore are many and varied (Yonge 1949). The plankton and nekton associated with the bentnos include many species not common to the oceanic biome.

Zonation

Vertical zonation of species on rocky shores is usually conspicuous, although individual species may extend widely into adjacent areas (Hewatt 1937, Yonge 1949, Stephenson 1949, Southward 19°8).

Beginning on the landward side there is a supralittoral zone mostly above the action of tides and inhabited as much by land as by marine animals. This is followed seaward by a supralittoral or Littorin fringe which is wetted by the highest tides and by the splashing of waves. Because of the presence of either Myxophyceae or lichens, this zone is often discovered; commonly, black. The fringe is especially characterized by large numbers of small snails and sometimes isopods.

Next below this fringe is the midlittoral or balanoid zone. It is strictly intertidal being covered and uncovered every day, and is occupied characterically by acorn barnncles. This zone is often divided into subzones with the barnacles predominate in the upper portion, while polychaets, colonial hydroids, or other forms are relatively more important in the lower part. The subzonation of algae as often also well marked.

The lowest zone over exposed, and then only at extreme low tides, is called the infralittoral fringe. It is a transition area. The entire area between extreme high and low tides, including the mid-littoral fringes, when considered as a unit may be referred to as littoral, eulittoral, or tidal zone to distinguish it from the infralittoral or sublittoral zone that extends from the lowest of low tides to the edge of the continental shelf.

Littoral Zone

Brown algae from thick masses and give protection to those animals that find shelter in or under them. A fauna of copepods, ostracods, water mites, and young littorinids inhabit these seaweeds. In England, the numbers of individuals per 100 g of seaweed vary from about 44 on brown algae to over 13,000 on lichens (Colman 1940).

The animal life on rocky shores is varied and luxuriant. Several species of acorn barnacles, snails, marine limpets, marine mussles, goose barnacles, sea anemones, chitons, sponges, hydroids, bryozoans, flatworms, annelids, isopods, crabs, sea urchins, starfishes, tunicates, and insects are present. Total abundance of animals may run into tens of thousands of individuals per square meter.

Sublittoral Zone

This community is not subjected to exposure by tides or to the pounding of surf, but is affected considerably by wave action and the complete circulation of water. Animals move around somewhat more freely and there is less need for strong holdfast structures. Most organisms lack physiological tolerance for long exposure to the air and hence differ fundamentally in structure and mores from the community described above.

Laminarias or kelps are the largest of the brown algae and occur commonly in this community. They have root-like holdfasts attached to the bottom and their stalks, which are often several meters long, bear leaf-like branches that float at the surface in the larger species. A long list of animals find shelter and food in the kelp beds and especially in the protection of the holdfasts (Andrews 1945), Polychaet worms are particularly abundant in these holdfasts (Colman 1940). Filamentous red algae (Rhodophyceae) are also prominent.

Abundant characteristic animals on the Pacific coast are sea urchins, sea cucumber, starfishes, snails, rock oyster, chitons, li pets, scallops, mussels, nudibranches, barhacles, crabs, hermit crabs, hydroids, tunicates, shrimps, and various fish.

Distribution of fish species correlates strongly with the type of bottom or benthos that is present.

Tidal Pools

Seawater is often retained as depressions or pools in the littoral zone and hence organisms here are never completely exposed to the air. They are however, subject to high light intensity an increase in the temperature between tides (Klugh 1924). Tidal pools are usually rich in both plant and animal life, and some species are largely restricted to them. Red algae and kelps prefer the more shaded, cooler pools; the green algae and some of the smaller brown algae prenominate in the well-insolated pools. Animals of both the sublittoral and littoral zones are found here.

PELECYPOD ANNELID BIOME

Habitat

This biome develops on depositing sand and mud bottoms in contrast to the biome just described that occurs on eroding-rocky shores. There is still a good deal of wave action over sandy bottoms. Fine sand particles shift about almost continuously, and animals have difficulty in preventing their burrows from collapsing. In general, the water over muddy shores is shallower, quieter, and warmer. The mud forms a soft, compact bottom, but is also easily moved or shifted around by storms and wave action. Animal burrows in mud are more permanent. Species tend to segregate depending on the amount of organic matter present. Shores of high mud content may be low in oxygen because of decaying organic matter, so animal populations tend to be largest and most varied in a mixture of mud and sand. Tidal currents are weaker, and change in the level of water is less pronounced on sand and muddy shores than on rocky ones.

Composition and Characteristics

Important plants in this biome are the marine eelgrass, which is a seed plant and green algae, particularly the sea-lettuce, which grows in sheets either attached to the substratum or lying fragmented over large areas, and Enteromorpha, which grows in tufts or tangles. Occuring on eelgrass and sea-lettuce may be several kinds of epiphytic algae. These plants form extensive stands and are important to animals for attachment, shelter, and food. Eelgrass was almost eliminated from the Atlantic coast in 1931-32, possibly because of a protozoan disease. This disturbance had a profoundly deleterious effect on the abundance of many animals, including the brant; a bird that depended on it almost exclusively for food, and on scallop and other coastal fisheries. Twenty years later there was evidence that eelgrass was recovering much of its former abundance (Cottam and Munro 1954).

Predominant animals are pelecypods, polychaete worms, particularly Arenicola and Nerels; starfishes, brittle-stars, sea cucumbers, crabs, amphipods, and snails. Populations may run to several thousands of individuals per square meter. A variety of small fish occur here. Birds include sandpipers, plovers and herons.

The biome is worldwide in distributior, but the characteristic life-forms are represented by different species locally Thus a number of secondary communities (Biociations) may be recognized (Petersen 1914, Jones 1950, Thorson in Hedgpeth 1957).

Many of the animal constituents in this biome are burrowing forms The sub-stratum of mud and sand holds considerable water and when the tide is out on exposed flats, pelecypods, worms and other animal constituents retract their fleshy organs into their burrows shells and remain in a water saturated environment (Hesse, Allee and Schmidt 1951). They are thus not exposed to the atmosphere with changes in the tide. Furthermore, most forms are generally tolerant of low oxygen and high carbon dioxide concentrations. In order to maintain respiration when retracted in their underground burrows these animals have long siphons, sometimes longer than their bodies, or long tubes or canals that extend to the surface. Through these they maintain a circulation of water, often by means of special pumping organs.

Coral Reef Biome

Coral reef are formed by the accumulation of the calcareous skeletons of myriads of organisms. They extend from the sea bottom at depths of 46 m or rarely 74 m. to slightly above low-tide level. The best formation of coral reefs is confined to warm waters above 10 C, although individual species may extend into colder regions (Vaughan 1919, Wells in Hedgpeth 1957).

Predominant organisms involved are commonly the anthozoan stony corals and organ corals and the hydrozoan milliporids. Some reefs however are formed principally by foraminifera and still others by calcareous algae. All massive coral structures employ calcareous algae as cement, these algae not only thrive in the pounding surf on the windward side of the reef, but by their growth are able to repair damage to the reef caused by storms. Most typical reef-building animals are colonial and of shapes varying from closely compact, globose, or encrusting, to loosely branched or dendritic, depending in part on their exposure to wave action. Each polyp in a colony secretes its own calcareous skeleton and when it dies the next generation builds on top of the old so that the accumulation of a lime structure is fairly rapid (Yonge 1963).

The bright yellow or red colors or corals near enough to their water's surface for adequate light penentration are the result of algae, the zooxanthellae, which are either embedded in the body wall or free in the internal cavities. In addition, there are bands of green filamentous algae growing to a depth of 2 or 3 cm in the pores or the insert coral skeleton that may have a biomass 16 times that of the zooxanthelate. In their photosynthesis these algae may absorb dioxide and nutrients derived from animals of the coral reef and liberate oxygen of value to the animals (Odum and Odum 1965). Perhaps because of this symbiotic relationship which requires solar radiation, living corals are largely confined to the upper, shallower waters. Coral animals actively ingest zooplankton, but apparently not phytoplankton, from the surrounding water.

Succession to Land

The three great biocycles-ocean, freshwater, and land-come into contact with each other around the margins of the seas. The change in the physical nature of the habitat from salt water to fresh water is a drastic one, but not more drastic than the change from salt water to land : The transition of animal and plant life is abrupt, and a zonation or physiographic succession of communities can be recognized. This transition from the ocean to fresh water and from the ocean to land as we see it today is of special interest since it parallels the probable evolution and dispersal of life in past ages.

Life is generally believed to have originated in the littoral region. Apparently no great group (phyla) of animals originated except in the ocean. The routes by which animals probably left the ocean and reached fresh-water and land have been various. Some animals probably migrated directly across sea branches; other probably ascended rivers, passed through marshes and swamps, or burrowed through soil. Some animals were transferred from the ocean by land elevations which isolated them in bodies of water which gradually became fresh Immigration from the sea did not take place at one time. It has occurred many times in the past and is slowly progressing on many shores today .. The most successful animal colonizers of the land have been : (1) the arthropods, which have in many cases developed booklungs or tracheae for breathing air; (2) the vertebrates, with lungs and dry skins; and (3) the snails, with slime and spirally coiled shells to prevent desiccation .. There are at present many examples of animals which are in the midst of their transformation from marine to fresh-water animals, or from marine or fresh-water into land animals. Not only have plants and animals emigrated from sea to land, but there are countless instances when migrations have taken and are taking place in the opposite direction. Grasses, insects, reptiles, birds and mammals have left the land for the sea... Fishes began in fresh water, but now range through the ocean at all depths.

On rocky shores and cliffs there is a splash or supralittoral zone above high tide level. Green algae occur here and scattered individuals of marine snails, acorn barnacles, limpets, amphipod sandfleas and flatworms, as well as insects, especially. Diptera and other forms that come from the land. Above the influence of splashing, the rocks may be covered with lichens and mosses, representing the initial stages in the terrestrial rock sere. However, salt spray is often blown inland a considerable distance to affect conspicuously the development of normal terrestrial vegetation and its accompanying animal life. Cliffs along the ocean, as well as sandy beaches and islands, are favorite nesting places for large numbers of pelagic birds.

Succession to Fresh Water

Where rivers flow into the ocean on low coastal plains and there are extensive embayments or estuaries as long the Atlantic Coast, there is a very gradual change from salt water to brakish water (salinity; 0.5-30%) to entirely fresh water. This habitat gradient fluctuates back and forth with the tides. Since fresh water is less dense and often warmer, it flows over the top of the salt water, with the result that strata with different physical characteristics are formed and these different strata are inhabited by different kinds of fish and other organisms, influx of fresh water is one of the principal sources of dissolved nutrients, and the gradient of salinity is dependent upon continuous inflow of fresh water. Any reduction of inflow, as by damming of streams, will allow salt water to penetrate further inland.

APPLIED ECOLOGY

Food Production

Alrhough 71 per cent of the earth's surface is occupied by oceans and only 29 per cent by land, nearly all of the food and raw materials used by man is derived from the latter. This is in spite of the fact that agricultural soil is only a few inches thick and must be cultivated, protected from erosion, and fertilized, while the ocean with its chemical fertility, its photosynthetic production of basic plant food, and its great fisheries is an entirely natural resource ready to be harvested. However, fish harvesting in the ocean has definite limits determined by photoplankton primary productivity. It is estimated that maximum sustained yield to man is of the order of 100-150 million metric tons per year and in 1967, 6000,000 tons were being harvested. The ocean is relatively infertile, yet it covers most of the area; much more productive are the coastal areas, particularly the areas of upwelling but these are of comparatively small size. A large part of the production is taken by predators other than man and part of it must be left to maintain the breeding stock. The possibility of the ocean serving as an abundant future source of food for man is probably exaggerated. Seafood is important mostly as a supplementary source of protein. Man must look to other resource for his main energy requirements.

The plankton of the sea represents a possible food supply for man (Davis 1955). Its energy value is approximately 4 kcal/g dry weight, and it is more or less palatable (Clarke and Bishop 1948). However the expense involved in filtering and concentrating it is too great to be economical; poisonous species sometime occur, it is not easily digested and assimilated and consequently it has not as yet proved to be a feasible diet. The energy value of the plankton is used by man at the present time primarily as it is transferred into higher links of the food chain. Aside from the fishes, the chief marine organisms used as food are the oysters and other mollusks, shrimp, crabs, lobsters, and sea turtles. These are mostly animals of the continental shelf and estuaries.

There are a number of problems in the use and conservation of marine organisms. Natural beds of American oysters on the Atlantic coast have nearly all been exhausted through overfising and pollution. Because of heavy erosion of the land, silt deposition has become excessive in most of the bays and estuaries and there is increasing difficulty for oyster spat to find clean hard surfaces on which to set. Surfaces that are loose or covered with silt are not suitable since the spat is very small and easily smothered. A common practice is to return to suitable areas all shells of mollusks removed or to introduce other suitable hard objects to furnish the necessary substratum for oyster setting. Control of erosion over the watershed would greatly alleviate the problem. The trend is increasing to lease suitable areas of water and to farm oysters in the manner of an agricultural crop.

In spite of their position at or near the top of the food chain, the greatest utilizable food resource of the sea is its fishes.

Ocean "farming" is largely limited to estuaries and salt mashes. Yields in the Orient occasionally reach of even surpass 1000 kg/hectare-yr (880 lb/acre-yr). Principal species are milkfish, grey mullets, eels, salmon, sea trout, tilapia, oysters, and shrimp. Conversion of marsh into ponds where water level, fertility, and cropping can be controlled has met with varying success in defferent parts of the world, but may be expected to expand as fish harvesting in the ocean itself approaches its yield limit.

Summary

Geographic distribution of marine organisms depends on their responses to current, temperature, and physical barriers; their local distribution is affected by waves and tides, type of bottom, salinity, and depth. Major division of the marine bioycle are pelagic (open water) and benthic (bottom). Major communities recognized are the oceanic plankton and nekton biome in the open sea, the balanoid-gastropod-thallophyte biome on rocky shores, the pelecypod-annelid biome on sand and mud bottoms, and the coral reef biome.

Organisms making up the oceanic biome are widely distributed around the world but may be divided into warm-water, arctic, and antarctic faunas. Coral reefs are found only in the tropics. The two biomes on the continental shelf subdivide into warm-water, temperate, arctic, and antarctic faunas and into more restricted regions and subregions. The warm-water faunas are richest in species, especialy in the Indo-Malayan and West Indian subregions.

Marine plankton include a greater variety of forms that does fresh-water plankton, although rotifers are nearly absent; cladocerans, less important. They possess various unique mechanisms for flotation. Although abundance varies greatly from place to place and from season to season, plankton is generally much more numerous in neritic coastal waters than in the open sea. Diel movements between the surface at night and greater depths during the day are pronounced.

Mollusks (squids), fishes, birds, and mammals constitute the nekton. The eaxonomic composition of the fish fauna varies with depth. Biolumines ence is exceptionally well developed among deep sea nekton and benthos.

Benthos includes a great variety of sessile, creeping, and burrowing forms. It is very abundant in the littoral zone, and decreases in numbers with depth, although individuals are found in the deepest ocean trenches. There is considerable difference in the life-form and species composition of benthos occurring on rocky shores and on sand and muddy ones. Zonation of species is more prominent on rocky than on depositing shores. Succession and dominance occurs in some situations, but is less impo tant than in terrestrial communities. Coral reefs have many special features, but are now exposed in the Pacific and Indian Oceans to damage by a species of starfish.

Food chanis in the sea are similar to those in fresh water but the number of links and species composition varies in different communities. Productivity is especially high in regions where upwelling and turbulence bring nutrients from deeper levels up to the surface.

The three great biocycles of ocean, fresh-water, and land come into contact around the margins of the seas. The succession from the ocean to land is abrupt and from the ocean to fresh water through estuaries only slightly less so.

Effective use of the ocean resources as food for man is largely limited to the continental shelf, regions of upwelling, estuaries, and coastal marshes. Plankton is abundant and has high productivity in these regions but is likely to be useful to man only as its nutrient material and energy are transferred with considerable loss into the higher food chain links of mollusks, larger arthropods, fishes, and other vertebrates.

Coastal regions need protection and management for good production and all waters kept clean from pollution of all sorts.

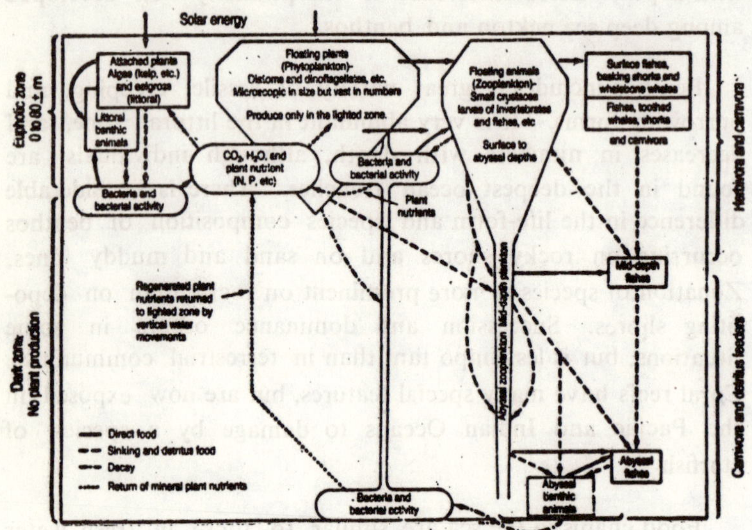

Interrelations of marine organisms (Sverdrup et al. 1942)

Water Circulation

The three great water reservoirs of the earth—the seas, the continents and the atmosphere are not in any sense self-contained units but are in constant communication with one another. The relationships take the form of a circulation. Under the influence of solar radiation, water is constantly vaporized and emitted into the atmosphere in the form of water vapor. This process can occur in a great variety of ways. On the one hand, water evaporates directly from the surface of seas, lakes and rivers, from glaciers and snowfields, or straight out of the ground. On the other hand, in the process of breathing, all living organisms, animals and plants alike, emit both carbon dioxide and water vapor into the atmosphere. A third process is the emission of water vapor by the combustion of organic materials such as wood, coal and oil, which are to be found all over the earth. Easily the highest proportion of vaporized water emanates directly from the oceans, however.

The water suspended in the atmosphere in the form of water vapor is of the greatest importance to the climatic conditions on earth. It conditions the composition of the air masses, exerts an influence on the energy conditions of the atmosphere, and substantially governs and sustains the water circulation.

The water content in the atmosphere is measured in terms of the relative humidity of the air. Whereas some portions of the vaporized water masses remain permanently suspended in the atmosphere in the form of moisture, others are condensed back by the cooling down of ascending airstreams and emerge in the form of clouds, fog, rain or dew. If the water cools still further, snow or hailstones may build up in the clouds. When the clouds get too heavy, precipitation begins and the moisture returns to the earth in the form of rain, snow or hail. If the precipitation goes straight into the sea or into lakes having no outlet, the water circulation will be complete. If it falls on land, some of it will accumulate by surface drainage in brooks, streams and rivers and so return to the ocean. Other forms of precipitation seep into the earth and replenish the groundwater, or if retained at an upper ground level as trap water will evaporate from there. The trap water is also available to sustain plant life, which absorbs it through its roots and returns it to the atmosphere as water vapor by respiration and transpiration.

This circulation, like all others on the earth, cannot occur in the absence of some motive force. The entire cycle is maintained by the regular inflow of solor energy. Of the total amount of energy absorbed by the earth, about one-third is utilized in maintaining the water circulation. The temperature, humidity and movement (wind) in the atmosphere together determine the level of evaporation.

Although the total volume of atmospheric moisture is very small in comparison with the total hydrosphere, owing to the circulation of the atmosphere an enormore amount of water movement takes place in the course of a year. To produce the annual precipitation on the earth of about 470,000 cubic kilometers, the water in the atmosphere about 12,300 cubic kilometers) must be replaced 35 to 40 times a year.

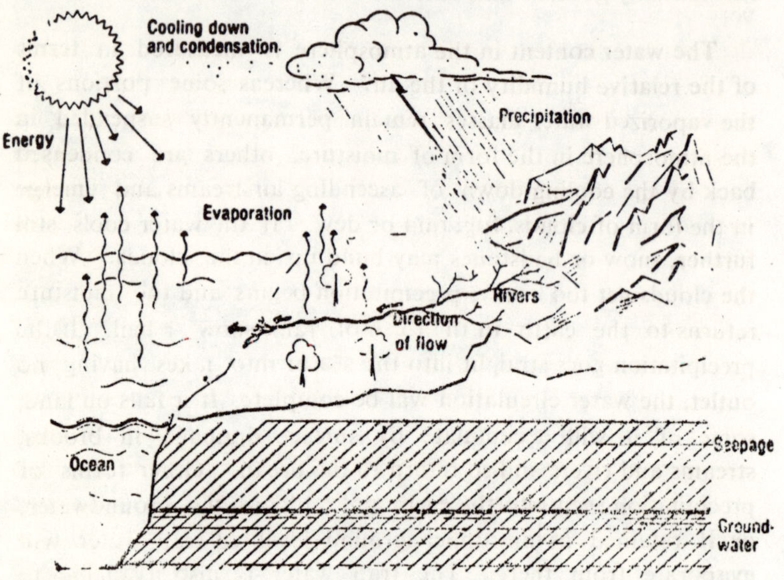

Fig. 1.1. Diagrammatic presentation of water circulation in nature.

Life in the Deep Sea

Sunlight penetrates the sea to a depth of about 1000 m (3000 ft). Animals living in this twilight zone consequently have very big eyes and exceptionally wide pupils. Like many nocturnal animals on dry land, deep-sea animals have all the sensory cells of their retinas protruding on rods. These rods, which serve to pick up what little light there is and convert it into nerve impulses, are unusually long and large. A nerve cell from the optic nerve is linked simultaneously to several rods. Under this arrangement an extremely high sensitivity to light is achieved.

At a depth of below 1000 m (3000 ft) or so, at which almost total darkness prevails, the fish have either no eyes at all or only very small eyes of limited capacity. It is now known that such deep sea fish find their way in the dark with the aid of sensory organs with which they are able to detect vibrations in the water. Many deep-sea fish have very long organs of touch of a most remarkable kind : tentacles of great length with feeler-type floating ends and extensive tail ends. Many fish have long feelers furnished with claws and sharp points, which also serve to locate and trap their prey.

Certain sea organisms are able to illumine their paths of their own accord or to radiate more or less intensive light (bioluminescence). In many cases a glow is cast by certain cells which are surrounded by reflecting cell groups. Other animals can emit luminous substances into the surrounding water which provide light away from the animal concerned for some time and probably serve to camouflage its activities. In particular cases a symbiosis is established between luminous bacteria and fish whereby the luminous bacteria are in effect kept in a tissue culture by the larger animal. Some varieties emit projector like light beams that probably help to locate the prey. Other deep-sea fish have luminous bait at the end of long extensions, which take various forms and colors. In some varieties the luminous bait even hangs from an enormous jaw. In other cases light organs may help the male and female of a particular species to locate one another on the seabed for mating purposes. Many sea organisms can switch their light beams on and off, as it were, so as to confuse their opponents.

Many deep-sea fish have enormous teeth and jaws. And their maws are often extremely flexible. This points to the fact

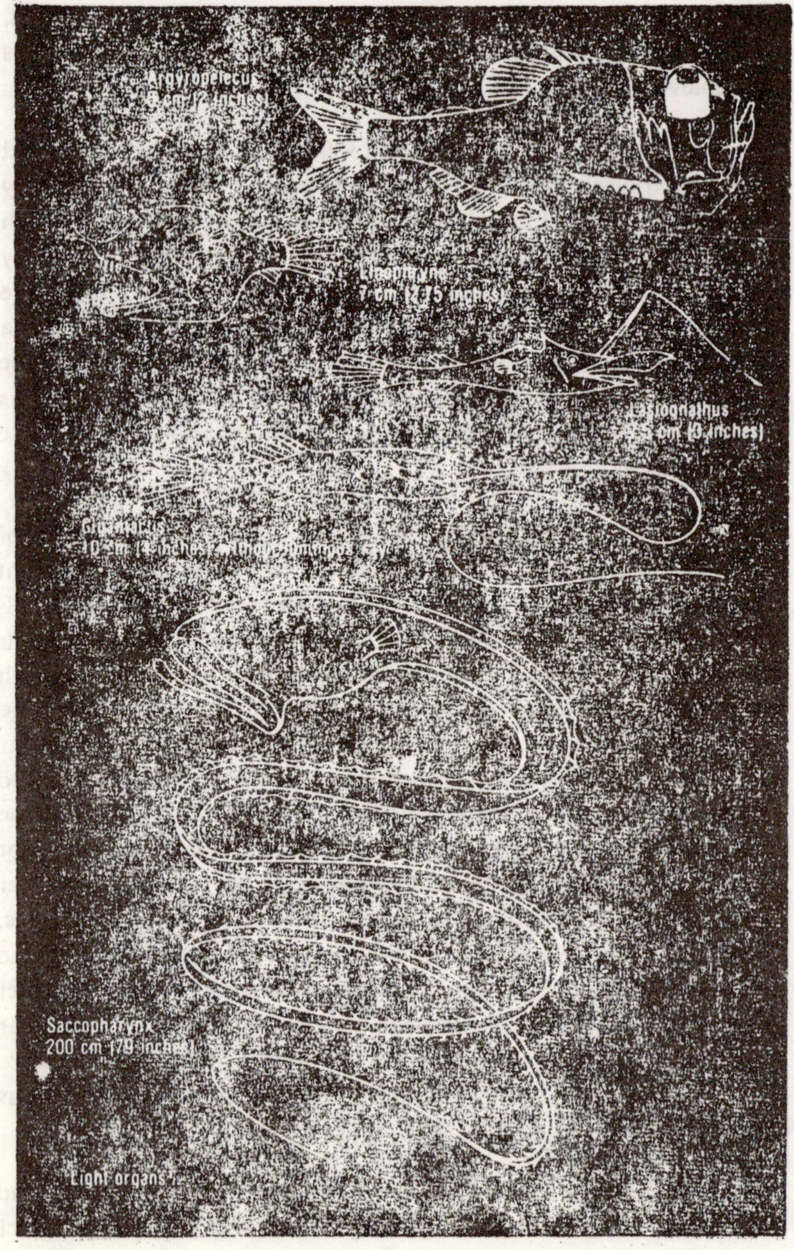

Fig. 1.2. Morphological features of deep-sea fish

that their nutriment may be found only at rare intervals, and it may then be very bulky and have to quell the animal's hunger for long periods.

A number of aspects regarding deep-sea fish still remain to be clarified, however. We often have to depend on chance discoveries, and animals that are brought to the surface are apt to die quickly, so that intensive investigations are not possible.

The Sea and its Temperature

Like the mainland and inland waters, the oceans of the world are also subject to seasonal temperature variations. In the sea, however, these changes are more limited. This is due to the water circulation that takes place constantly within the oceans, coupled with the extremely high specific heat of salt water and the capacity that goes with it for storing energy. Except in the shallow shelf that surrounds the continents, the temperatures in the seas are consequently very uniform. In low geographical latitudes on each side of the equator, temperatures of up to 30°C (86°F) are recorded in the surface waters, while in shallow and enclosed waters they may rise in coastal regions to as high as 50°C (122°F). Except in extreme cases the temperature variations between the coldest and warmest areas are in the 30° - 35°C (54°-63°F) range. In polar regions and in equatorial waters the temperatures over the year remain remarkably uniform. As for deep-sea water, a constant water temperature can be assumed in all the oceans. The lowest temperatures are to be found in polar sea regions, where they can come close to the freezing point of seawater (– 1.9°C, or 28°F).

Whereas in the lower latitudes seawater absorbs warmth from the atmosphere, at higher latitudes it emits warmth into it. The cooling of the water surface caused in this way leads to the formation of convection currents, which results in the intermingling of the water masses and the equalization of temperature between surface and deep water. This phenomenon arises from the fact that seawater (salt content 35%) attains its maximum density at − 3.5°C, or 25.7°F (compared with 4°C, or 39°F, for pure water). In this respect seawater behaves quite differently from freshwater. It freezes on cooling before it

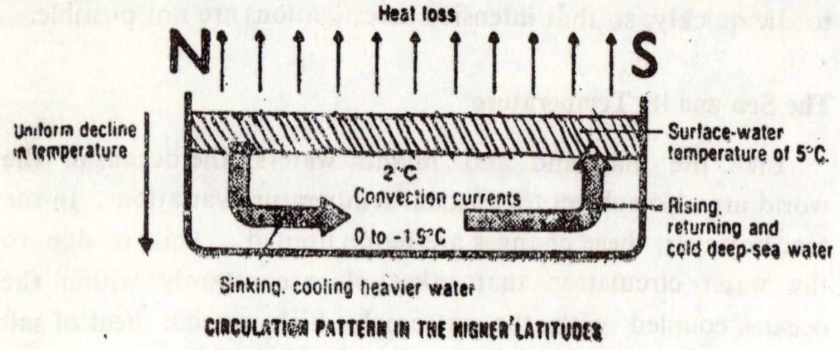

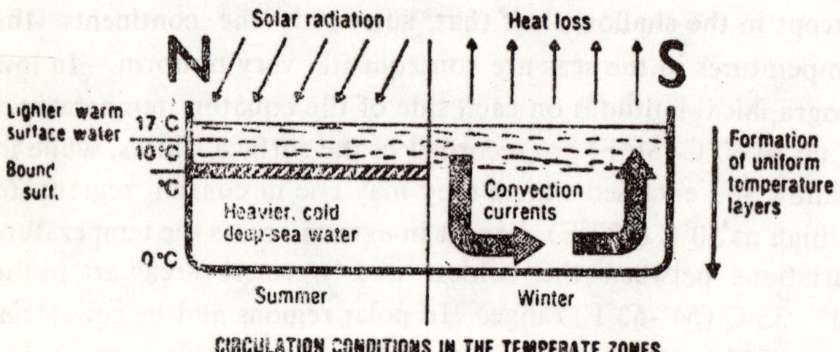

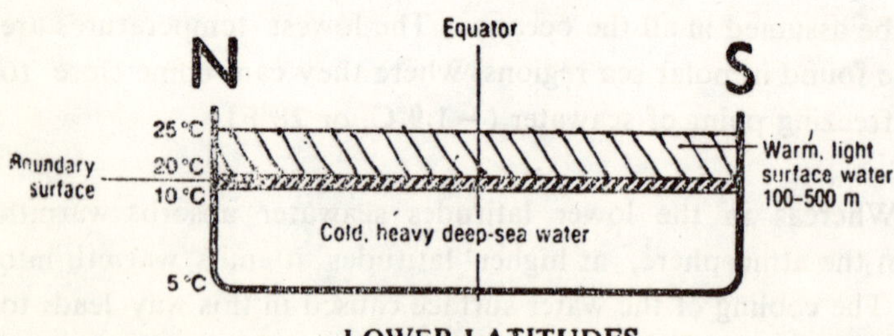

Fig. 1.3. Formation of convection currents and boundary surfaces.

reaches its maximum density. From this it follows that no stable temperature stratification takes place in winter or in arctic regions, as in the case of freshwater, but that the intermingling in the sea is not interrupted. The heat accumulated in seawater is emitted into the atmosphere as the water cools, not as in freshwater where below a shallow surface layer the water maintains a constant temperature of 4°C (39°F). It is from this property that the sea acquires its importance in moderating the climate.

Because of its lower specific gravity, at lower latitudes the warm surface water cannot pr mote convection currents. This gives rise to considerable drops in temperature between the surface and deep-water levels and to the development of so-called boundary surfaces between the two layers, which occur at depths of 100-500 meters (328-1640 feet). In temperate latitudes a seasonal change takes place in the formation of convection currents and boundary surfaces. During the summer months, when the surface water is warmed by increased solar radiation, the boundary surfaces form at a depth of 15-40 meters (49-131 feet). In the autumn, when the water is gradually cooling off, the boundary surfaces disappear and convection currents build up.

Composition of Seawater

Seawater is a complex solution of various salts, trace elements and gases. There is a measure of equilibrium between the input of soluble matter by the rivers, elutriation (or removal of suspended particles) from the atmosphere by rain, and the loss by precipitation and absorption of nutrients. The bulk of the soluble matter is washed into the sea through the weathering and erosion of rocks from the solid crust of the earth. Much of this matter is soon precipitated to form new rock deposits on the seabed, which become stratified over geological periods and can form new mountains again as a result of pressure movements in the earth's crust.

In shorter periods, variations can be caused in the composition of seawater by biological processes (occasioned by the temperature, for instance) and today in particular by the deposit of waste and toxic substances in the sea. In general, the quantity of inorganic material dissolved in seawater amounts to 35 grams per kilogram of water. This represents a solution of 3.5%.

To come down to details, seawater contains the following elements (average concentration) ;

Substance	*Concentration (milligrams per litre)*
Sodium	10,600
Chlorine	18.990
Magnesium	1,350
Sulfur	885
Calcium	400
Potassium	390
Cabon (as carbonates and carbon dioxide)	23—28
Strontium	8.1
Bromine	65
Boron	4.6
Silicon	0.02 – 4
Fluorine	1.5
Nitrogen	0.02—0.8
Rubidium	0.12
Aluminum	0.01
Lithium	0.18

Barium	0.05
Iodine	0.05
Phosphorus	0.0001–0.1
Arsenic	0.003
Iron	0.002–0.02
Manganese	0.001–0.01
Copper	0.001–0.01
Zinc	0.005–0.01
Lead	0.00003
Selenium	0.00009
Cesium	0,0004
Uranium	0,003
Silver	0.0003
Thorium	0.00005

Most of these elements are present in seawater in the form of salts, and a smaller portion in the form of dissolved gases. The most important of these are oxygen and carbon dioxide. The oxygen content fluctuates between 0 and 8.5 milliliters per liter. The high concentrations occur near the surface of the water, where the oxygen is in equilibrium with the oxygen in the atmosphere. A second source of the oxygen dissolved in the sea comes from the photosynthesis of phytoplankton, the drifting oceanic plant life. At great depths it may happen that (owing to the intense activity of bacteria and animals that absorb oxygen) the oxygen content of the seawater falls to zero. In many places, however, owing to the downward trend of the convection currents, a large quantity of dissolved oxygen from the surface water is carried to considerable depths in the sea.

An important part is played by carbon dioxide gas, which is present in considerable quantities in seawater. Since the basic ions of sodium, potassium and calcium are also present in large quantities in seawater, this facilitates the solution of a relatively high percentage of carbon dioxide. Carbon dioxide is one of the basic substances for photosynthesis (see Part Six). The plants living in the sea (especially plankton) take the carbon dioxide they need for photosynthesis directly out of the surrounding water. The second important effect of carbon dioxide in seawater is its function as a buffer (dissolved matter which keeps the pH value of the solution practically constant over wide areas). Normally the pH value of seawater lies between 7.5 and 8.4. As carbon dioxide and its associated marine chemicals are in equilibrium, the pH value of seawater is approximately constant as regards the input of both acids and bases.

The other gases from the atmosphere are dissolved in seawater in much lower concentrations than oxygen and carbon dioxide. The concentrations are as follows :

Substance	*Concentration (milligrams per liter)*
Nitrogen	between 8.4 and 15
Helium	0.000005
Neon	0.0001
Argon	0.6
Krypton	0.0003
Xenon	0.00005

A particular phenomenon is the enrichment of seawater by trace elements that occur in considerable concentrations in living organisms. An example is provided by the ascidian (a tunicate), a small, mostly clinging animal that increases the element vanadium in seawater up to 50,000 times its normal concentration. It is known today that many other trace elements such as iodine, arsenic, nickel, zinc, titanium, chromium and strontium are also very much increased in the water by decaying organisms. Certain fish are known to contribute chromium, nickel, silver, tin and zinc. Similarly, some of the substances produced by humans get into the sea as waste substances. As such a buildup of substances in the food web takes some time, the damage caused by them is often not noted until too late. The increase of chlorinated hydrocarbons, for instance (especially pesticides such as DDT), reaches its maximum concentration in fish only after a period of 11 years from its production.

Also of great importance in its effects on life in the sea is the content of ammonium compounds, nitrates and phosphates. As these are absorbed by plants to build up their bodies, their content in seawater varies considerably according to the presence of plant life. The following concentrations in seawater have been established :

Substance	*Concentration (milligrams per liter)*
Ammonia	0.4—5.0
Nitrate	1—600
Nitrous oxide (particularly NO_2)	0—15
Organically combined nitrogen	30—200
Phosphates	1—100
Organically combined phosphorus	1—30

The Sea and the Seabed

The oceans cover nearly 71% of the earth's surface, or about 361 million square kilometers. This enormous volume of water is not spread evenly over the earth's surface, but varies sharply in area and depth. Three extensive oceans separate the main land masses of the American, Eurasian and African continents from one another. With an area of 180 million square kilometers the Pacific Ocean accounts for nearly half the total sea surface of the world. It is followed in size by the Atlantic Ocean with a surface area of 106 million square kilometers, and the Indian Ocean with 75 square kilometers. The other seas (Mediterranean, Black Sea, North Sea, Baltic Sea, etc.) are included in the Atlantic area.

There are also substantial differences in the matter of sea depths. The greatest known sea depths are in the Pacific Ocean, where they extend at some points to over 10,000 meters (6.2 miles), whereas the average sea depth is no greater than some 3700 meters (2.3 miles).

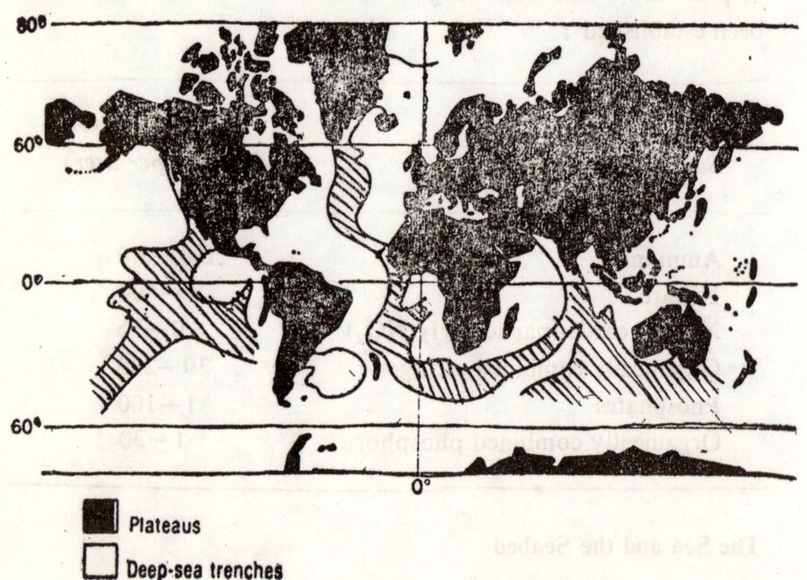

Fig. 1.4. The Principal Oceans. Deep-sea Trenches and Ocean Plateaus.

Near the coast the sea is generally quite shallow, and the seabed declines gently to an average depth of 200 meters (656 feet). The shallow coastal ledge surrounds almost all the coasts of the continents like a girdle. This girdle of shallow seabeds is known as the continental shelf. The sediment that is carried down into the sea by the rivers all the year round is deposited primarily in this area The continental shelf is bordered by the continental margin, from which the continental slope drops away. From this point the seabed falls sharply to greater depths. This often provides gradients of 1 : 15 and angles of gradient of over 45°. Occasionally a vertical face is found in this region. At about 3000 to 6000 meters (1.8 to 3.7 miles) from shore the continental slopes give way gradually to the deep-sea bed. The decline to the deep-sea bed seldom occurs in the continental slope in a uniform manner, however; it is often punctuated by hollows and ravines. The deep sea bed proper is uniform and even over wide areas. But in certain sectors the seabed is intersected by still deeper troughs, the deep-sea trenches. At these points it may drop to a depth of 7000 meters (4.3 miles) or more. Most of these deep-sea trenches are to be found on the fringe of the Pacific adjoining Asia.

In order sea regions, on the other hand, the seabed rises to form big plateaus, which cover wide areas of the oceans. These plateaus, or submarine ridges, can be likened to the mountains on the continents, though they are much more sharply delineated. The biggest known sea obstacle is the Mid-Atlantic Ridge, which stretches in the shape of on S from north to south midway across the Atlantic Ocean and roughly follows the coastline of the American continent. Such submarine ridges and plateaus play a very important part in setting the pattern of ocean currents and the exchange of waters between the individuals regions of the sea.

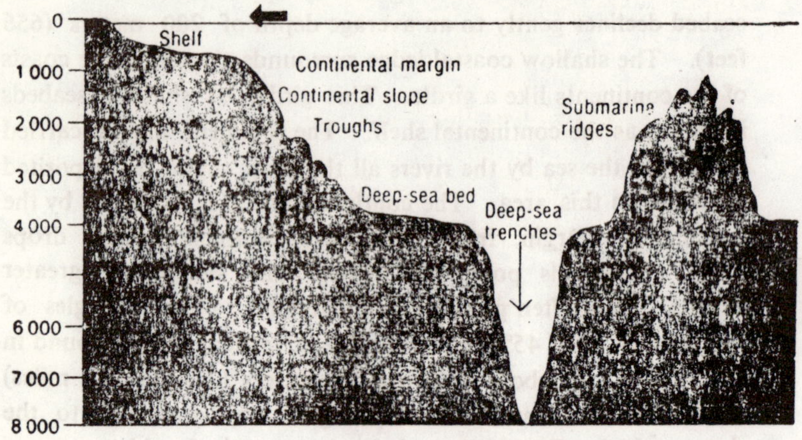

Fig. 1.5. Profile of the Seabed.

Sea Currents

The water masses in the oceans are not dormant bodies but are in constant motion. If the movements of the water are on established lines they are referred to as marine currents. The causes of these currents are very different. The most important factors affecting marine currents are wind, density variations within the water masses, and differences in the heat flow between water and atmosphere. When these factors occur in combination they may serve to reinforce one another as well as to neutralize one another.

For the most part the direction of individual ocean currents is determined by the earth's rotation, the shape of the continents, submarine ridges, and tidal currents. Owing to the multiplicity of determining factors, any estimate of the direction of the resulting marine current is extraordinarily complicated. The velocity of the ocean currents compared with those in rivers is substantially lower.

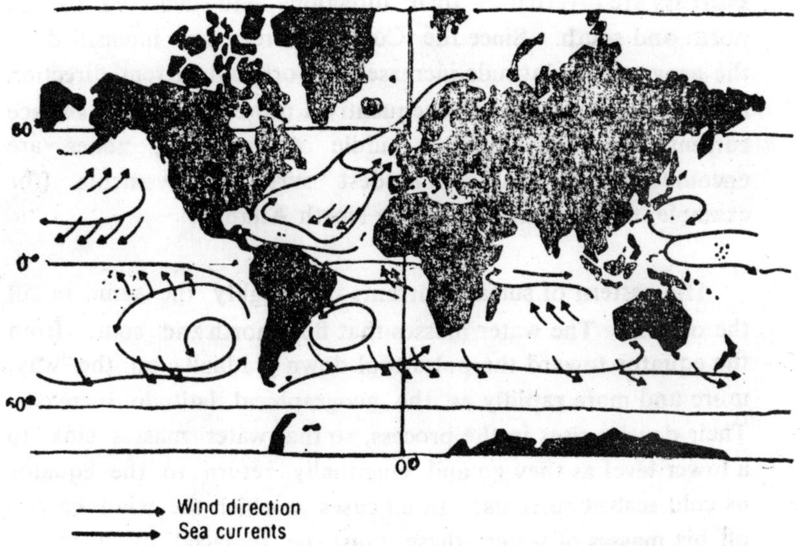

Fig. 1.6. The Principal Sea Currents and Direction of Winds.

It the wind sets the surface water in motion, the direction of the current does not necessarily follow that of the wind. Owing to the rotation of the earth and the Coriolis forces generated thereby, the currents in a particular sector are linked to the direction of the wind. In the northern hemisphere all the currents are deflected clockwise to the right, and in the southern hemisphere to the left. Since at the same time the prevailing winds are deflected likewise, the deflecting forces receive additional reinforcement. The deflection of the water currents is thus all the stronger the deeper the water columns are below the surface.

Basically, two types of marine currents are distinguished: surface currents and underwater currents. The most important surface currents are found in the equator belt between the northern and southern tropic zones. The northeast and southeast trade winds provide the motive force for these big equatorial currets. Between the individual continents these currents are diverted in their directions and deflected to the north and south. Since the Coriolis forces are intensified as the geographical latitude increases, the original current direction is gradually reversed. Consequently a powerful flow of surface currents develops. In the middle of the cycle, zones are encountered with relatively modest surface movements (for example, the Sargasso Sea in the North Atlantic).

The pattern of surface currents is roughly the same in all the oceans. The water masses that flow north and south from the equator toward the poles cool down gradually on the way, more and more rapidly as the geographical latitude increases. Their density rises in the process, so that water masses sink to a lower level as they go and enentually return to the equator as cold scabed currents. In all cases in which the wind carries off big masses of water, these must be replaced by a return fiow. This happens as a result of either an influx of surface water or an influx of water from a lower level. Water masses flowing toward the poles and so becoming cooler set off the deep-water currents.

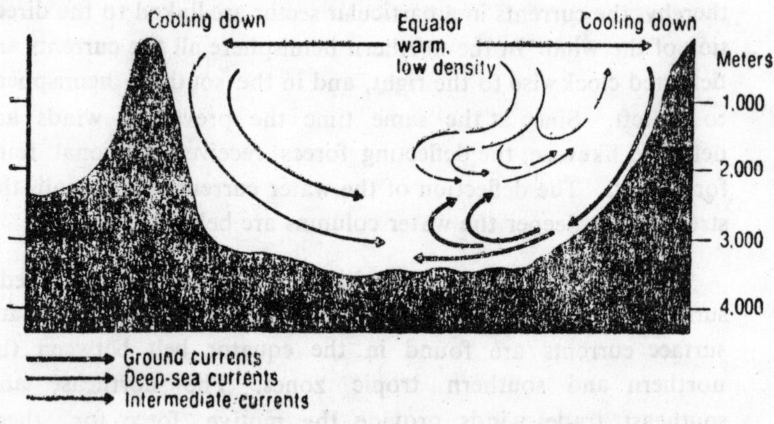

Fig. 1.7. Principal Currents Below the Surface (the Atlantic is taken as an example).

Regions in which surface currents combine to produce deep-water currents are known as convergence areas. Under the influence of surface, deep-water and seabed currents, a constant exchange of water masses develops in the course of time in all the big oceans.

Energy from the Sea

If it were possible to utilize a mere 0.5% of the head stored in the form of temperature differentials in the oceans of the world, man's energy problems would all be solved. This concept, however utopian it may sound, is not in fact utterly unrealistic. Sea-heat power plants fall within the field of technical possibility. The idea of utilizing the energy stored in the ocean is not new. It was first suggested in 1881 by the French physicist Jacques d' Arsonval. His fellow countryman George Claude erected the first sea-heat power plant in Cuba in 1929. Its power output then amounted to 22 kilowatts. Its performance was satisfactory, but it was uneconomical, as Claude's technical resources were inadequate. American environmental engineers have now developed the idea. Design work has begun at the University of Massachusetts for a sea-heat power plant to be erected in the Gulf Stream off the coast of south Florida.

The theory of a sea-heat power plant is as follows : between various water depths there is normally a temperature differential which can be utilized for energy production. In the tropics, that is between the celestial spheres of Cancer and Capricorn, the surface waters of the oceans have an almost unvarying temperature of 25°C (77°F) over the whole year. At a depth of 1000 meters (3200 feet) or so, on the other hand, the prevailing temperature is only 5°C (41°F). This temperature differential can be utilized as in conventional power plants by letting the liquid on the "warm side" evaporate or simmer. The steam drives a turbine and is condensed on the "cold side,"

As the heat differentials are in a narrow range, water is not suitable as a medium. First calculations indicate that propane gas would be a very suitable gas for circulation in seawater power plants. It boils at temperatures of under 25°C, and can return to liquid form at 5°C. The power plant could be installed on a floating island in the open sea.

Power plants of this kind could provide a realistic technical solution for the utilization of solar energy, for the water is heated by the sun, and the oceans serve as energy stores. The temperature differentials arise as a result of circulation between the poles and the tropics (see "Sea Currents" in Part Two).

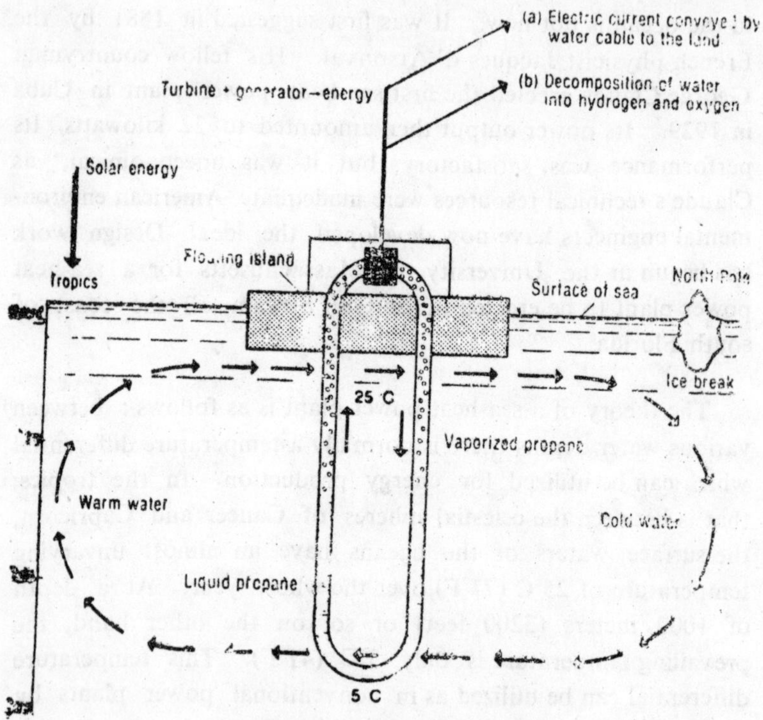

Fig. 1.8. Energy from the Sea.

Sea-heat power plants could also acquire much greater importance. The cold water pumped up from the depths of the sea could serve to do more than just cool the turbines. It still remains cool enough to condense water vapor drawn off from seawater into a vaccum chamber. In this way the power plant can extract drinking water from the sea. It is estimated that a plant with an output of 100 Mw of electric power could provide some 200 million liters of drinking water a day.

In contrast to the development of nuclear energy, especially by fast breeder reactors, no serious new technical problems are posed by this form of utilization of solar energy.

Tides

The periodic alternation of ebb and flow on the seacoast is caused by forces that, in addition to wind and the earth's rotation, are exerted by the influence of sun and moon on the water masses of the oceans.

The flow of the tides is highly complicated, and varies from place to place. Since the days of Isaac Newton the attraction forces of the sun and moon have been recognized as the cause of the movement of the tides. Their influence is vastly different in strength, however, and the stronger effect must be attributed to the moon.

Two separate lunar forces have to be distinguished; the attraction power of the moon and the centrifugal force arising from the rotation of the moon and the earth (at the same point of concentration). Whereas the centrifugal force remains constant at each point of the earth's surface, the attraction force of the moon changes in inverse ratio to the square of its distance from the earth. This means that the attraction force of the moon on the side of the earth facing away from the moon is less than that on the side of the earth facing it. The result of this is a horizontal force that tends to concentrate the water masses of the earth at two specific points, of which one is directly facing the moon and the other is on the precisely opposite side of the earth. At these two points (A and B in the diagram) tidal crests are thus produced. In consequence of the earth's rotation and of lunation (the approximately 29-day period between two successive new moons) in an ideal situation, these would travel round the earth in a period exactly corresponding to the length of a lunar day (24 hours 50 minutes).

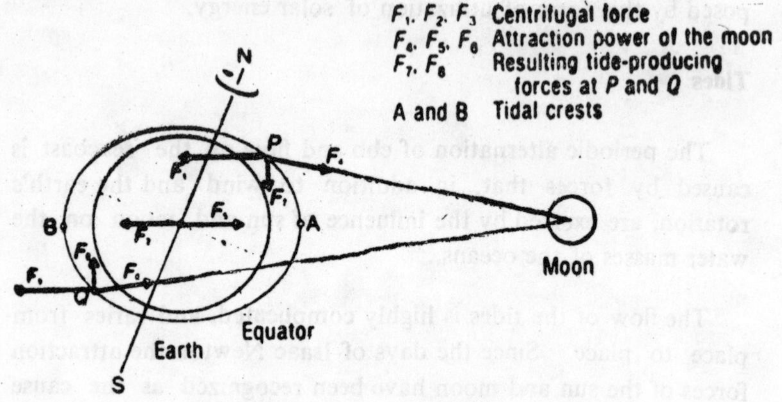

Fig. 1.9. Tide formation.

The sun two exerts tidal forces on the earth. The sun's mass is, of course, substantially greater than that of the moon, but it is also at a very much greater distance from the earth. Because of this, the tidal forces of the sun amount to only 46% of those of the moon.

The change of tidal forces in the course of a month emerges from the interplay of the forces of the sun and moon. Thus, the pull from the sun and the moon reach their peak at times of full and new moon and combine to produce spring tides. In the first and last quarters of the moon the orthogonal directions of their forces are directly opposed to one another, and so lead to a reduction of the tidal forces and result in the occurrence of neap tides. Spring tides and neap tides occur twice in the course of a lunar month.

The position of the continents prevents the tides from registering ideal periodic changes and so produces many irregularities. As the vast water masses, once they are in motion, record a natural period of oscillation, the periodic changes in the tides and the natural motion of the water can overlap and so produce very complicated tidal phenomena. On occasion this can result in resonances, which will produce a maximum expansion of the tidal range (up to 14 meters), as can sometimes happen on the coast of Brittany. In tidal power plants an attempt is made to use this energy for human needs.

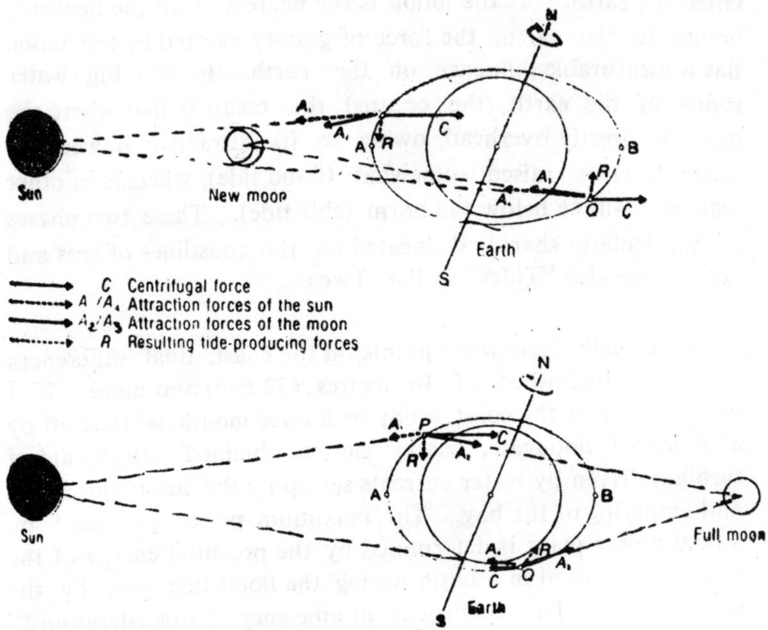

Fig. 1.10. Causation of spring tides by influence of the sun and moon.

Apart from the tidal forces, wind and air pressure have considerable influence on the extent of the tidal variations. Thus constant wind pressures are capable of producing independent tidal ranges of about 1 meter. Storm conditions sometimes give rise to extreme anomalies which manifest themselves as storm tides.

Tidal Power Plants

Tidal power plants are a particularly attractive way of utilizing the regenerative forces of nature for purposes of power production. Solar energy and lunar energy can be converted into electric power by this means in the same way as in a waterworks. The process extends over a period of 12 hours and 24 minutes, that is, half the period it takes the moon to circle the earth. As the moon is the nearest of all the heavenly bodies to the earth, the force of gravity exerted by the moon has a measurable influence on the earth. In the big water zones of the earth (the oceans) the result is that where the moon is directly overhead, owing to its attractive power, the water level is raised somewhat (flood tide), whereas in other regions it will be below the norm (ebb tide). These two phases are particularly sharply delineated on the coastlines of seas and oceans (see also "Tides" in Part Two).

At specially favorable points on the coast, tidal differences can be distinguished of 10 metres (32 feet) and more. If at such a point on the coast, a bay or a river mouth is shut off by a sluice of floodgate, energy can be obtained with the aid of turbines driven by water currents set up by the alternate filling and emptying of the bay. The maximum power produced by a tidal power plant is determined by the potential energy of the water mass stored in a basin during the flood tide and by the tidal period. The coefficient of efficiency of this energy utilization lies between 20% and 25%.

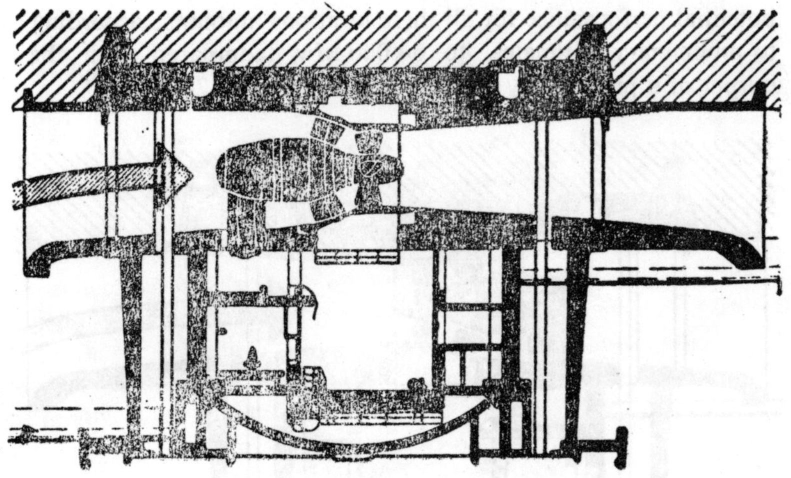

Fig. 1.11. Operation of a tidal power plant on a rising tide.

The pioneer in the erection of tidal power plants was West Germany. In the First World War a small tidal power station was in operation in Husum, using the flow and ebb of the current, in a former oyster-culture basin, in order to supply houses in the neighbourhood with electricity. The first big tidal power station came into operation in 1966 at the mouth of the river Rance in France. Today its output amounts to 240 megawatts, and should be raised eventually to 320 Mw, Altogether 10 tbrbines are set in a dam 750 meters long, and they work in both directions, using both the incoming and outgoing tides. The tidal range (the difference between high and low tide) averages about 10 metres, with a maximum of 13 meters. In 1968 a small plant of 400 kilowatts was started up in the USSR at the mouth of the Kislaya, 80 km northeast of Murmansk. A larger plant of 320 Mw is projected for the Lombowska River on the northeast coast af the Kola Peninsula.

The following table shows part of the power available on the earth from tidal energy. Possible performance in the various locations ranges from 2 to 20,000 Mw. The total potential performance for all these locations amounts, according to preliminary estimates, to 64.000 Mw (compared with the output of a present-day nuclear power plant of 1200 Mw).

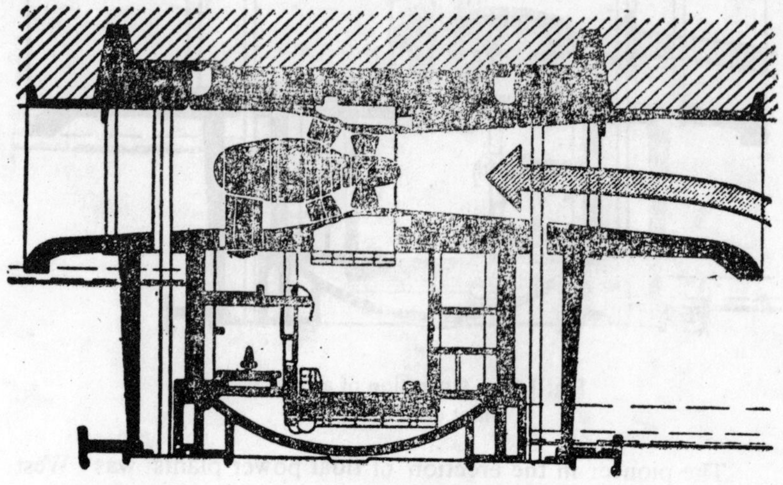

Fig. 1.12. Operational of a tidal power station when the tide begins to EBB.

Place or region	*Avevage potential output (Mw)*	*Possible annual power production (Mwh millions)*
North America		
Bay of Fundy (9 locations)	29,000	255
South America		
Argentina (San Jose)	6,000	52
Europe		
England (R Severn)	2,000	15
France (9 locations)	11,000	98
USSR (4 locations)	16,000	140

Glacier Power Plants

After many years research work in Arctic stations, where he was conversant with the structure and dynamics of the Greenland ice sheet, a Swiss hydrobiologist came up a short time ago with an unusual project for energy production. Enormous quantities of ice melt in Greenland every summer and run down into the sea from land 2000-3000 m (6500-9800 feet) lakh. If normal power stations were built on the coast in Greenland, enormous quantities of electric power could be produced by this means. The technology of the necessary hydraulic power stations would be standard, but the construction material for the dams and the supply and pressure, ducts would be something quite new, namely rock-hard glacier ice.

As the buggest island in the world, Greenland has a surface area of about 2 million sq km ((760,000 sq mi). On a conservative estimate something like 500,000 sq km (90,000 sq mi) would be available for the installation of storage basins. With the sun shining for about 2000 hours per annum, some 8 kwh of energy could be produced each year from 1 sq m of storage lake area. From the estimated 500,000 sq km of storage lake area, about 4000 billion kwh of useful energy should be obtainable each year. This represents an electric power output of about 200,000 Mw, approximating the output of 200 large atomic power stations. During the summer an extensive canal system, corresponding to a network of streams, would have to be built inside Greenland The ice melted by the suns heat would run along these canals into big storage lakes. In the course of the flow of the melted ice water, which would be warm compared with the ice it came into contact with the streams would expand of their own accord, so that relatively little technical energy would be required for the construction of the canal system. Owing to the differences in elevation from 2000 to 3000 m, the melted ice water would shoot through ducts from the storage lake down to normal, big hydraulic power stations installed on the coast. The storage lakes are required mainly to ensure that energy production will be available also in winter. In the winter a layer of ice 1 to 2 meters thick forms on the surface of the storage lakes and protects the water below from further freezing. The water below the layer of surface ice could thus be drawn off for energy production as required.

The necessary barrages, and the supply and pressure ducts, can be modeled by suitable techniques with the aid of the ice. Tested procedures already exist for the construction of ice channels in glaciers. By means of a circular cutting guide (a steel tube with an interfacing rotating saw tooth rim), cylinders, can be cut out of the glacier ice having a diameter of about 10 m (33 feet). With a subsidiary circular saw appliance the ice cylinder cut out lengthways can be split up into semicircular portions and lifted out on to the canal bank by means of a rotating table turned at an angle of 180°. These segments can be stacked together quite easily to form dams, whereupon they rapidly freeze up again.

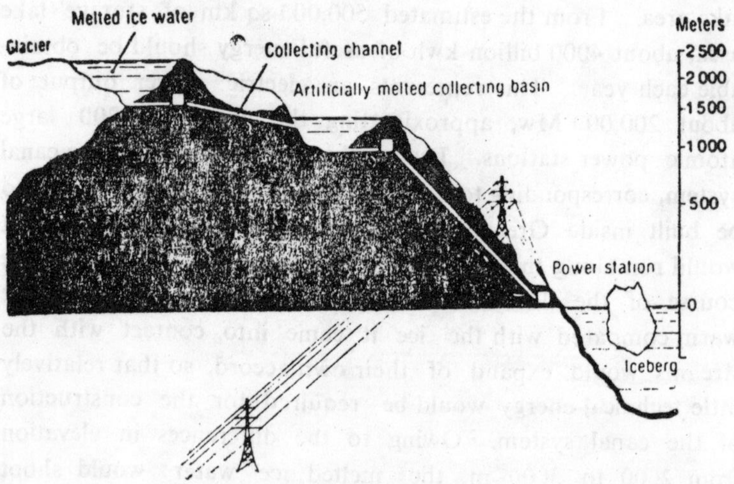

Fig. 1.13. Gracier power plant.

By means of such glacier power plants, cheap energy could be produced in large quantities without causing any pollution of the environment and without the consumption of law materials. For transmission of the energy there are two possibilities :

(1) The electric current produced can be conveyed directly by directly by submarine cable to North-America and Europe ; or

(2) this is probably the better solution, with the aid of the electric energy produced in the hydraulic power station the water can be split up into hydrogen and oxygen, and the hydrogen can be liquefied and conveyed by tanker to the country of consumption. It could then be used for heating, for driving advanced motor vehicles, or in fuel cells for electricity production.

Petroleum and Natural Gas -Their Origin and Formation

Petroleum and natural gas are the most important sources of energy and are the raw materials most in demand by the chemical industry today.

For the most part, petroleum comprises a mixture of several hundred or even thousand hydrocarbon constituents. In many cases these are the only constituents, while in others a large number of other organic compounds are present, such as oleic acid, asphaltene, gums and a variety of sulfur and nitrogen compounds. The vast proliferation of hydrocarbons stems from the tetravalence of carbon and its many possible compounds – in the form of chains of different lengths with single, double and triple bonds, of rings of different bond types and sizes and of the most varied bonding with one another: and it also allows the formation of side chains. Gums and asphaltenes are high-molecular-weight organic compounds, which give to the oils their dark color and increase their viscosity. The sulfur and nitrogen compounds are in the form of chains or rings, in which carbon atoms are replaced by sulfur or nitrogen atoms.

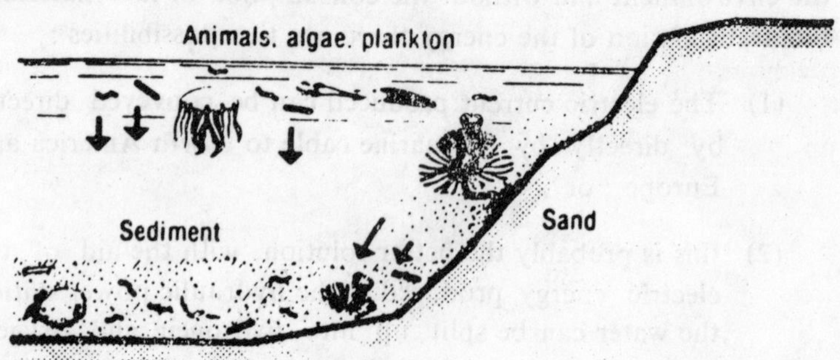

Fig. 1.14. Sedimentation

The explanation of how petroleum is formed is one of the most difficult problems encountered in geological research. Almost all the facts point to its organic development from decomposition products of p'ant and animal organisms that were deposited in the mud beds of waterways, were preserved there from immediate putrefaction by the lack of oxygen, and then formed rock bitumen. One problem regarding this explanation of the origin is that organisms are composed to a large extent of oxidized compounds, whereas petroleum consists of reduced (oxygen-free) compounds. Reduction is conceivable, however, only as a result of energy input. In the first phase of transformation at least, the necessary energy could not have been derived from the heat of the earth. as the petroleum would then still contain elements from the chlorophyll and blood pigment, which will not sustain a higher temperature than 200°C (424°F) and will persist only in an oxygen-free environment. One possible reaction. which also occurs in lower temperatures and is anaerobic (without free oxygen) is biological reduction by bacteria. In the sediment in water and in oil a whole series of anaerobic bacteria can be recognized that are able to reduce organic substances and to transform them into fatty acids, methane, and ethane, and also into other hydrocarbons. The hydrocarbons in question do not form petroleum, however.

The further transformation of the long-chain compounds (fatty acids) into petroleum with its light paraffins (5 - 7 carbon atoms) can occur only as lower temperatures and in the absence of active clays as catalyzers or at great depths under high pressures by thermal decomposition. Under this thermal decomposition or fission, long-chain hydrocarbons will be split up into methane and other light gaseous hydrocarbons.

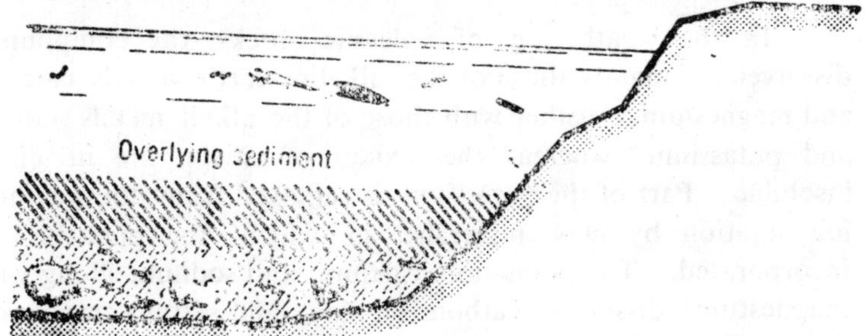

Fig. 1.15. Anaerobic Bacteria Decompose the Organisms Deposited

Natural gas is produced in the same way, but contains carbon dioxide, nitrogen hydrogen sulfide, and mixtures of rare gases in addition to hydrocarbons. A distinction is made here between dry gases, which consist almost exclusively of methane, wet gases (ethane, propane, butane. etc.), and acid gases with mixtures of hydrogen sulfide.

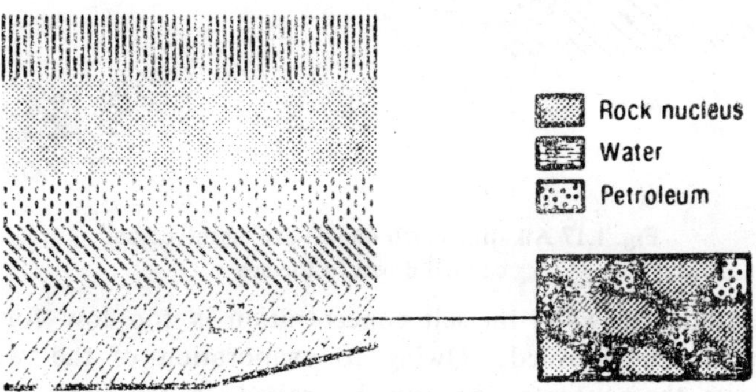

Fig. 1.16. Different deposits intensify the pressure

The formation of petroleum and natural gas thus pussibly represents a process that embraces some very different reactions (bacterial and thermal decomposition or fission) and extends over long periods. The formation of the most reeent petroleum fields dates back roughly one million years.

Salt Deposits

In the weathering of volcanic rocks, the compounds dissolved are mainly those of the alkaline-earth metals caicium and magnesium, together with those of the alkali metals sodium and potassium, whereas the oxides of silicon are in effect insoluble. Part of the potassium is removed from the weathering solution by clay minerals, in which the potassium is incorporated. The potassium, calcium and sodium, along with magnestum, dissolved carbon dioxide, and sulfur compounds, are carried down the rivers into the oceans, where they eventually form salts.

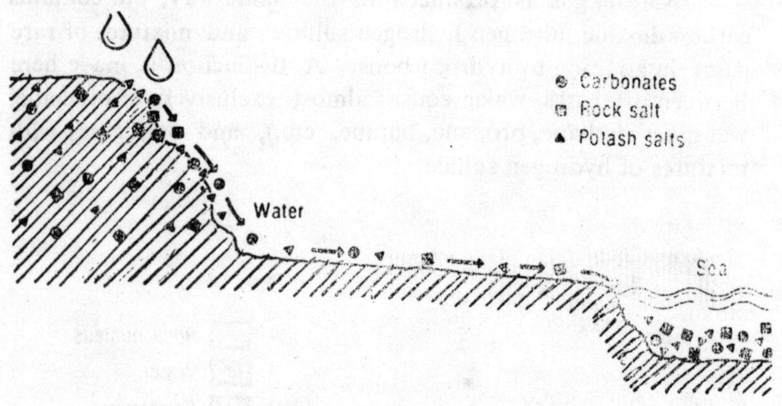

Fig. 1.17 Alkaline-earth metals are dissolved and carried down to the sce

In open seawater the salt concentration is too low for the salts to be deposited. Owing to evaporation of the water, howeve, the concentration can be raised to the limit, which results in the deposit of the precipitated salt. This presupposes the delimitation of sea basins, in which certain conditions must be present. The loss by evaporation must exceed the inflow of water. And the shores of the inlaud lake or of the sea bay must be so flat that no more material is fed into the basin from the land.

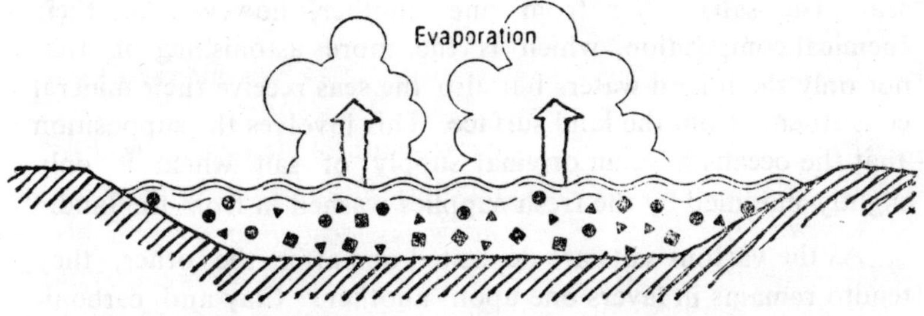

Fig. 1.18. A High Evaporation rate produces concentration of salt in waters with limited inflow

The first substances to settle are the least soluble carbonates and sulfates. This can also occur in very small concentrations biogenetically in the case of marine organsims which by their metabolism absorb the lime as a stroma (supporting tissue substance in their scales. Some 40 % of the seabed is covered with what is known as foraminiferal ooze, formed from the shells of dead protozoa and from clay substances. In the further process of deposit and sedimentation, rock salt is produced, and finally the most easily soluble potash salt.

The sinking of the bed of the basin, a rise in its shoreline and an inflow of new water masses will mean that the water formation process is repeated. The salt formation thus occurs only during a static phase in part of the earth's crust. In many regions several such cycles can occur in succession. The clays

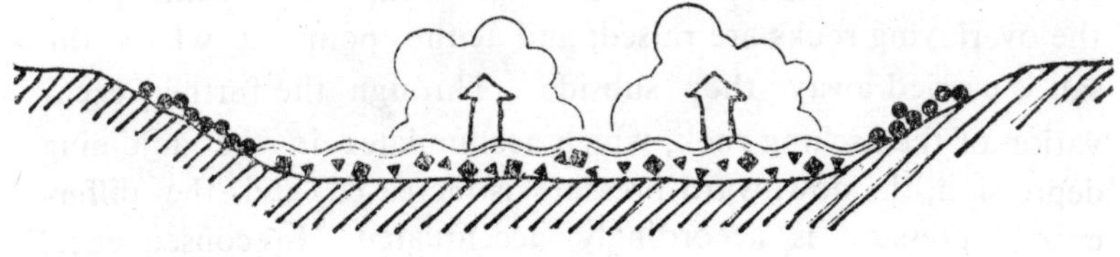

Fig. 1.19. Sedimentation of carbonates that are difficult to dissolve on the banks of the waters

washed into the basin at times of increased erosion of the surrounding land surfaces protect the salt deposits from being washed away.

Salt formation is possible both in inland waters and in the sea. The salts differ from one another, however, in their chemical composition, which is the more astonishing in that not only the inland waters but also the seas receive their mineral constituents from the land surface. This involves the supposition that the oceans have an original supply of salt which is only slightly modified by the fresh supplies washed in from the land.

As the various salts are deposited one after the other, they tendto remains in layers one upon another. Clay and carboniferous rocks are deposited first from the shore of the basin into the middle; sulfates and chlorides are deposited in the basin's interior. In this way salt basins are formed with their typical salt distributions.

Fig. 1.20. Complete sedimentations in zones of different Solubility.

From salt deposits, which are overlaid by sediment, salt masses can form. This depends on the fact that salt begins to flow even when there is very little difference in tension in the sediment. Differences in tension are produced, for instance, by movements in the earth's crust or differences in erosion levels in the overlying rocks. The salt then flows into zones of lower pressure, and accumulates to form salt cushions. At this point the overlaying rocks are raised; and at the point at which the salt is carried away they subside. Through the further excavation of the arching rock, which accumulates in the adjoining depression, the downward pressure is increased and the difference in pressure is accordingly accentuated. In consequence, further salt flows into to salt mass. This process can continue until such time as the salt has penetrated to the earth's surface.

2

Nature of the Oceanic Life

Introduction

The organisms of the sea are bore, live breathe feed, excrete, move, grow, matereproduce, and die within a single interconnected medium. Thus interactions among the marine organisms and interactions of the organisms with the chemical and physical processes of the sea range across the entire spectrum from simple, adamant constraints to complex effects of many subtle interactions. A general discussions of a living system should consider the ways in which plants elaborate basec organic material from inorgansc substances and the successixe and ofen highly intricate steps by which organisms then return this material to the inorganic reservoir. The discussion should also slow the forms of life by which such processes are conducted.

Some organic material is carried to the sea by rivers and some is manufactured in shallow water by attached plants. More than 90 % of the basic organic material that fuels and builds the life in the sea, however, is synthesized within the lighted surface layers of open water by the many varities of phytoplanleton. These sunny pastures of plant cells are grazed by the herbivorous zooplanteton and by some small fishes. These in turn are prey to various carnivorous creatures, large and small, who have their predators also. The debris from the activities in the surface layers settles into the dimly lighted and unlighted midlayers of the sea, the twilight mesopelasic zone and the midnight bathypelagic zone, to serve as one source of food for their strange inhabitants. This process depletes the surface layers of some food and particularly of vital plant nutrients, or fertilizers, that become trapped below the surface layers, where they are unavailable to the plants. Food and nutrients are also actively carried down ward from the surface by vertically migrating animals. The depleted remnants of this constant "rain" of detritus continue to the sea floor and support those animals that live just above the bottom, on the bottomand burrowed into the botrom. There filter-feeding and burrowing animals and bacteria rework the remaining refractory patricles.

The more active animals also find repast in mid water creatures and in the occasional falls o` carcasses and other larger debris. Except in unusual small areas there is an abundance of oxygen in the deep water. And the solid bottom presents advantages that allow the support of a denser populations of larger creatures than can exist in deep mid water. In shallower water such as banks, atolls, continental shelves and ahllows seas conditions ociatedted with a solid bottom and other regional modifications of general regime enable rich populations to develop. Such areas constitute about 7% of the total area of the ocean. In some of these regions added food results from the growth of larger fixed plants and from land drainage.

The cycle of life in the sea, llke that on land, is fueledby the sun's visible light acting on green plants. Of every million photons of sunlight reaching the earth's surface, some 90 enter into the net production of basic food Perhaps so of the 90 contribute to the growth of the land plants and about 40 to the growth of the single-celled green plants of the sea, the photoplankton. It is this minute fraction of the suns radiant energy that supplies the living organisms of this planet not only with their food but also with a breathable atmosphere. The terrestrial and marine plants and animals arose from the same sources, through similar evoluttionary sequence and by the action of the same natural laws.

In some important respects this imaginarys condition is not unlike that of the dominant, food web of the sea, where almost all marine like is substained by microscopic plants and near-microscopic harbivore 45 and carnivorous, which pass on only a greatly diminised supply of food to sustain the larger, more active and more complex creatures. In other respects the analogy is substantially inaccurate, because the primary marine food production is carried out by celles dispresed widely in a dense fluid medium this fact of an initial dispersal imposes a set of profound general conditions on all forms of life in the sea. In modrately rich areas of the sea, food is 100th times more dilute in volume and hundreds of thousands of time more dilute in relative mass. To cropthis meagre both a blind herbiuore or a simple pore in a filtering structure would need to process a weight of water hundreds of thousands of times the weight of the cell if eventuarlly captures. In even the densest concentrations the factor execds several thousands and with each further step in the food wed dilution increases. Thus from the beginnings of the marine food web we see many adaptations accommodating to this dilution: eyes in microscopic herbivorous animals. Filters of exquisite design, mechanisms and behavious for discovring local concentrations, complex search gear and, on the bottom. Attachments to elicit the aid of moving water in carring out the task of filtration. All these adoptations stem from the conditions that limit plant life in the open sea to microscopic dimentions. It is in the sunlight near surface of the open sea that the unique nature of the dominant system of marine life is i revocably molded. The near-surface, or mixed, layer of the sea varies in thickness from tens of feet to hundreds depending on the nature of the general circulation, mixing by winds and heating. Gear the basic food production of the sea is accomplished by single-called plants.

One common group of small phytoplankton are the coccolithophores, with calcareous plants. A swimming ability and often an oil droplet for food storage and bouyancy. The larger microscopic phytoplankton are composed of many species belonging to several groups : naked algal cells, diatoms with complex shells of silica and activity swimming and rotating flagellates. Very small forms of amny groups are also abundant and collectively are called nannoplankton. The species composition of the phytoplankton is everywhere complex and varies from place to place, season to season and year to year. The various regions of the ocean are typified, however, by dominant major groups and particular species, seasonal effects are often strong, with dense blooms of phytoplankton occuring when high levels of plant nutrients suddenly become usable or available, such as in high latitudes in spring or along coasts at the on set of upwelling. The concentrations of phytoplankton varies on all dimensional scales, even down to small patches.

In addition the large scale circulation of the ocean continuously sweeps the pelagic plants out of the region to which they are best adapted. It is essential that some individuals be returned to renew the populations. More mechanisms for this essential return exist for single-celled plants than exist for large plants or even for any conventional spores, seeds or juveniles. Any of these can be carried by oceanic gyres or diffused by large-scale motions of surface eddies and periodic counter flow, but single-celled plants can also ride submerged counter currents while temporarily feeding on food particles or perhaps dissolved organic material. Other mechanisms of distribution undoubtely are also occasionally important. For example, living marine plant cells are carried by stormborne spray. In bird feathers and by wellfed fish and birds in their undigested food. No large plant has solved the many problems of development, dispersla, and reproduction. There are no pelagic trees, and these several factors in concert therefore restrict the open sea in a prodound way. They confine it to an initial food web composed of microscopic forms, whereas larger plants live attached only to shaollow bottoms. Attached plants, unlike free-floating plants, are not subject to the afore mentioned limitations. For attached plants all degrees of water motion enhance the exchange of nutrients and wastes. Although species of phytoplankton will populate only regions with conditions to which they are adapted, factors other than temperature, nutrients and light levels undoubtedly are important in determining the species composition of phyteplankton populations. Little is understood of the mechanisms that give rise to an abundance of particular species under certain conditions. Grazing herbivores may consume only a parts of the size range of cells. Allowing certain sizes and types to dominate temporarily. Little is understeed of the mechanisms that give rise to an abundance of particular species under certain conditions, Chemical by-products of certain species probably exclude certain other species. Often details of individual cell behavior are probably also important in the introduction and success of a species in a particular area. In some cases we can glimpse what these mechanisms are for example, both the larger diatoms and the larger flagellates can move at appreciable velocities through the water. The diatoms commonly sink downward, whereas the flagellates actively swim upward toward light. These are probably patterns of behavior primarily for increasing exchange But the interaction of such unidirectional motions with random turbulance or systematic convective motions is not simple, as it is with an in a inactive particle. Rather, we would expect diatoms to be statistically abundant in upward moving water and to sink out of the near surface layers when turbulance or upward convection is low.

Conversely, flagellates should be statistically more abundant in down welling water and should concentrate near the surface in low turbulance and slow sownward water motions. These effects seem to exist. Of some continental coasts in summer flagellates may eventually collect in high concentrations. As they begin to shade one to another from the light, Each individual struggles close to the lighted surface. Producing such a high density that large areas of the water are turned red or brown by their pigments. The concentration of flagellates in these "Red Tides" sometimes becomes too great for their own survival. Several specia of flagellates also become highly foxic as they grow older. Thus they sometimes both produce and participate in a mass death of fish and invertibrates that has been on own to give rise to such a high yield of hydrogen sulfide as to blaken the white houses of castal cities. Large diatom cells, on the other hand, sperd a disproportionately greater time in upward moving regions of the water and an unlimited time in any region where the upward motion about equals their own downward motion. Diatom cells are there statistically abundant in upwelling water, and the distribution of diatoms probably is often are flection of the trubutant-convective region of the water. Sinking and the dependance of the larger diatomes on upward convection and turbulance for support aids item in reaching upwelling regions, where nutrients are high, it helps to emplain their dominance in such regions and such other features of their distributions as their high proportion in rich ocean regions and their frequent inverse occurance with flagellates. Differences in adaptations to the physical and chemical products, probably reinforce such relations.

In some areas, such as parts of the equatorial current system and shallow seas. Where lateral and vertical circulation is rapid, the species composition of phytoplankton is perhaps more simply a result of the inherent ability of the species to grow, survive and, reproduce under the local conditions of temperature, light, nutrients, competitors and herbivores. Elsewhere second-order effects of the detailed cell behavior often dominate. Those details of behavior that give rise to concentration on any dimensional scale are particularly important to all subsequent steps in the food chain. The grazing of the phytoplankton it principally conducted by the herbivorous members of thet zooplankton. A hetrogenous group of small animals tha carry out several steps in the food web as herbivores, carnivores and detrital feeders. Among the important members of the zooplankton are the arthopods, animals with external skeletons that belong to the same broad groups as insects, crabs and shrimps. The planktonic arthopods induce the abundant copepods, which are in a sense the maring equivalent of insects. Copepods are represented in the sea by some 10,000 or more species that act not only as herbivores. Carnivores or detrital feedeıs but also as external or even internal parasites' two or three thousand of these species live in the open sea. Other important arthropods are the shrimp like euphausidis, the strongest vertical migrators of the zooplankton. They compose the vast shoals of krill that occur in high latitudes and that constitute one of the principal foods of the baleen whales.

The zooplankton also include the strange bristle-jawed chateognaths or arrow worms, carnivores or mysterious origin and affinities know only in the marine environment. Widely distributed and abundant. The chaetognaths are represented by a surprisingly small number of species. Perhaps fewer than 50. Larvae of many types, worms, medusae, ctenophores, gastropods, pteropods and heteropods, salps, unpigmented flagellates and many others are also important components of this milieu. Each with its own remarkably complex and often bizarre life history, behavior and form. The larger zooplankton are mainly carnivores, and those of herbivores habit are restricted to feeding on the larger plant cells. Much of the blood supply, however, exists in the form of very small particles such as the nanoplankton, and these appear to be available almost solely to microscopic creatures. Eyesight has developed in many minute animals to make possible selective capture. A variety of vebs, bristles, rakes, combs, cilia and other structures are found, and they are often sticky. Stickiness allows the capture of food that is finer than the interspaces in the filtering structures, and it greatly reduces the expenditure of energy. A few groups have developed extremely fine and apparently quite effective nets. One group that has accomplished this is the "Larvacea". A larvacian produces and inhabits a complex external "House", much larger than its owner. That contains a system of very finely constructed nets through which the creature maintains a gentle flow. The larvacea have apparently solved the problem of energy loss in filtering by having proportionalely large nets; fine strong threads and a low rate of flow.

The composition of zooplankton differs from place to place, day to night, season and year to year, yet most species are limited in distribution, and the members of planktonic communities commonly show a rather stable representation of the modes of life. The zooplankton are, of course, faces with the necessity of maintaining breeding assemblages and like the phytoplankton. With the necessity of establishing a reinoculation of parent waters. In addition, their behavior must lead to a correspondense with their food and to the pattern of large-scale and small scale spottiness already imposed on the marine relean by the phytoplankton. The swimming powers of the larger zooplankton are quite adequate for finding local small-scale patcho of food. That this task is accomplished on a large scale is indirectly demonstrated by the observed correspondence between the quantities of zooplankton and the plant nutrients in the surface waters. There are many large and small puzzles in the distributions of zooplankton. As an ex-dense concentra tions of phytoplankton are often associated with low populations of zooplankton. These are probably rapidly growing blooms that zooplankton have not yet invaded and grazed on, but it is not completely clear that this is so. Chemical repulsion may be involved. The concentration of larger zooplankton and small fishes in the surface layers is much greater at night than during the day, because of a group of strongly swimming members that share their time between the surface and the mesopelagic region. Many small zooplankton organisms also make a daily migration of some vertical extent.

In addition to its primary purpose daily vertical migration undoubtedly served the (migration) migrating organisms in a number of other ways. It enables the creatures to adjust their mean temperature. So that by spending the days in cooler water the amount of food used during rest is reduced. Perhaps such processes as the rate of egg development are also controlled by these tactics. Convincing arguments have also been presented to show that vertical migration serves to maintain species so that they will be more successful under many more conditions than if they lived solely in the surface layers. This migration must also play an important part in the distribution of many species. Interaction of the daily migrants with the water motion produced by daily land-sea-breeze alternation can old the migrants offstore by a kind of "Rectification" of the oscillating water motion. More generally descent into the (water) lower layers in creases the influence of submerged counter currents. There by enhancing the opportunity to regions and hence to find high nutrient levels and associated high phytoplankton productivity. Even minor details of behavior may strongly contribute to success. Migrants spend the day at a depth corresponding to relatively constant low light lwves, where the moment of water commonly is different from that at the surface. Most of the members rise some what even no the passage of cloud shadow.

The principal food supplies of the pelagic populations are passed on in incremental steps and rapidly depleted quantity to the larger carnivores, zooplankton, then to small fishes and squids, and ultimately to the wide renge of larger carnivores of the pelagic realm.

The pelagic region contains some of the largest and most superbly designed creatures ever to inhabit this earth : The exquisitely constructed pelasic tunas. The multicolored dolphin fishes, capturers of flying fishes; the conversational purposes; the shallow and deep feeding swordfishes and toothed whales, and the greatest carnivores of all, the baleen whales and some plankton eating sharks. Whose prey are entire schools of krill or small fishes. Seals and sealions feed far into the pelagic realm. In concert with these great predators, large cornivorous sharks a wait injured prey. Marine birds, some adapted to almost continuous pelagic life, consume surprising quantities of ocean food, diving, plunging, skimming and gulping in pursuit. These larger creatures of the sea commonly move in schools, shoals, and herds. In addition to meeting the needs of mating such grouping is advantageous in both defensive and predatory strategy. Small fishes of several species commonly school together. Diverse predators also form loosely cooperative groups, and many species of marine birds depend almost whooly on prey driven to the surface by submerged predators. At night, schools of prey and predators are almost always spectacularly illuminated by bioluminescence produces by the microscopic and larger plankton. The reason for the ubiquitous production of light by the micro-organisms of the sea remains obscure, and suggested explanations are controversial. It has been suggested that light is a kind of inadvertent byproduct of life in transparent organisms. It has also been hypothesized that the emission of light on disturbance is advantageous to the plankton in making the predators of the plankton conspicuous to their predators.

The fall out of organic material into the deep dimly lighted mid water supports a sparse population of fishes and invertibrates with in the mesopelagic and bathypelagic zones are found some of the most curious and bizarre creatures of this earth. These range from the highly developed and powerfully predators intruters, toothed whales and sword fishes, at the climax of the food chain to the remarkable squids, octopuses, euphausidis, lantern fishes, gulpers and angler fishes that in habit the bathypilagic region. In the mesopelagic region, where some sunlight penetrates, fishes are often countershaded, that is, they are darker above and lighter below. As are surface fishes. Many of the creatures of this dimly lighted region participate in the daily migration. Swimming to the upper layers at evening like bath emerging from their caves. There are some much larger stronger and more active fishes and squids in this region, although they are not taken in trawls or seen from submersibles. Knowledge of their evidence comes mainly from specimens found in the stomach of sperm whales and sword fish. There is evidence that the sperm whales posses highly developed long-range hunting sonar. They may locate their prey over relatively great distances. Perhaps miles, from just such an extremely sparse population of active bathypelagic animals. Although many near-surface organisms are luminescent. It is the bathypelagic region that bioluminescence has reached a surprising level of development. With at least two-thirds of the species producing light. Clearly bioluminessence can be valuable to higher organisms, and the creatures of the bathypelagic realm have developed light-producing organs and structures to a high degree.

Strong fishes may confuse predators by "target alteration" effects or by producing residual images in the predators vision. Some squids and shrimps are more direct and discharge luminous organs are arrangedon some fishes so that they can be used to countershade their siltouettes against faint light comming from the surface. Lights may also be used for locating a mate. A problem of this vast, sparsely populated domain that has been solved by some angler fisnes by the development of tiny males that live parasitically attached to their relatively huge mates. Light level in the bathypelagic region can be much lower. This is most probably the primary difference that accounts for the absence of bioluminescence in higher land animals and the richness of Il's development in the ocean forms. There are some 2000. Species of the larger invertibrates lenown to inhabit the bathypelagic zone. But only 4 few of these species appear to be widespread. The barriers to distribution in this widely interconnected mid-water region are not obvious. The floor of the deep sea constitutes an environment quite unlike the mid-water and surface environments. There are sites for the attachment of the larger invertebrates that filter detritus from the water. Among these animals are representatives of some of the earliest multicelled creature to exist on the earth glass sponges, sea littles -- once thought to have been long extinct -- and lamp shells.

Larger numbers of active fishes and other creatures are attracted to the bait almost immediately. It is prosaldy 1 fue that several rather independent branches of the food web coexist in support of the deep-bottom creatures : one the familiar rain of fine detitus, and the other the rare, widely separated falls of large food particles that are in excess of the local feeding capacity of the broadly diffuse bathypelagic population. Such falls would include dead whales, large sharks or other large fishes and fragments of these, the multitude of remnants that are left when predators attack a school of surface fish and now. Undoubtedly, garbage from ships and kills from underwater explosions. These sources result in an influx of high-grade food to the sea floor, and we would expect to find a population of active creatures adapted to its prompt discovery and utilization. Other sources of food materials are braided into these two extremes of the abyssal food web. There is the rather subtle downward diffusion of living and dead food that results initially from the daily vertical migration of small fishes and zooplankton near the surface. This migration appears to impress a sympathetic daily migration on the mid-water population down to great depths, far below the levels that light penetrates. Not only may such vertical migration bring feeble bathypelagic creatures near the bottom but also it accelerates in it self the flux of dead food material to the bottom of the deep sea.

Benthic animals are much more abundant in the shallower mater off continents, particularly offshore from large rivers. Here there is often not only a richer near-surface production and less hazardous journey of food to the sea floor but also a considerable input of food conveyed by rivers to the bottom. The deep slopes of river sediments wedges are typified by a comparatively rich population of burrowing and filtering animals that utilize this fine organic material. The shallo regions of such wedges are highly productive of active and often valuable marine organism. The botom is much more variable than the mid-warer zone is. There are as a result more environmental riches for an organism to occupy, and hence we see organisms that are of a wider range of from and habit. Aside from the wide range of form and fraction the benthic environment elicits from its inhabitants, there are more fundamental conditions that influence the nature and form of life there. For example—the dispersed food material setting from the upper layers becomes much concentrated against the sea floor.

In the mid-water environment most creatures must move by their own energies to seek food, using their own food stores for this motion. On the bottom, however, substantial water currents are present at all depths, and creatures can await the passage of their food.

Here large organisms can grow by consuming microscopic or even submicroscopic food particles. Clams, scallups, mussels, tube worms, barnacles and a host of other creatures that inhabit this zone have developed a wide range of extremely effective filtering mechanisms. Although the benthic environment enables the creatures of the sea to develop and major branch of the food web that is emancipated from succesive microscopic steps. This makes little difference to the food economy of the sea. The sea is quite content with a large population of tiny organisms. From man's stand poin, however, the shallow benthic environment is an unusually effective producer of larger creatures for his food, and he widely utilizes these resources.

In short, their is, of course, much to learn about all marine life. The basic processes of the food web, productivity, populations, distributions and the mechanisms of reinoculation, and the effects of intervention into these processes, such as pollution, artificial upwilling, transplantation, cultivation and fisheries.

To learn of these processes and effects we must understand the (structure) nature not only of strong simple actions. But also of weak complex interactions, since the forms of life or the success of a species may be determined by extremely small second and their order effects.

In a synopsis wap we can also say that the possible benefits of broad marine-biological understanding are endless Man's aesthe tic, advanturous, recreational and practical proclivities can be richly served.

3

Concepts in Marine Pollution

Introduction

The International Oceanographic Commission (IOC) for the United Nations Educational and Scientific Commission (UNESCO) defines marine pollution as : "Introduction by man, directly or indirectly, of substances into the marine environment (including estuaries) resulting in such deleterious effects as harm to living resources, hazards to human health, or hindrance to marine activites and reducti~n of amenities. " If we allow broad interpretation of the word "substances" this definition appears to be all-encompassing. Note however the strong contrast between the dictionary and UNESCO definitions. The connotation of the oceanographers is that unless man introduces the pollutant, there is on pollution. Apparently the inference is that if pollution is man-caused it can be man-cured.

Nearly 71% of the earth's surface is covered by oceans, which together comprise a total of approximately 1.37×10^{39} litres, weighing about 1.40×10^{36} metric or long tons. This is the tremendous amount of water and consequently for many years the oceans are regarded an ideal place to dump all of man's wastes. For example, the rivers of the world discharge close to 2×10^{14} metric tons of water into the ocean every year but this is much smaller than the water already into the oceon. Carried along with the water each year are 4.5×10^{11} metric tons of dissolved matreials. Although this is a large amount of material compared to that already present it is literally a drop in the bucket. Unfortunately, the ocean does not receive all of its dissolved material input form the world's rivers. Some comes from the atmosphere as it is washed by falling rain. Most of the pollutants placed into the atmosphere and up in the oceans either directly or indirectly form precipitation. This also is a sizeable amount of material. It is to be noted that this is larger than the amount of sediment plus the amount of dissolved materials carried to the oceans by rivers.

The more important reason for being concerned about marine pollution stems form the fact that materials put into the oceans by man's activities is not evenly spread throughout the oceanic volume, pollution is generated where man lives and works and therefore finds its way for the most part into the oceanic areas that are closest to their activities. Consequently, the dilution factor is very small and the concentrations of these pollutants build up in coastal regions. They are increased to a much higher level than would be the case if the material were distributed throughout the entire oceanie volume.

Coastal are dumping grounds area having a much higher pollution concentration not only because the material is being put into these relatively shallow areas much more rapidly than it is being carried away by natural weve nations but also because the normal structure of the oceans tends to prevent the mixing of these inputs with the rest of the oceanic volume.

The oceans are not dead from pollution, not are they insensitive to the effects of pollutants. As long as we find it necessary to use the sea for a world dump, and there is no reason to believe we will ever stop, we must learn as much as we can about oceanic processes so that the assimilative capacity of the oceans is never exceeded.

Strictly speaking marine pollution may also be of natural origin. For example, it may be caused by underwater gas and oil eruptions, or by the intensive growth and subsequent death of certain micro-organisms, which are responsible for the familiar disastrous 'red tides' However, such processes and effects are not regarded as 'pollution', even though the are often studied by methods similar or those used for investigaing pollution effects caused by man.

Ecological studies on marine pollution fall into three principal categories :

(1) Biogeochemistry of pollutants.

(2) Marine ecotoxicology.

(3) Biological principles of anti-pollution measures.

The biogeochemistry of toxicants includes the investigation of the sources of pollutants, the pathways along which they enter the marine environment, patterns of accumulation in the biotic and abiotic components of ecosystems, mechanisms and rates of migration of pollutants, their transformations and other processes which determine the fate of toxicants in the sea. An important, thogh not decisive stage in such investigations is the determination of the cotent of toxicants in marine organisms and communities; this is a difficult analytical problem because the chemical composition of matter is complex, while the concentration levels of pollutants are low. The methods of chemical oceanography are used in order to obtain and analyse samples, the results being interpreted in a biogeochemical sense.

The second type of research work carried out on this problem, which is best described as 'marine ecotoxicology', involves the study of biological effects and consequences of human interference with the composition of the marine environment. Finding answere to such questions, is not by itself tantamount to solving the problem of pollution, but nevertheless yields an odjective evaluation of present-day ecological anomalies in the World Ocean and prediction of those likely to occur in the future. These investigations provide a scientific fnoudation on which to base national or international efforts to preserve the seas from pollution.

Solutions of the immediate practical problems concerning pollution of the sea must be based on the results of closely interlinked ecotoxicological and biogeochemical studies.

Marine Pollutants

In Table 2.1 a list of common pollutants associated with the marine environment have been given These are not listed in any particular order of importance because it is found that in certain areas certain pollutants arc more worrisome than others, while the opposite condition may be true in other areas. This differenc in importance comes from local conditions like population pressure, flushing, and climate.

Theoretical calculations of the concentrations of the principal toxicants in epipelagic waters of the World Ocean indicate that considerable pollution (lead pollution, in particular) of surface waters by atmospheric pollutants may have taken place. This is true of inland seas.

The global pollution zone of the marine environment may be characterised as follows: highest pollution levels in the euphotic layer; high pollution levels in the neritic zone and

TABLE 2.1

Pollutants Associated with the Marine Environment

Pathogens	Toxic organics
Sediments	Petroleum
Solid wastes	Nutrients
Heat	Radioactive materials
Fresh water	Oxygen demand materials
Brine	Acids and bases
Toxic inorganics	Aesthetically displeasing materials

inland seas; latitudinal distribution of toxic pollutants; a mosaic distribution pattern of toxicant concentrations in water; localisation of toxicants in the hyponeuston and benthos biotope; and a coincidence of the maximum pollution zones with zones of high biomass and high productivity.

Before we discuss the marine pollutants one by one, we shall give some general conclusions about these :

(1) The rate of biological accumulation and migration of micro-amounts of metals and radionuclides in the World Ocean is directly correlated with their physichcocmical properties and with the specific surface area of aquatic organisms.

(2) Concentrations of metals in sea water and in plankton tend to decrease with increasing atomic number of the metal.

(3) The relative content of artificial radionuclides in oceanic seston does not exceed 1 per cent of their total content in water; the corresponding figure for heavy metals and transition is 1 – 10 per cent, while in inland seas it may be as high as 25 per cent.

(4) The forms of microcomponents in sea water are largely determined by the supersaturation of surface water by calcium carbonate, since the suspended and the colloidal forms of this compound are strong sorbents.

(5) Self-purification of surface waters by biosedimentation of impurities is mostly due to their accumulation in aquatic organisms at low trophic levels. If the accumulation factor in seston is 1000-10000, the rate of vertical biogeochemical migration of a given impurity is of more or less the same order of magnitude as the rate of its hydrological transport (for biomasses and productivities considered as average for the World

Ocean). This is true of many radionuclides (^{144}Ce, ^{95}Zr, ^{106}Ru, ^{65}Zn, ^{54}Mn, etc.), of heavy metals and transition metals present in microamounts (mercury, leads, cadmium, iron, zinc, etc.) and chloro-organic compounds (DDT, PCB, aldrin, lindane, etc.).

(6) The rate of input of petroleum and chloro-organic toxicants into the World Ocean is faster than their rate of decomposition under natural conditions. The degradation processes are particularly slow at great depths, and the latter must be considered as a depot of toxic substances and their metabolites.

(7) A typical feature of the geochemical behaviour of petroleum and chlorinated hydrocarbons in the World Ocean is that their distributions in biotic and abiotic components of the same ecosystem are altogether different.

(8) The contemporary radio-ecological status of the World Ocean is distinguished by the relatively stable contents of ^{90}Sr and ^{137}Cs in surface waters and in aquatic organisms. Another typical feature is the gradual increase of radionuclide contents in the ecosystems of inland seas.

(9) The concentration levels of artificial radionuclides (^{90}Sr and ^{137}Cs), heavy metals (mercury, lead and cadmium) and chloro-organic compounds (DDT, polychlorinated biphenyl, etc.) in commercially important marine products vary with the degree of pollution of marine biotopes, taxonomic identity of the organisms, and their ecological and physiological characteristics (trophic level in the community, diet, age, zinc, etc.).

The most variable concentrations in industrial species are typical of substances with cumulative properties, DDT and DDT metabolites, polychlorinated biphenyls and other chloro-organic compounds, and methyl mercury.

(10) There is a generally valid relationship (a direct collelation in the case of radionuclides) between the concentration levels of toxicants in commercial animals and the pollution level of the marine environment as shown by the increasing sequence of pollutant concentrations : pelagic ocean waters, neritic zone, inland seas, freshwater basins.

(11) Typical accumulation factors of ^{90}Sr and ^{137}Cs in comercial species are of the order 10^1-10^2 for heavy metals 10^0-10^3, and for chloro-organic compounds 10^3-10^4. The food chain effect - *i.e.*, the dependence of the toxicant concentration in a given organism on the trophic level of the organism in the community— is definitely present only in the cases of mercury, polychlorinated biphenyls, DDT and other chloro-organic compounds. The contents of mercury and of chloro-organic compounds in fish show a regul r increase with the size (weight, age) of the animal.

(12) The selective, irreversible accumulation of high concentration of mercury in pelagic predatory fish and marine mammals is a natural process, and is not usually due to human factors.

(13) The distribution of taxicants in the organs and tissues of commercial fish species is typically non-homogeneous. ^{90}Strontinum, lead and cadmium become preferentially concentrated in ligaments and bones; chloro-organic substances and methyl mercury concentrate in the liver and in the lipid fractions; ^{137}caesium concentrates in muscles. Chloro-organic compounds concentrate in facty tissuer.

(14) Global concentration levels of radioactive and chemical toxicants in commercial marine products are usually much lower than the national and international norms for maximum permissible concentrations, and thus present no danger to human health. However, in view of the possibility of local pollution and human interference with the natural background of micro-components in individual regions, concentrations of toxicants in commercial species and marine products must continue to be constantly monitored, especially for heavy metals and chloro-organic compounds.

(15) Generally speaking, monocellular algae my react to the presence of toxic components in the aqueous medium in two different ways :

(a) By inhibition of vital processes and production.

(b) By stimulation of cell development and cell division, which is usually followed by imapired vital activities.

The development of micro-algae is relatively independent of the presence of the toxicant in the medium.

(16) The inhibitory effect of the pollutants increases in the following sequence : oil, detergents, metals, (arsenic, iead cadmium, copper, mercury, methyl mereury), chloro-organic compounds. The most highly toxic compounds are DDT, polychlorinated biphenyls, mercury and methyl meecury, which inhibit photosynthesis in long-term experiments at concentration as low as 1–10 μg/l. Arsenic, when present as arsenate ion in concentrations of up to 1—10 mg/l, had no effect on the rate of division of algae cells.

(17) Low concentrations of toxicants (0.1–10μg/l) acting for a short period of time tend to stimulate photosynthesis

and the rate of cell division in algae. This may be caused by the overall activation of vital processes by small doses of poisons or by an alteration of the metabolic interrelationships with the cells of the microflora. In the case of petroleum products such a stimulation may be due to the presence of biologically active substances in petroleum.

(18) Toxic (algicidal) and threshold concentration ranges are determined for various types and species of monocellular algae. Out of the several combinations of the effects of several factors studied, synergistic effects were observed for the combinations of petroleum with DDT, and combinations of certain metals with a detergent. A combined effect of several metals may be additive, or else may be manifested by a dominant inhibitory effect of the most tovic one (mercury, copper).

(19) The varying respones of different monocultured species to toxic impurities in short-term experiments (less than one day) are probably due to the differing rates of absorption and penetration of toxicants into the cells. In long-term experiments the specific differences are usually much smaller and depend on molecular, cellular and tissue level mechanisms. A general characteristic is the better resistance of freshwater protococcal algae to most pollutants, as compared with cultured marine phytoplankton forms.

(20) Of the species studied, Gyrodinium fissum in highly sensitive to mercury, the response being irreversible; the same applies to diatomous algae acted upon by a mixture of DDT and petroleum products.

(21) The inhibition of photosynthesis is a more sensitive reactions of monocellur algae to toxicity than is the decrease in the rate of cell division.

(22) The general picture of the effects and relative toxicities of the most common toxicants on natural communities of marine phytoplankton does not significantly differ from that obtained for cultures of single species.

(23) In a number of cases the intensity of photosynthesis of natural phytoplankton communities decreases in the presence of lower toxicant concentrations than in experiments carried out on monocultures. The higher sensitivity of natural phytoplakton to contaminats is probably due to interference with the interspecies relotionships in the community.

The considerable geographic, seasonal and other fluctuations in the reaction of natural phytoplankton to the presence of toxicants are caused not only by the environmental factors, but also by the special features of its specific composition. This composition undergoes significant changes if the action of the contaminants on the phytoplankton is sufficiently prolonged. Nitzschia diatoms in marine phytocoenoses are more resistant than other species to certain heavy and transition. metals,

Pathogens

The pathogenic materials are the living organisms that can produce sickness or biological unbalance in either plants or animals within the ocean itself or in humans who either come into contact with oceanic waters or eat the organisms caught in the water. These include a wide variety of bacteria, protozoa, viruses and fungi. The most common of these are normally found in sewage. However, other pathogens may occur in non-waste disposal areas where environmental conditions are such that the proper conditions exist for growth and reproduction.

Sediments

Sediments are always present to some extent in the marine environment. These sediments have a marked effect on plant growth because they block out a large portion of the light normally reaching greater depths and therefore decrease photosynthetic activity. In some case rooted plants get completely destroyed by this process.

As sediments are deposited on the bottom they will cover up bottom dwelling organisms (benthos) such as oysters and may even smother them under extreme conditions. The deposited sediments tend to make the water shallower so that, in regions traversed by ships, periodic dredging is needed.

Solid Waste

The disposal of solid waste has been a critical urban problem because areas suitable for the dumping of these valuminous materials are becoming scarcer. Due to this reason the ocean has been used as a dumping ground for solid waste. The solid waste most frequently marine dumped is sludge material left over as a byproduct from domestic sewage treatment. However, the unused products of industry and the used-up products of society are also put into the sea. If the product discharged at sea contains materials which may be leached into the oceanic environment, a serious problem could arise especially when the materials are toxic. However, when the solid materials are inert, a little forethought may result in some benefit to the marine environment. Artificial fishing reefs, for example, have been found to be very successful in certain areas, serving to enhanee the habitat area, especially for small fish.

Excess Heat

Excess heat, if added to the marine environment, alters ambient conditions, and these changes may be detrimental to the organisms present. The amount of heat that is detrimental and the extent of the degradation is determined by a number of factors. The primary source of this heat has been of course, from electrical generating plants, whether they be fossil fueled or nuclear powered (see Thermal Pollution).

Fresh Water and Brine

Although fresh water may be in great demand ashore, too much of it in the ocean obviously will produce a marked environmental change within a small area. This change may occur due to poorly designed storm drainage systems, water diversion networks associated with dams, and effluent of some industrial processes. Excessive fresh water usually is not a critical problem.

The introduction of brine into the marine environment is similar in its effect to that of fresh water except in the opposite direction. The organisms acclimated to a particular salinity now find themselves in a more saline environment which could make permanent damage. Brine is a byproduct of desalination. plants.

Toxics

Toxic inorganies have been materials commonly used in industry, many of them are relatively harmless; however, in larger quantities they may be quite destructive. There are perhaps, 35 to 40 commonly used toxic inorganics and these should be very closely controlled by the user.

The toxic organics have been the most disturbing of the modern day chemicals commonly discharged either purposefully or accidently into the marine environment. These include the biocides such as fungicides, herbicides, insecticides, rodenticides, and also the additional organics including halogenated hydrocarbons, petroleum and industrial chemicals.

The most disturbing toxic organics have been the pesticides such as DDT and kepone which have the unfortunate characteristic of being more soluble in oil than in water so that they tend to collect within the fatty tissues of marine organisms. They have been also very stable compounds which do not deteriorate very easily over a long period of time.

These find their way into the ocean both as manufacturing effluent and as runoff after utilization. Their long term effects are unknown upto this fine.

Petroleum

Although petroleum may be classed as a toxic organic, it is a naturally occuring material and is biodegradeable, given enough time. Its effects are not too well known. Petroleum enter into the marine environment due to accidents such as tanker damage or transfer loss, natural scepage, off shore production losses, losses associated with refineries, from runoff originating as drippings or disposal of used automobile lubricants, and unburned hydrocarbons emitted into the atmosphere a; internal combustion exhaust.

Nutrients

Nutrients (commonly called fertilizers) are those chemicals which are required by plants. The activities of man have added to the total nutrient load of almost all coastal areas. When nutrient levels becomes out of hand, plants grow unchecked so that decaying plants exist in such great numbers that the oxygen supply becomes rapidly depleted. These nutrients are present in domestic sewage effluents, agricultural runoff, and the little understood but apparently important non-point source runoff from urban areas.

Radioactivity

Radioactive material have been not only discharged to the marine environment by nuclear power plants, nuclear power plant fuel production and reprocessing plants, and uranium activities of all sorts, but also result from more common activities of burning of coal, When coal is burned it gives out radioactive particles to the atmosphere which are the washed into the sea at a greater rate than any known nuclear power plant at this time. Other sources of radioactivity include the natural back-ground, weapons testing, mine drainage. accidental spillage, and a few isolated industries.

One of the partially unsolved problems associated with the use of nuclear energy for electrical power has been the long term storage or disposal of spent fuels. This storage must be in an area such there have been no pathways back to man, and the deep oceans have been suggested as meeting this criterion.

Oxygen Demand

Oxygen demand materials have been those which need oxygen for degeneration and therefore steal oxygen which would normally be utilized by marine animals. Thus if too many oxygen demand materials are kept in the marine environment, the animal population will be markedly decreased due to the lack of oxygen. Sewage sludge and any other organic waste material, even that resulting from excessive plant growth due to an over supply of nutrients have examples of common oxygen demand materials.

Acids and Bases

The discharge of acid and bases to the marine environment is quite disturbing to the natural ecological balance of the system. The normal pH of oceanic water has been somewhere around 8.0, slightly basic. This is maintained by the carbonate system. If a large amount of acid or base is introduced into the system, the carbonate reactions will be offset and an important element of the environment will get affected. In addition, there are large synergistic effects associated with pH,

Most toxic materials, for example, increase their toxicity under conditions of low pH.

The sources of acidic or basic material have been primarily industrial with some of this material reaching the marine environment from accidental discharges and the rupturing of tankers.

Aesthetic Considerations

Aesthetically displeasing material include all the stuff one finds in the ocean which is unpleasant to look at or to smell. Tar balls, floatables, gas (often hydrogen-sulphide-) producing materials, and coloring agents are some examples of pollutants offending the senses. Although in some cases these materials do not pose any real threat to the ecology of an area, when the area is being used for rocreation, the quality of the surroundings becomes some what important.

Management Problems

Although the major pollutants are delineated, the management of marine pollution is quite complex. The reason for this is that the marine environment is used by man in many different ways and this multi-use is having a number of ramifications. In the first place each oceanic activity pursued by man may produce a whole range of pollutants. A moving ship, for example, may not only discharge pollutants in the form of waste products from the people living aboard, oil from pumping its bilges, and heat from the discharge of its condensers, it may also need deepening of a harbor channel. This may generate a salinity change in addition to sedimentation problems associated with the maintenance dredging required.

Each pollutant may come from many different users. The nutrients which primarily appear to come from the effluent of sewage disposal plants also may come from storm drainage of urban areas in the form of waste products of domestic animals, along with runoff from agricultural areas that have been fertilized by either commercial fertilizers or farm animals.

An example of the effect of one pollutant on another has been the attraction of heavy metals to suspended sediments. Most of the heavy metals in coastal waters are swept out of the water by sinking sedimentary particles and end up in the bottom deposits. If the heavy metals then enter their way into bottom dwelling organisms which, in turn, find their way into a food chain pathway to man, thed this obviously is not desirable.

Another example of this synergistic effect of two or more pollutants has been the effect of oil on Pesticides, combined with sediments. The pesticides are more soluble in oil than they are in water so that if there is oil present in oceanic water, it will tend to concentrate any pesticides that also may be present. Oil is also having an affinity for sediments and as it collects on the suspended particles, their weight gets increased to the point where they sink to the bottom. Portions of the inshore marine environment thus are covered with sediments very rich in both oil and pesticides.

The introduction of foreign material into the marine environment has been not always detrimental to man or to the environment either. In many areas the increased erosion produced by construction activities in large areas of siltation where these eroded sediments have been deposited in the shoreline areas. After stablization, populations of marsh grass have been seen to spring up in many of these newly created areas. In the main there is no planning for this type of rehabilitation, but recent experimental work reveals that production of marshlands may very well be a common tool of the estuarine planner of the future.

Sources of Marine Pollutants

Now that the pollutants are delineated and described very briefly, we will concern ourselves with the activities involved in the production of these pollutants in an attempt to pinpoint the source of the problem. These activities are outlined in Table 5.2.

Table 5.2.

Pollution Producing Activities

Marine Commerce
Industry
Electrical power generation
Sewage treatment
Other non-industrial
Recreation
Construction

Let us discuss their one by one.

Marine Commerce

Marine commerce has been deeply involved with ships, and ships require a deep enough water environment so that they can pass to from on their appointed rounds. This usually requires continuous dredging. Dredging is an expensive proposition requiring large expenditures of money. Once the sediments are extracted from the bottom and the channel is cut to the desired depth, the problem becomes one of disposing of the dredge spoils, the material dredged from the bottom. Various solutions have been suggested but the problem is still one that has not been adequately solved.

Another aspect of the ship problem has been oil. Whether these ships has been transporting oil or using it for fuel and lubrication, there always seems to be some lost to the sea.

Most harbors are having large storage areas open to the atmosphere so that a certain amount of leaching into the marine environment is inevitable. Lastly, there has been a whole family of pollutants associated with any ship. A ship is just a little city afloat and any problems found in urban areas will be found on ships also.

Industry

Whenever one mentions pollution to the average individual the first source of pollution that pops into mind has been industry. Most industries require the use of water. This water has either heat or some chemical added to it before being discharged into the environment. These chemicals may be anything from toxic substances to harmless coloring agents.

Electrical power generation is responsible for waste heat and certainly this is one of the by products of producing electrical power whether it be from the burning of fossel or nuclear fuels.

An additional problem involved with heat exchahgers has been the fact that many of these are made from copper, a toxic material which is used in anti-fouling paints on boats for many years. Sometimes these heat exchangers are allowed to remain in an unused condition for extended periods of time with water sitting in the heat exchanger tubes. Some copper leaches into this water from the tubes and when the plant gets turned on again this copper-rich water is pumped into the environment where it may bring about some consternation among the local marine organisms.

Large amounts of water pumbed at high speeds from a coastal regions are able to trap or entrain small of sometimes even large organisms. These creatures may suffer mechanical damage as they go through the system, or they may get exposed to large amounts of heat for a short period of time.

Radioactive wastes are considered as one possible disadvantage of nuclear power plants, but the amount of radioactive waste actually transferred by cooling water to the surrounding environment has been measured as extremely low. The spent fuel problem appears to be of more concern at this time.

The pollution problems associated with mineral extraction could not be documented due to the small opportunity for data taking, but it is expected they will be similar to marine construction. At this time the major oceanic mining effort has been directed toward the extraction of sand and graved in the near shore areas. Within the imminent future it is expected that a connected effort will be made to extract manganese nodules from the ocean floor, perhaps at depths as great as 3000 metres. This mining effort will be expected to have some effect on the environment but just how much has been not quite clear. The same can be said for the increase in activity connected with offshose oil drilling although it appears that there is less petroleum lost into the environment when the oil is obtained from an offshose well and transported to the continent by pipeline than when it is obtained from a land well and transported by means of tanker to its eventual user point. The spillage resulting from the use of tankers has been greater than that resulting from the use of pipe line.

Sewage Treatment Systems

The process treating human waste products has been quite successful in removing suggested materials and pathogens, but it has been extremely difficult to extract all of the nitrogen and phosphorous compounds. Consequently, sewage treatment facility effluent is having reasonably high amounts of these nutrients which push plants toward uncontrolled growth. In addition, when the facility gets overloaded, as during a heavy rain, it is often completely bypassed, discharging raw sewage directly into the water. This needs a great deal of oxygen for decomposition so that the biological oxygen demand is increased.

One aspect of sewage treatment neglected up to now, primarily because the costs have been so overwhelming, has been the treatment of storm runoff. Unfortunately the solution is not as straight-forward as simply increasing the capacity of existing plants to handle the heavy loads associated with storms, or even to add treatment to storm drainage systems when they exist separately Much of the urban and rural runoff does not go through conventional pipe systems, so additional systems would have to be built if all runoff has to be treated. Storm drainage washes urban streets clean. All material deposited on the streets, including crankease drippings, rubber worm from auto tires, and bird, dog, and cat droppings are washed to sea. Modern studies have indicated that this 1 unoff has been a very significant source of coliforms and petroleum, to name just two pollutants of some concern to man. How to handle these nonpoint sourees has been a task presently facing marine environment managers and one that appears to have no inexpensive or simple resolution.

With most large urban areas disposal of the solid residue from sewage treatment plants has been a solid waste disposal problem of the first magnitude. Ocean dumping in the near-shore coastal regime is utilized for many years and, to a certain extent, will probably continue to be. Either the sludge must get treated more thoroughly before it is dumped or new deep sea dumping means must be found. If new treatment or disposal techniques are not followed, the e may occur major changes in the coastal enviro ment.

Agricultural Sources

The largest single class of non-industrial polluters are farms. Agricultural pollutants have been commercial fertilizers, animal wastes, pesticides, herbicides, and sediments. In many cases the agricultural contribution of all these pollutants has been greater than any other single source. The pollution can be stopped, and there have been cases in the past where particularly bad problems have been solved,

Recreational Activities

Usually when we think of marine recreation we think of a non-polluted area since recreation is essentially limited by pollution. In shallow water motor boats stir up the sediment on the bottom, a condition which often persists for long periods of time. This increase in turbidity markedly influences the natural plant growth and probably has something to do with the decrease in the numbers of rooted plants reported in the last few yeas. The aspect of motor boating that has many investigators most concerned has been the discharge of petroleum products into the environment. There are some figures which indicate that recreational boats add as much petroleum and petroleum waste products to the environment as all other sourcer combined.

Construction

The last source of pollutants listed in Table 4.2 has been construction. By construction has been meant both that done at sea such as offshore oil rigs, and than done on land contiguous with the sea, such as port facilities. Implied here has been both the actual construction of the structure and the associated activities that go along with construction. There must be all sorts of support equipment, but most important, there must be support people. As in general, the amount of pollution gets directly related to numbers of people, any large construction effort will bring with it the usual people-waste products. The effect of a new physical slructure where one had not previously has been not too well known, but one thing is sure– the environment will never be the same as it was before. Some of these changes might be beneficial, but no matter how beneficial there have been always going to be some members of society who react to any change by claiming a degradation of the environment. Any marine construction project must get judged on the basis of the benefits to be derived by society as a whole rather than solely to those accruing to some small group.

EFFECTS OF MARINE POLLUTION

In this article, we shall attempt to get some idea as to what pollution does and why we consider it to be so undesirable. There have been three basic tppes of pollutants; the pathogenic, the aesthetic, and the ecomorphic. Pathogenic pollutants have been those which cause disease. This disease may be fatal if the pollutant is a fethal poison.

Aesthetic pollutants have been those pollutants causing a change in the environment displeasing to the eye, ear, or nose of man.

Ecomorphic pollutants, on the other hand, have been those pollutants which produce a change in the physical characteristics of the environment in such a way that there may be drastic changes in the structure or composition of the biosphere.

Obviously, these three tyyes of pollutants have been not of equal importance. Pathogenic pollutants have been certainly much more serious than the other two; however, ecomorphic pollutants are often an indicator of more serious types of pollution to follow. Furthermore, since pollution has been man-produced and the effects have been suffered by man, aesthetic problems are certainly of interest.

Acute Effects

The pathogenic pollutants have been obviously the most important. The effects of pathogenic pollutants are either acute or chronic.

The acute effects have been the easiest to determine because of the short time between administration and affliction. The easiest way of measuring acute effect has been by feeding the pollutant in question to test organisms, such as mice or selected fish, and observing the dosage required to kill 50% of the organisms involved. This is usually carried out by feeding a population of test organisms increasing amounts of the pollutant, and for each dosage the number of individuals that succumb is noted. When these data are plotted, an S-shaped curve results.

Another way of examining acute effect is to observe the effect of a given pollutant concentration on organisms over a somewhat longer period of time, noting how long it takes for a given dosage to produce mortalities. This may be done by giving a predetermined concentration of the pollutant to the test animals and observing how long it takes to kill half of them. When data from an experiment such as this are plotted, a curve similar to vertical asymptote results.

Chronic Effects

There appears to be a dose size for each pathogen below which the pollutant does not have any effect. The concern with threshold values for various pollutants has been one aspect of the study of chronic effects. Chronic effects are the most difficult to measure because of the time involved; in some cases cancerns have developed as long as 25 years after initial exposure to the carcinogenic agent. Nevertheless, measurements are made and for many materials a threshold value seems to describe the data reasonably well.

Most experiments require some measure of the effect on the organism other than death, so that many different measures are used. These are; deformity in the growth of organisms, damage to particular organs, change in heartbeat or breathing rate, genetic damage to individuals (rather than to the population as a whole), change in the rate of increase of a population, life expectancy of individuals within a particular population, and fecundity of females within the population. Unfortunately, an index may be very descriptive of a pollutant on a particular species, but it may be completely ineffective in describing what happens when this pollutant comes in contact with other species.

Synergism

Another complication in the examination and quantification of pathogenic pollutants has been the phenomenon of synergism. A synergistic effect takes place when the combined effect of two or more materials acting together has been greater than would be expected from the simple sum of the individual effects. Temperature, for example, has been a very strong synergistic parameter, generally enhancing most pollutant effects as temperature is increased. The same has been true of salinity and dissolved oxygen. Some pollutants, on the other hand, tend to decrease the effects of others, as might be in the case of a strong acid and a strong base present at the same time. Other pollutants may make strong pathogens to get precipitated out of the water column or to be collected on sediments, so that in either case they end up on the bottom. Thus it has been extremely important in the analysis of any pollutant to be aware of the other materials present and their synergistic tendencies.

Within the marine biosphere many organisms get affected by various pollutants. Whether or not a particular organism has been affected by any given pollutant will depend on many variables. For example, many pollutants occur only in the water column while others, such as some of the pesticides and heavy metals, are adsorbed into suspended sediments and usually find their way to the bottom within a relatively short period of time. Consequently, these latter types would tend to affect those organisms living on the bottom or feeding from bottom organisms more than they would influence the organisms living within the water column, like free swimming fish.

Also of importance in determining the effectiveness of a particular pollutant on living organisms has been its relative solubility in water and oil. Pollutants more soluble in oil will tend to find their way to organisms that have a larger content of oil in their body tissues. This has been particularly true of some of the pesticides which are more soluble in oil than water. The individual habits of marine organisms also influence their susceptibility to a particular pollutant. Feeding habits with respect to time of day, portion of water column foraged, type of material ingested, and the method of digestion utilized all determine to a great extent the types of pollutants the organism will be exposed to. Similarly spawning habits decide the type of area and time of year in which a species has been particularly sensitive to subtle changes in the environment. These changes influence not only the parents but also the offspring, and may be even their progeny.

Other habits not having to do with spawning also help to determine whether an organism will get exposed to particular pollutants. Whether the organism has been sensitive to light or sound, for example, will often determine whether it gets attracted to a particular out-fall. Thus we find that a pure and simple cause and effect relationship between a pollutant and an organism has been not enough to determine completely the actual response of the organism in the real world.

Pathways to Man

Once some of the pollutant gets ingested by marine organisms, the major concern of man has been the possibility of this pollutant appearing on his dinner table and causing a pathogenic response. Obviously if a fish ingests a pollutant and a human eats that fish, then that person will get ingested a dose of that pollutant and there will probably be some danger. The question is, "How much ?" In order to arrive at an approximation of the actual amount of undesired material finding its way into the reader's stomach, one must be able to follow the pollutant through a number of steps.

Most organisms living in the sea tend to concentrate materials existing in the sea to much greater values than they have been in the ocean itself. For example, a diatom, a small form of marine algae having a silicate frustule, is having a body concentration of silicon about 40 thousand times as great as the oceanic waters from which the organism derives all of its material. Thus the diatom concentrates silicon very effectively so that if we are diatoms, a large portion of our diet would be glassy. Similarly, other organisms, including fish, will concentrate other materials even if these do not naturally occur in the environment. But this amplification or concentration does not stop with one step. We must continually keep in mind the fact that an organism does not exist by itself in the marine environment. Any organism has been dependent upon many other organisms for its existence. An edible fish, for example, might very well subsist on smaller fish which, in turn, might subsist on small zooplankton (small floating forms of animal life), which, in turn, may subsist on phytoplankton (forms of floating plant life). There may be 5 to 10 individual links in a food chain leading to man, and there has been the distinct possibility that for each one of these links a concentration of the pollutant occurs. Hence, the total pathway to man for the pollutant might be a rather tortuous one, but it might result in a very high concentration of the pollutant material in the fish. This in itself may be of no concern to the individual unless he ingests the fish and if so, how often and how much he consumes. It has been not enough simply to know that there has been some pollutant present in marine organisms; one should also know how much is present, and in addition two other facts have been required. This first has been the accepted maximum level of ingestion of the pollutant before harm results, and the second has been the amount of fish that can be eaten before this level gets reached. In this way it might very well be possible to have a particular kind of fish one or two times a year with perfect safety, while if it has been eaten once a day, it might very well have a toxic effect.

Ecomorphic Pollutants

There are many different types of pollutants which may be classified as ecomorphic, while some pollutants fall into all three of the classes stipulated above and many fall into at least two. Sediment has been a pollutant whose effect has been primarily that of changing the environment since it is not pathogenic and very often is not aesthetically displeasing, although it can be. As it settles to the bottom, it will tend to bury the organisms that live on the bottom, such as oysters and clams, and eventually smother them. Sediment also tends to fill in marsh areas, killing the marsh grass, and completely changing the habitat. As marsh areas are breeding grounds for small fish and an important ecological link in most of the oceanic life, any destructive process such as this has been bound to markedly change the marine biological environment. On the other hand, in some cases where man's activities are able to produce large amounts of erosion and sediment has been brought down by rivers into estuaries, some estuarine areas have been filled enough to support marsh grasses. In same cases excess erosion can produce marsh lands rather than destroy them. Whenever there has been a depth change in an estuarine or coastal area, the effects have been many. They range from changing the biological environment so that larger fish will no longer live in the shoal areas to affecting the total circulation pattern of the area.

If the sediment has been in suspension it also has an effect on the ecosystem, the most obvious aspect being a change in transparency. By making the water more opaque, light will not penetrate as deeply as before so that the thickness of the layer of water in which plants grow (the euphotic zone) will get decreased. If the water has been fairly shallow to begin with, this decrease in transparency may very well result in the inability of rooted plants to grow and some marsh lands may be destroyed. The effect of sediment, then, has been two-fold;

changing both bottom and water properties. Both of these effects tend to change the physical characteristics of the ecosystem.

Another ecomorphic pollutant has been oil, although oil sometimes produces toxic effects The result of oil coating bird feathers has been a well known physical effect. The oil does not poison birds; it simply makes it impossible for them to fly, and consequently many of them die. A film of oil on the surface will also decrease the amount of sunlight entering the water and, similarly, will limit the exchange of oxygen from the atmosphere. In addition to the aesthetic and pathogenic effects of oil, there are thus also ecomorphic effects.

The toxic effects of various nitrogen compounds have been well known but fertilizers and other nutrients washed into the sea possess a nontoxic effect on marine waters. These materials will do just what they have been designed to do : make plants grow, whether these plants be terrestial or aquatic plants. Consequently, the first effect of a spike of fertilizer added to the sea has been an overstimulation of those plants normally there. Beyond that the undesirable plants (those that are not food for the edible types of marine animals) often get stimulated to grow and these marine weeds grow so rapidly that the overwhelm the other types of plants. As plants have been at the bottom of the food pyramid, the structure and characteristics of the ecosystem have been completely changed, even to the extent of markedly altering the species composition.

Once these plants have started to grow at greatly accelerated rates, they may completely cover the surface of the water, disallowing any light from penetrating more than a few centimetres. Those plants on the bottom of the blanket will die, due to lack of light, and those rotting plants will use oxygen in their decay processes. Even though there have been more plants than before, producing more oxygen in the process of photosynthesis, so many of them are dying and decaying the result has been to decrease the dissolved oxygen. This phenomenon is termed as eutrophication.

Solid waste has been another type of pollutant very often disposed of in oceanic areas. In some cases they tend to completely destroy the natural habitat and the result has been not only ecomorphic but also aesthetically displeasing. However, in some cases, the ocean dumping of waste products such as old automobile tires and even automobile bodies has produced an artificial habitat for many organisms that were not endemic to the region previously. However, there are cases where nontoxic solid waste materials have destroyed desirable habitats. Sometimes the dumping of solid wastes makes a change in water flow patterns producing changes in salinity and temperature which influence the biosphere markedly. This usually takes place when the water is reasonably shallow and the volume of solid waste products dumped is relatively large.

Another ecomorphic pollutant that seems to be receiving a lot of attention lately is heat which is supplied to the marine environment from electrical power plants or other industrial sources. This heat will increase the water temperature and may result in different kinds of damage to marine organisms. As most mutations have been caused by thermal activity under normal conditions, the possibility of genetic damage has been real. It is estimated that about 90% of the mutations occurring normally have been thermally caused, while only about 10% have been caused by radiation. Thus with an increase in the temperature, one can expect greater mutation rates or more genetic damage.

In addition to genetic damage, heat can cause both acute and chronic problems. Animals can be killed by extreme thermal shock or they can suffer lingering effects and finally expire by being unable to acclimate to the new surroundings. More subtle changes are also noticed as growth rates are changed with increase or decrease in temperature. Normally a small increase in temperature will make a small increase in growth rate; however, if the temperature change in extreme, this may be reversed. Changes in spawning patterns have also been noted in which fish that normally move upstream to spawn are unable or unwilling to cross a thermal barrier associated with a heated effluent. This may cause the cessation of spawning for a large portion of the species population. Another effect of temperature increase has been to cause certain organisms to grow more rapidly than others, upsetting the previous ecological balance and eventually causing a change in species composition.

A similar range of effects to that produced by heat has been caused by salinity changes. These might be produced from the input of rich brine solutions resulting from the effluent of water desalination efforts or a fresh water outfall such as a raw sewage treatment plant. A marked change in salinity will bring about damage similar to that produced by heat, including genetic damage growth rate changes, spawning pattern changes, and changes in species composition. All organisms are used to living within some range of salinity and if this range gets exceeded, they will either die or move some place else.

Aesthetic Pollutants

The last type of pollutant mentioned above was aesthetic pollutants. Aesthetic pollutants have been those which offend the human senses and as such are regarded by many to be unimportant. In many environmental problem areas, though, the aesthetic considerations often receive more attention by environmentally oriented citizens than some of the pathogenic pollutants. This is simply because the aesthetic pollutants have been visible and what can be seen, smelled, or heard appears much more bothersome than that which is hidden, even though the hidden pollutant might be much more dangerous to life. Consequently, any scheme for controlling marine pollution must include some consideration of the aesthetic pollutants if it is to succeed. An excellent strategy seems to be to focus on the aesthetic pollutants and use them as a mechanism to gather momentum to clean up the rest of the pollution problems.

Solid waste material, when piled in shallow areas where it can be seen, has been a typical aesthetic pollutant. Building activities also may be regarded to be sources of aesthetic pollutants. Power transmission cable has caused more than one power company grief because of the environmental consideration given the local citizens who are concerned about the appearance of power cables running across the countryside. Oil wells, especially the offshore variety visible from resort areas, have been of great concern to most environmentalists. The same thing has been true of equipment required for dredging operations and the spoil areas resulting from these operations. To some people, especially those in living relatively pristine environments near the water, boats can also be an aesthetic pollutant, especially those that cause waves and noise. Effluents that make the color of the sea to change or increase the amount of suspended sediments also may be regarded aesthetic pollutants. It simply has been not as pleasant to go swimming in water that is cloudy or contains coloring material different from what one would expect in a normal, natural body of water.

In essence, any change from the pristine environment appears to many to be aesthetic pollution. Obviously, we are living in an unreal world if we think the marine environment can be maintained in an unspoiled form. It should be kept in mind that many complaints about aesthetic pollution come from individual who would rather live in the primeval environment not realizing that it would not be available to them unless the commercial world about them supported it. There appears to be a dichotomy wherein we try to maintain the unspoiled environment in certain areas while letting others become overutilized. Nevertheless, there has been a growing movement to include in the cost of every project a relatively small sum to improve its aesthetic qualities. This is, of course, exactly the same philosophy that has been applied to the control of other forms of pollution. Additional money has been spent in a chemical process, for example, to control the pollution-producing properties of the effluent because society believes that this additional sum of money has been a desirable expenditure. It may be similarly be maintained that the expenditure for aesthetic pollution control is desirable as it also will tend to increase the quality of life.

CONTROL OF MARINE POLLUTION

Now that the nature of pollution and some of the sources of this undesirable product of society have been considered, we will now concern ourselves with some of the avenues open to us to accomplish some sort of control. The most obvious control strategy that can be used has been to some-how or other completely prevent the introduction of the pollutant into the environment. This can be carried out by not producing the pollutant or by restructuring the process so that the pollutant is no longer a by product. Let us consider a few major sources of pollutants and some possible methods of control in these particular cases.

Dredging

Maintenance dredging, that is, dredging required to maintain a particular depth, adds sediment to the water column and would not be needed if there were no sediment supply to shoal up major channel areas. This type of dredging has been not a one shot affair, but it has been almost always necessary to periodically redredge the accumulated sediment from these channels and harbor areas. This continual sedimentation has been a normal process wbich occurs whether man is present or not. In some instances the activities of man tend to accelerate the sedimentation process but this has been not necessarily always true. For example, coastal plain estuaries, often the result of river basin flooding, tend to be a rather ephemeral event in geologic time. They get formed when water level rises, and they disappear with the continual process of deposition of material eroded from the higher reaches of the water shed.

Another example of natural erosion has been found on the west coast of the United States in the westernmost portion of California (that portion where more than 90% of the population lives). This area was formed by erosion of the Rocky Mountains and deposition of the eroded material at the base of the mountains.

The most obvious solution to the problem of maintenance dredging has been to cut off the sediment supply to the areas where sedimentation has been a major problem. This can be carried out in a number of different ways. The most effective of all has been to prevent upstream erosion, but at the same time this is perhaps the most difficult The entire watershed must be policed very carefully to make sure that the natural landscape gets changed to such an extent that erosion no longer takes place. This implies extensive terracing and replanting of areas that have been denuded for one reason or another. Of course, this also implies that extreme measures must be taken in areas that do not have natural cover, such as agricultural areas or areas where construction is underway. A certain amount of this is being done.

Another method of preventing sediment from reaching the undesired are has been to provide settling ponds. The water is released after it has dropped the major portion of its load and is allowed to proceed downstream. The major disadvantage of this system has been that it is essentially a temporary solution since the ponds will fill up rather rapidly, needing either building of new ponds or dredging of some sort.

Sometimes the sedimentation that takes place in a channel area is a result of sediment loads that are introduced into the marine environment from nearby rather than those carried from far up-stream. This takes place for example, when a channel gets dredged with unstable sides so that the material just tends to slough into the deeper regions. This needs continual dredging as the removed sediment has been almost immediately replaced by bottom material from the sides. One method of correcting this situation is by stabilizatlon of the bottom. Adding larger, more dense material such as gravel to the bottom has been a technique utilized occasionally, although this has been usually more expensive than dredging so that it has been not done too often. Bottom stabilization, however, is a technique that is being used more and more to prevent the movement of bottom materials within relatively small contiguous areas.

Another possibility for preventing the accumulation of sediments in undesirable areas has been to change the natural circulation patterns so that so that sediments get deposited in an area where they do no damage. This may be carried out in various ways : by changing the physical dimensions of estuarine areas, by putting dams in selected areas, and even by changing the circulation pattern by planting grasses to increase bottom friction,

Another method to be considered in decreasing the amount of suspended sediments has been that involved in controlling the numbers and types or water craft allowled in particular areas. In regions that have been relatively shallow and narrow, high speed vessels tend io churn up the bottom, putting sediments back into the water column that had previously settled out. In addition, large wakes are generally produced that tend to erode the sides of the waterway by the mechanical action of these relatively high energy waves breaking on the shoreline. Both these effects can get decreased by the simple expedient of limiting the speed of boats in certain areas. It has been a fairly effective method; however, if the traffic is extremely heavy it may be necessary to limit the total number of vessels, in addition to their speed.

In addition to the general clarity aspect of pollution caused by dredging, there has been also a toxic one. Sediment rstrieved from harbor bottoms has been especially likely to contain a relatively high concentration of industrial pollutants such as oil and heavy metals. During the dredging operation there has been a likelihood of some of this material's finding its way back into the water column, but of more concern has been the long-time leaching from dredge spoil dumping areas. Various methods, such as diking and the construction of artifical islands, are utilized to minimize this leaching but their performance under all conditions has been not too well known. Further research in the handling of dredge spoil gets needed at this time.

Oil Pollution

Another problem that, to a certain extent, appears amenable to prevention at the source is that involving oil. Unforunately, the sources of oil in the marine environment have been extremely difficult to delineate.

All the experts agree that the greatest terrestial source of petroleum products in the ocean is used crankcase oil. Some go so far as to indicate that this source supplies more petroleum to the sea than *any* other source. This may be true because within the last decade or so the habits of American motorists are changed markedly to the extent that a large portion of them now change their own oil, discarding the used oil in a manner that probably makes it to end up in storm sewers. The major reason for this probably has been the almost complete disappearance of the used lubricating oil re-refining industry in recent years since it was not economically feasible to re-refine oil. However, with the modern continual increase in the price of new oil, the re-refining industry has been having a rebirth so that a large portion of the oil previously thrown away will now be reused.

Another entirely different source of oil in the marine environment has been that resulting from accidents that take place during shipping and transferring processes. Generally speaking, the more handling steps involved, the more accidents and associated losses can get expected. The figures as to how much has been actually lost in handling accidents compared to that lost in normal ship procedures, such that as pumping bilges, has been not well known, but there has been no doubt that a very large portion of the oil reaching the marine environment has been the result of poor handling procedures in both the operation of vessels and the transfer of oil from one carrier to another. Better procedures are required, but perhaps even more than better procedures, stricter enforcement of accepted safe procedures would go a long way to decreasing the amount of oil that enters the ocean each year.

When a tanker empties its load of oil, the dynamic characteristics of this vessel get markedly changed. Its weight gets decreased about a thousand times and therefore it becomes extremely difficult to drive the ship, because it was designed to be driven with a full load. Therefore, when most tankers do not have a load of oil, they will fill their tanks with water for ballast. When they return for a fresh cargo of oil, they mustl pump this water from the tanks, releasing large amounts of oie as the residue left in the tanks gets washed out. There ar many schemes which are suggested for decreasing the amount of oil that is wasted in the ballasting-unballasting process; however, it is not clear at this time how effective these processes have been or how effectivély any requirements can be enforced.

Modern supertankers have been extremely large vessels and therefore have major structural weaknesses, so that occasionally they will break up in unusually hesvy seas. They have been simply not designed to be utilized under unusual storm conditions, so that there will continue to be losses of this type in rough weather. In passing, it should be mentioned that once oil gets spilled at sea under large wave conditions (usually) the case when accidents occur, there has been no way for this oil to be retrieved. On the other hand, oil may be retriered in harbor areas where the sea surface is relatively clam, but only when there are waves no higher than approximately 1 metre. The obvious way the only way - to prevent oil from getting to the marine environment when a ship founders has been to prevent the accident from occurring in the first place. Alternatively. once the accident has taken place the oil must be prevented from escaping from the ship. It has been somewhat doubtful whether these solutions will ever be possible.

Industrial Pollutants

Most industries are using large amounts of water for cooling purposes or as an integral part of the manufacturing process. Consequently, industrial effluents may be having waste products, heat, leached material from heat exchangers, or even incidental house-cleaning wastes. If the industry, for example, has been using water as a coolant, the heat exchangers must constantly be cleaned to keep the heat exchange efficiency high. These cleaners may be more toxic than process wastes. Consequently, it has been extremely desirable to treat all industrial effluents.

Some industries have tried to modify the entire process rather than just clean up the effluent. This often causes an increase in efficiency with a lower overa'l production cost. If this expenditure can be recouped in a relatively short period of time. this obviously might be expected to be a very cost-effective method of handling unwanted effluents. However, in many cases, there has been no increase in operating efficiency, with the net result being an increase in manufacturing costs passed on to the consumer. Society must then make a decision as to how much it has been willing to pay for a particular product *vis a vis* the amount of pollution introduced in the manufacture of this product.

Antifouling Paint

Sometimes pollution comes from the use of antifouling paint on boats. During the summer time in temperate waters the growth rate of marine organisms get increased markedly, especially those organisms setting on fixed surfaces. An untreated boat hull left in the water for a period of just a few weeks will need enough growth to cut the available speed for a given power input by fifty per cent. Consequently, all owners of boats left in the water have been very careful to apply some coating to the underside to prevent the accumulation of marine organisms. For large cargo ships or tankers, this could make savings of thousands of dollars in fuel costs. Common practice has been to paint the bottom of the boat with antifouling paint.

Antifouling paint has been so used to leach a toxic material into the water in just the proper amounts so that all organisms setting on the hull will get killed. However, the older types of antifouling paints, those that use copper as a toxin, released enough material to the environment not only to kill possible fouling organisms bat also to be harmful to other marine creatures at some distance from the boat. Thus there has been a movement of to improve the quality of antifouling paints by adrastically reducing this leaching to toxic material into the water. The solution that has been suggested has been to use new paint vehicles in conjunction with new toxic materials so that the toxic material has been almost completely retained within the vehicle, requiring oganis as to come within a very short distance of the boat to be affected. One result of recent research is to develop a family of paints using acrylic resins as vehicles and tri-butal tin flouride (TBTF) as the primary antifouling ingredient. In the first few years of use this paint holds great promise because it is less toxic in the water, lasts longer, and does not allow bottom growth more effectively.

In their very effectivenss these new paints pose a problem, because the toxin gets retained within the paint for a longer period of time. Paint scrapings have been now more toxic than they were with the old copper bottom paint. This means that it has been somewhat more dangerous to strip the paint from the bottom of the boat when applying a new coat and precautions must be used to prevent the old paint from getting back into the water environment. When sandblasting large ships, for example, precautions have to be taken to retain the sandblasted material rather than allowing it to be simply washed away. Thus the solution of one problem presents another, but these problems have been solvable if some care has been taken to see that additional health hazards do not get created.

Pesticide and Herbicide Pollution

Some of the juicier pollution scandals that have taken place in recent years have involved various pesticides and the problem has been that many of the chemical compounds get introduced for public sale before the total effects of these materials have been known. It seems to be almost an insurmountable problem to determine what the total effects of a new compound will be before it has been put on the market because so many new products are introduced every year. However, a large portion of the problem has been undoubtedly due to basic carelessness. In both the manufacturing and use of these materials proper precautions are not being taken into consideration. Many users, for example, undoubtedly believe that if a certain amount per unit area will suffice, twice as much will produce twice as much control of either weeds or bugs. This excess toxin is washed into the streams and ends up killing marine organisms rather than protecting plants. It would be evident that more effective control of both the manufacture and use of pesticides and herbicides would go a long way toward eliminating undesirable side effects.

Solid Waste Pollution

The disposel of solid waste has been very necessary and there even seems to be a fear that if the solid water problem is not solved, eventually there will be no room left for people. Because of this fear, large amounts of solid waste get dumped in the ocean. Some of these solid wastes take the from of sludge from sewage treatment plants whereas others consist of large pieces of discarded consumer products. In the latter case the problem might very well solve itself as the cost of scrap metal continues to increase.

One possible use for sewage treatment sludge has been in refurbishing land disfigured by strip mining. Often the overburden removed to get at the coal seam has been not capable of supporting life nor it has been even particularly stable. The addition of sludge from sewage treatment plants is considered as a mathod of soil treatment to make it possible to support a viable plant population. It is a concept that has not been tried yet but one which will be tried when it becomes economically feasible to transport the sludge to the strip mine. Another possibility for using the sewage sludge, if it contains oely nutrient materials, has been suggested and has been considered by some of the Middle Eastern oil producing countries. The idea has been that empty tankers be filled with sewage sludge for the return voyage rather than with ballast water. This sludge will then be utilized to bring the desert regions back to a point where they have been capable of supporting a large agricultural industry.

Other forms of solid waste being dumped in nearshore areas have been dumped there primarily because there has been no other acceptable depository. One method of decreasing the severity of this problem has been simply to decrease the amount of solid waste produced by society. Packag ng of consumer items, for example, seems to be a good place to start. From a disposal point of view the catsup bottle is probably the worst possible package. The package weighs more and takes up more space than the contents. The Navy has done excellent work in decreasing package size and weight because there are definite limitations aboard ship, but not too much has been done with the private sector of society simply because there hasn't been enough action on the part of consumers to insist upon small volume and weight packages. One possible exception to this has been the introduction of lightweight plastic bottles for large size drinks to replace the heavyweight glass variety, They are somewhat thinner than glass, weigh less, and may be incinerated, so the disposal problem has been somewhat alleviated. However, with the continuing increase in petroleum costs, plastics might not remain economically feasible in the future.

Recycling and Reclamation

It has been found that biological communities living in the sea need a certain amount of physical shelter. Some species just like to be alone, whereas in other cases the young of the species require places to hitde to protect against predation. A marsh or wetlands area has been a good breeding place because both of these conditions prevail. It is found that in many cases these conditions can be created artificially by introducing large junk articles such as old automobiles or worn out ships to form effective artificial fishing reefs.

There has been disadvantages to using waste products for this sort of activity. One has been that in many cases these junk, objects get transported to undesirable areas by dynamic ocannic forces. Pollution has been not controlled when automobile fenders and doors wash up on swimming beaches. When creating a finishing reef, steps must be taken to retain the integrity of these reefs for a iong period of time If proper attention has been paid to the magnitude and nature of oceanic forces, artificial reefs night he made relatively permanent.

With the present state of the economy where things are some what more expensive, it appears that more items will find themselves in the near future on the list, of materials to be recycled or reclaimed. Industrial processess will alter as it becomes more feasible to extract materials from the waste stream from a cost standpoint and, at the same time industrial. Waste streams wlll become less and less polluted. Even in the area of multiple waste product use, like the combination of waste heat from either manufacturing or electrical power generation and waste nutrients from sewage treatment plants for the purposes of aquaculture, cost will always be the controlling factor.

It is known that elevated temperatures and the artificial addition of nutrients will increase growth rates of many organisms markedly. The choice of which organism to grow has been involved not only with which would be best to grow, but also which there has been a market for. Setting up an aquaculture system involves picking organisms which respond favourably to the environment, developing a system by which the optimum growth rate can get produced, developing a marketing system so that the end product will be sold at the maximum possible price, and assuring the continuing existence of a market for everything produced. Not only has been science included but also sociology and economics must be considered, and it is probably in these latter two areas that the major difficulties reside. Hence, no sophisticated aquaculture systems employing both waste heat and nutrients have besn developed at this point, but it has been probably only a matter of time before we will have extensive aquaculture using man's waste products.

Storage of Pollutants

Another method of controlling pollution has ,been is to store them at some distance from man's activities so that they have been as inaccessible as possible to the major fraction of the population and pathways to man. Occasionally nuclear waste products are being dumped in deep oceanic areas in the hope that when they do break out of their canisters, they will not find an easy pathway back to man because the deeper life forms have been probably not in any food chain involving man. Perhaps not so well known has been the fact that deep ocean disposal is used for other materials such as average ordinance and poison gases for which the military has no further use.

In the case of nuclear products, there has been a very vociferous school of thought that believes storage facilities should allow waste retrieval if a technological break through is ever accomplished that would allow these nuclear waste products to be profitably utilized.

Asimov's suggestion has been to implant our hazarodus waste products in the oceanic trench areas so that within a few thousand years they will get carried into the interior of the earth and no longer be bothersome. The only problem with this suggestion has been that the exposure time before the canister having the waste products is effectively buried in the crust is relatively long. During this time the canister seal has to be absolute. Whether this can be accomplished with present technology of presently being debated within the scientific community.

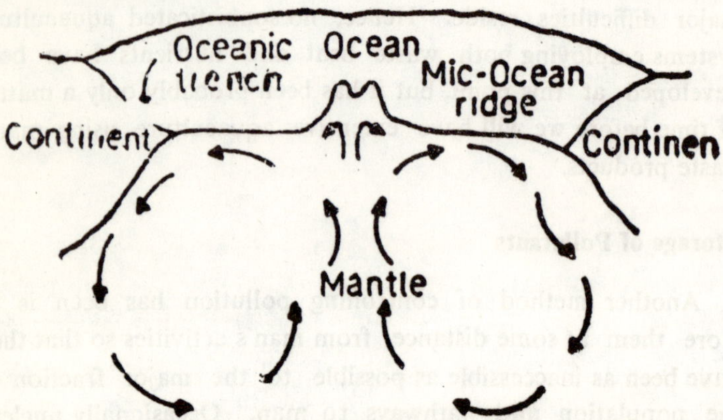

Fig. 3.1. Convection currents in the mantle resulting in mid-ocean ridges and oceanic trenches.

Nevertheless, storage has been still a viable method of controlling pollution, especially for the more toxic materials. At least theoretically, one knows where they are. The major concern with storage of toxic material has been accidental release, and the chances of this taking place always remain within the realm of possibility.

Controlling Pollution by Zoining

Another method of controlling pollution has been by specifying certain areas that can be utilized for effluent discharge and other areas that cannot. Although we are even starting to convert our city dumps into usable areas, such as golf courses or ski slopes by covering, planting, and land-scaping as rapidly as possible, but it will be some time before ocean dumping areas are reclaimed in this fasion.

Certain coastal regions would be reserval for industry, others for sewage treatment, while still others would be set aside for recreation. Some of these activities have been such that they may get pursued in conjunction with one another, whereas others cannot. The idea has bcen for every coastal area to try to get the optimum utilization of marine resources available. In order to accomplish this type of zoining most effectively, a great deal more knowledge is needed than is presently available about the synergistic effects of various types of activities. One of the major advantages of optimum zoining has been that it would allow maximum avoidance of undesirable synergistic effects.

The biggest stumbling block to coastal zoining probably has been inovercoming entrenched interests in regions where the optimum activities have been found to be different from those presently underway : a socio-economic problem rather than a technological one.

The concept is some what interesting one, because it essentially permits some pollution of certain areas while refusing to permit any pollution of other locals. This has been different from the way pollution has been presehtly controlled, where the effort has been made to limit pollution in all areas to the minimum possible amount. With the joining concept pollution would still be limited as much as possible, but it might permissible to allow the water quality of ocean to degrade below the mean in some places, because in others it would be higher than the mean.

Controlling Pollution by Taxation

One last method of pollution control is taxation which can be utilized to encourage or discourage certain activities in addition to raising funds to support government programs. Pollution would be allowed, but it would be taxed at a rate proportional to the environmental insult.

Some economists suggest that a tax on pollution will simply be a license to pollute and will therefore encourage pollution rather than discourage it.

From a management point of view there have been a number of different directions that can be taken to control pollution, including both technological and socio-economic alternatives. So far society has tended to aim more in the direction of the technological alternatives, but there appears to be a definte swing toward other methods. In the years to come it might be possible that more and more emphasis will be kept an these non-technical methods, especially as the tradeoffs, costs, and benefits become better understood.

FINAL RIMARK

It has been said that pollution is a biological problem that can be solved by the application of physical and chemical methods. Whether this is a completely true statement is often a moot point, however, because the opportunity to apply any solution is usually won only after the employment of politics. Thus the study of pollution is a truly interdisciplinary one, including as it does the three Ps – pollutants, processes, and people.

IMPORTANT CONCLUSIONS

(1) Effective control of marine pollution requires further research work aimed at evaluating the extent of pollution of marine ecosystems, determination of the biological effect of toxicants and prediction of biological consequences. However, such an approach alone is inadequate, since the problem is urgent and suitable measures must be taken as soon as feasible.

(2) Small marine organisms have a low resistance to toxicants. This fact was utilised to develop a system of rapid bioassays for immediate evaluation of the harmful effects produced by any given substance present in sea water.

(3) The more promising applications of the results and methods toxicological research to the protection of the marine environment from pollution include : standardisation of the components of various toxicants in the sea based on biological criteria; ecotoxicological characterisation of sewage effluent and its components, for the determination of methods and norms of permissible dumping; recommendations on the priority and stepwise sequence of reducing the volume of sewage discharged by various industries; rapid tests of comparative toxicities of different substances, in order to select those which are ecologically safest; development and realisation of regional plants for protecting the marine environment from pollution.

4

Marine Pollutants and Their Sources

Introduction

Once we have agreed on what pollution is, we can proceed with the specifics of the problem. Let us than in this chapter list and briefly discuss the more common pollutants appearing in the ocean, along with their sources. As the list of pollutants is perused, it will immediately by seen that many of these are not necessarily uniquely produced by man but occur normally in nature. However, in most cases, the activities of man have exaggerated the problem in the sense of causing a marked increase in the amount of pollutant present.

The Pollutants

In Table 2.1 a list of common pollutants associated with the marine environment will be found. These are not listed in any particular order of importance since it is found that in certain areas certain pollutants are more worrisome than others, while the opposite condition may be ture in other areas. This difference in importance results from local conditions such as population pressure, flushing, and climate. In later chapters the problem of why particular pollutants are more worrisome chapters the problem of why particular pollutants are more worrisome in some areas than in others will be addressed.

TABLE 4.1

Pollutants Associated with the Marine Environment

Pathogens	Toxic organics
Sediments	Petroleum
Solid wastes	Nutrients
Heat	Radioactive materials
Fresh water	Oxygen demand materials
Brine	Acids and bases
Toxic inorganics	Aesthetically displeasing materials

Pathogens

The first entry in Table 4.1. is pathogenic materials. These are the living organisms that can produce sickness or biological unbalance in either plants or animals within the ocean itself or in humans who either contact oceanic waters or eat the organisms caught in the water. These include a wide variety or bacteria, protozoa, viruses and fungi. The most common of these are normally associated with human waste products and are found in sewaee. However, other pathogens may occur in non-waste disposal areas where environmental conditions are such that the proper conditions are present for growth and reproduction

Sediments

Sediments are always present to some extent in the marine environment. Generally speaking, concentration of suspended solids increases with proximity to the coast, with the maximum occuring in the riverine and estuarine environment. As man impinges on the coastal regions, his construction and agriculture efforts generally tend to increase erosion and therefore increase the amount of sediment in suspension. These sediments have a marked effect on plant growth since they block out a large portion of the light normally reaching greater depths and therefore decrease photosynthetic activity. In some cases rooted plants are completely destroyed by this process.

As sediments are deposited on the bottom they will cover up bottom dwelling organisms (benthos) such as oysters and may even smothes them under extreme conditions. In addition to destroying bottom dwelling life, deposited sediments tend to make the water shallower so that, in regions traveled by ships, periodic dredging is required. Dredging and the disposal of dredged material have their own set of environmental problems which will be discussed later.

The sediments of concern are primarily inorganic silts and clays since the larger particles such as sand and gravel do not remain in suspenion for any monegligible peroid of time. They result from soil being washed from land areas into sea, in many cases because man has changed the character of the affected area by agricultural or construction activities. Once the sediments settle to the bottom they may be resuspened in shallow water by natural causes, such as strems, or by man as an operator of a power boat. The relative importance of recreational vessels in maintaining turbid conditions in shallow water is not well known at this time.

Solid Waste

The disposal of solid waste is a critical urban problem at the present time primarily because areas suitable for the dumping of the sevoluminous materials are becoming scarcer, especially when transportation costs are considered. Due primarily to low transporation costs the ocean has been used as a dumping ground for solid waste for centuries. The solid waste most frequently marine dumped is sludge materials left over as a byproduct from domestic sewage treatmeut. However the unused products of industry and the used-up products of society are also discharded into the sea. If the product discharged at sea contains materials which may be leached into the oceanic environment, a serious problem could develop, especially if the materials are toxic. However, if the solid materials are inert, a little forethought may result in some benefit to the marine environment. Artificial fishing reefs, for example, have been very successful in certain area, especially for small fish.

On the other hand, solid waste materials also can serve as a pollutant in the sense of destroying habits when this materials is dumped into marsh or wetland area. Until recent years marshes and wetlands were assumed to have no practical value, but recently we have found these areas to serve as breeding grounds for most of the commercial species of fish along with many other organisms important in the food chains of all marine creatures. Thus there is a growing movement not only to save the wetlands from further destruction but also in many cases to attempt to rehablitate these areas of extreme biological importance.

Excess Heat

Excess heat, when added to the marine environment, changes ambient conditions, and these changes may be deterimental to the organisms present. The amount of heat that is detrimental and the extent of the degradation is determined by a number of factors to be discussed later. The primary source of this heat is, of course, from electrical generating plants, whether they by fossil fueled or nuclear powered.

Fresh Water and Brine

Although fresh water may be in great demand ashore, too much of it in the ocean obviously will produce a marked environmental change within a small area. This change may be caused by poorly desinged storm drainage systems, water diversion networks associated with dams, and effluent of some industrial process. Excessive fresh water usually is not a critical problem but it could be one if the effluents were directed into a sensitives area.

The introductoin of brine into the marine envirnoment is similar in iis effect to that of fresh water except in the opposite direction. The organisims acclimated to a particular salinity now find themselves in a more saline envoirnment which could cause permanent damage. Brine is a byproduct of desalination plants, but changes in the salinity regime also can produced by changes in estuarine channel depths necessated by shipping considerations.

Toxics

Toxic inorganics are materials commonly used in industry, many of them primarily to control the growth of algae or to destroy pathogens. Chlorine is an excellent example of this. In larger quantities this material is relatively harmless; however, in laeger quantities it may be quite destructive. The key here apparently is how much and how often. There are perhaps 35 to 40 commonly used toxic inorganics and these should be very closely controlled by the user.

The toxic organics are the most disturbing of the mordern day chemicals commonly discharged either purposefully or accidentally into the marine environment. These include the biocides such as fungicides, herbicides, insecticides, rodenticides, and also the additional organics including halogenated hydrocarbons, petroleum and industrial chemicals. The most disturbing toxic organics are the pesticides such as DDT and ketone which have the unfortunate characteristic of being more soluble in oil than in water so that they tend to collect within the fatty tissues of marine organisms. They are also very stable compounds which do not deteriorate very easily over a long period of time.

These find way into the ocean both as manufacturing effluent and as runoff after utilization. Perhaps the most disturbing aspect of there toxic organics is that there are hundreds available with many more being produced by the chemical industry without any rela knowledge of their long term effects.

Petroleum

Although petroleums may be classed as a toxic organic, it is a naturally occurring materials and is biodegradeable, given enough time. Petroleum in its natural state is a very complex organic materials containing a large number of seperate compounds, each of which seems to have it own effect on the biosphere. These effects are not too well known and opinions within the scientific community range from one extreme to the other with respect to the toxicity of the material. It is a aesthetically disleasing of nothing else. Petroleum finds its way into the marine environment due to accidents such as tanker damage or transfer loss, natural seepage, offshore production losses, losses associated with refineries, from runoff originating as drippings or disposal of used automobile lubricants, and unburned hydrocarbons emitted into the atmosphere as internal combustion exhaust.

Nutrients

Nutrients are what are commonly called fertilizers, those c' emicals required by plants. The most common of these are the compounds of nitrogen and phosphorous. They exist in the natural environment at all times and some of them are recycled naturally by decaying living organisms. However, the activities of man have added to the total nutrient load of almost all coastal areas. When nutrient levels get out of hand, plants grow unchecked so that decaying plants exist in such great numbers that the oxygen supply becomes rapidly depleted. These nutrients are present in domestic sewage effluents, agricultural runoff, and the little understood but apparently important non-point source runoff from urban areas.

Radioactivity

Radioactive materials are not only discharged to the marine environment by nuclear power plants, nuclear power plant fuel production and reprocessing plants, and uranium activities such as the burning of coal, when coal is burned it emits radioactive particles to the atmosphere which are then washed into the sea at a greater rate than any known nuclear power plants at this time. Other sources of radioactivity are the natural background, weapons testing, mine drainage, accidental spillage, and a few isolated industries.

One of the partially unsolved problems associated with the use of nuclear energy for electrical power is the long term storage or disposal of spent fuels. This storage must be in an area such that there are no pathways back to man, and deep oceans have been suggested as meeting this criterion.

Oxygen Demand

Oxygen demand materials are those which require oxygen for degeneration and therefore steal oxygen which would normally be utilized by marine animals. Thus if too many oxygen demand materials are placed in the marine environment, the animal population will be markedly decreased due to the lack of oxygen. Sewage sludge and any other organic waste materials, even that resulting from excessive plant growth due to an over supply of nutrients, are examples, are examples of common oxygen demand materials.

Acids and Bases

The discharge of acid and bases to the marine environment can be quite disturbing to the natural ecological balance of the systems. The normal pH of oceanic water is somewhere around 8.0, slightly basic. This is maintained by the carbonate system wherein carbon dioxide is moved back and forth through a chemical reaction to bicarbonate and carbonic acid. If a large amount of acid or base is introduced into the system, the carbonate reaction will be offset and an important element of the environment will be affected. In addition, there are large synergistic effects associated with pH. Most toxic materials, for example, increase their toxicity under condition of low pH.

The sources of acidic or basic material are primar'ly industrial with some of this material reaching the marine environment from accidental discharges and the rupturing of tankers.

Aesthetic Considerations

Aesthetically displeasing materials include all the stuff one finds in the ocean that is unpleasent to look at or to smell. Tar balls, floatables, gas (often hydrogen sulphide) producing materials, and coloring, agents are some examples of pollutants affending the senes, although in some cases these materials presents no real threat to the ecology of an area, when the area is being used for recreation, the quality of the surroundings becomes very important. Thus even though an aesthetically unpleasant area may still be useable for many activities, it is one which probably generates the most public response because no special instruments are required to measure the degradation; it is obvious. We thereafter find that aesthetic considerations very often are more important to the average person than those that may be more damaging from an ecolygical point of view.

Management Problems

Even though the major pollutants have been declineated the management of marine pollution turns out to be quite complex. The reason for this is that the marine environment is used by man in many different ways and this multi-use has a number of ramifications. In the first place each oceanic activity pursued by man may produce a whole spectrum of pollutants. A moving ship, for example, may not only discharge pollutants in the form of waste products from the people living aboard, oil from pumping its bilges, and heat from the discharge of its condensers, it may also require depending of a harbor channel. This may produce a salinity change in addition to sedimentation problems associated with the maintenance dredging required.

Each pollutant may come from many different users. The nutrients which primarily seem to come from the effluent of sewage disposal plants also may come from strom drainage of urban areas in the form of waste products of domestic animals, along with runoff from agricultural areas that have been fertilized by either commercial fertilizers or farm animals. Complicating the situation still further is the fact that pollutants sometimes affect each other. An interesting example of this occurs in baltimore. Maryland, a rather large, industrial city located on a small arm of the Chesapeake Bay. A significant portion of the effluents. It turns out that the waste ferrous sulphate from the steel plant combines with the phosphate in the sewage plant effluent to form a precipitate. Thus the phosphate ends up on the bottom of Baltimore Harbor rather than dissolved in the waters of Chesapeake Bay. In this case it appears that an industrial; effluent is utilized profitably (although accidentally) to decrease the input of a pollutant comprising one of the larger pollution problems in the Chesapeake Bay.

Another example of the effect of one pollutant on another is the attraction of heavy metals to suspended sediments. Most of the heavy metals in coastal waters seems to be swept out of the water by sinking sedimentary particles and end up in the bottom deposits. This may or may not be desirable. If the heavy metals then find their way into bottom dwelling organisms which, in turn, find their way into a food chain pathway to man, then this obviously is not desirable. A third example of this synergistic effect of two or more pollutants is the effect of oil on pesticides, combined with sediments. As indicated previously, pesticides in the main are more soluble in oil then they are in water so that if there is oil present in oceanic water, it will tend to concentrate any pesticides that also may be present. Oil also has an affinity for sediments and as it collects on the suspended particles, their weight is increased to the point where they sink to the bottom. Portions of the inshore marine environment thus are covered with sediments very rich in both oil and pesticides. Any management activity therefore must be very careful in controlling one pollutant not to disturb the conditions of another so that a greater problem is not generaged as a result of some "solution".

The introduction of foreign material into the marine environment is not always detrimental to man or to the environment either. The constrnction of fishing reefs was mentioned previously as one example of man's improving the environment by introducing foreign materials. Another example of this is the generation of wetlands in some instance due to man's carelessness. In many areas the increased erosion produced by construction activities has resulted in large areas of siltation where these eroded sediments have baen deposited in the shoreline areas. After stabilization, populations of marsh grass have been seen to spring up in many of these newly crated areas. In the main there has been no planning for this type of rehabilitation, but recent experimental work indicates that production of marshlands may very well be a common tool of the estuarine planner of the future.

Pollution Control Costs

It should be constantly kept in mind that wastes are never destroyed. Waste materials, whether liquid, solid or gaseous, either can be moved from one location to a other or can have their form or chemical composition altered. But the material is still there. Some authors have suggested the term "waste placement" be used instead of "waste disposal". Nothing is ever consumed; it is just used for a while and then pushed aside. Entropy is increased but there is no decrease in mass, and there is usually on increase in the amount of energy required to keep the system going. This is why recycling is so attractive. The advantages in terms of energy and natural resource requirements, along with the usual decrease in pollutants, are very strong. This is why recycling is so attractive. The advantages in terms of energy and natural resource requirements, along with the usual decrease in pollutants, are very strong. The key appears to be cost, with must of the cost setting in the area of transportation. When the cost of recycled materials in low enough to be competitive with new material then recycling will be increased to the point where it becomes a common part of every product that we use. Cost is a major part of every pollution problem. For example, ocean dumping has been criticized by many to the point where the U.S. Environmental Protection agency is attempting to stop it completely. In this context ocean dumping usually means dumping in the near coastal zone : within 10 or 15 miles of the area where these waste are generated. One satisfactory solution would be to require a distance of a thousand miles from the coast before dumping could proceed. Here, the pathways back to man would be extermely difficult and highly improbable. However, the cost of transporting this material such a great distance is, at this time, more than society is willing to pay so that this does not appear to be a viable solution.

Pollution Sources

Now that the pollutants have been delineated and described very briefly, let us concern outselves with the activities involved in the production of these pollutants in an attempt to pinpoint the source of the problem. These activities are listed in Table 4.2.

TABLE 4.2

Pollution Produeing Activities

Marine commerce
Industry
Electrical power generation
Sewage treatment
Other non industrial wastes
Recreation
Construction

Marine Commerce

Marine commerce is deeply involved with ships, and ships require great many services. The first of these is a deep enough water environment so that they can pass to and for on their appointed rounds. This usually requires continous dredging, and in some cases plans are also to increasc the depth of the presently available channels so that larger ships can be accomodated. Dredging is an expensive proposition requiring large expenditures of money since the amount of material handled is large and the time in which this has to be done is relatively small in order to stay ahead of the sedimentation rate. Once the sediments are extracted from the bottom and the channel is cut to the desired depth, the problem becomes one of disposing of the dredge spoils, the material dredged from the bottom. As indicated previously, sediments tend to have an affinity for a number of toxic materials, heavy metals, oil and pesticides being just a few. Thus these spoils must be placed in an area where leaching back into the environment will be minimal. Various solutions have been suggested but the problem is still one that has not been adequately solved.

Another aspect of the ship problem is oil. Whether these ships are transporting oil or using it for fuel and lubrication, there always seems to be some lost to the sea. Even though pumping of bilges is illegal within the coastal areas, it may still be done at sea. The oil input to the ocean resulting from bilge pumping is considered by many to be a major fraction of the petroleum products found in the ocean. When the major purpose of the ship is t› transport oil, the oil must be transferred from the ship to the shore holding facilities and *vice versa* and this process is also one contributing significantly to the amount of petroleum products lost to the sea.

Whenever ships are handled in a port area, a port facility is required. This facility must be maintained, improved, and modified to handle modern methods such as containerized shipping. All this requires construction of one sort or another, and very often associated with this construction is some amount of pollution. Most harbars have large storage areas open to the atmosphere so that a certain amount of leaching into the marine environment is inevitable. Lastley, there is a whole family of pollutants associated with any ship. A ship is just a little city afloat and any problems found in urban areas will be runoff on ships also. These problems must be addressed, and solutions usually take the form of shipboard waste treatment or waste storage facilities capable of holding wastes until they can be transferred to shore facilities for treatment.

Industry

Whenever one mentions pollution to the average individually the first source of pollution that pops into mind is industry, and there is no doubt that industry does contribute some pollutant materials to the marine environment. Just how much and how serious its contribution is a matter of some debate, but nevertheless, most industries require the use of water. This water has either heat or some chemical added to it before being discharged into the environment. These chemicals may be anything from toxic substances to harmless coloring agents.

Electrical power generation bring forth vision of waste heat and certainly this is one of the byproducts of producing electrical power are other byproducts of electrical power generation not so well know but just as important in terms of degreading the environment. The cooling water utilized in electric power plants is sent through heat exchangers composed of many metal tubes. These tubes must be kept free of algal growth because if they are not, the amount of waste heat transferred to the cooling water will be drastically reduced, with an associated decrease in plant efficiency. In order to keep these heat exchanger tubes clean, various methods are ured. One of these is the occasional use of chlorine. If the chlorine is misused by employing large amounts in an attempt to overkill, this chlorine can very easily produce a large mortality of organisms other than algae in the area of the power plant. Present data indicate that more fish have been killed from excess amounts of chlorine that from heat discharged by electrical power plants.

An additional problem involved with heat exchangers is the fact that many of these are made from copper, a toxic material used in antifouling paints on boats for many years, sometimes these heat exchangers are allowed to remain in an unused condition for extended periods of time with water sitting in the heat exchanger tubes. Some copper leaches into this water from the tubes and when the plant is turned on again this copper rich water is pumped into the environment where it may cause some consternation among the local marine organisms.

Large amount of water pumped at high speeds from a coastal region can trap or entrain small or some times even large organisms. These creature may suffer mechanical damage as they go through the system, or they may be exposed to large amounts of heat for a short period of time. Large individuals are perticularly susceptible to the former conditions, while heat spikes seem to bother the younger ones the most. Thus mechanical and chemical as well as heat problems are associated with the running of the electrical power plant. All these problems must be considered together to produce a design solution resulting in an minimum effect on aquatic conditions. Many modern plants have done this. However some of the older plants continue to insult the environment.

Radioactive wastes have been cited as one possible disadvantage of nuclear power plants but the amount of radioactive wastes actually transferred by cooling water by the surrounding environment has been measured as extremely low and well within the limits set by the nuclear Regulatory Commission. The spent fuel problems appears to be of more concern at this time.

One industry presently relatively small but which promises to get much larger and spread itself out over much of the oceanic bottom is mineral extraction. The pollution problems associated with this endeavour have not been documented due to the small opportunity for data taking, but it is expected they will be similar to marine constructions. At this time the major ocean c marine effect is directed toward the extraction of sand and gravel in the near by areas. With in the imminent future it appears that a concerned effort will be made to extract the manganese noudles from the ocean floor, perhaps at depth as great as 3000 metres. This mining effort will have some effect on the environment but how much is not quite clear. Whether the bottom will be disturbed in areas important to the food chain of the fish eaten by man is still an unanswered question since, to a great extent, the bottom has not even been mapped for the major locations of those noudles. If nothing else, however, one chain of effects will be to increase the number of vessels going to sea, requiring more port facilities to service them, utilizing more petroleum. and producing more ship wastes. The same can be said for the increase in activity connected with offshore oil drilling although it appears that there is less petroleum lost into the environment when the oil is obtained from an offshore well and transported to the continent by pipeline than when it is obtained from a land well and transported by means of tanker to its eventual user point. The spillage resulting from the use of tankers is greater than that resulting from the use of pipe lincs.

Sewage Treatment Systems

The treatment of domestic sewage appears at first glance to be an easy hing; this is a process that has evolved over a period of many years and certainly by now one would expect the process to be reasonably well developed, The process treating human waste products is quite successful in removing suspended materials and pathogens, but it is extremely difficult to extract all of the nitrogen and phosphorous compounds. Consequently sewage treatment facility effluent contains reasonably high amounts of these nutrients which push plants toward uncontrolled growth. In addition, when the facility is overloaded, as during a heavy rain, it is often completely bypassed, discharging raw sewage directly into the water. This requires a great deal of oxygen for decomposition so that the biological oxygen demand is increased.

The largest problem facing sewage disposal plants at this time is probably that generated by the fact that many of the sewage system customers are not homes but industries. Some of the industrial effluents flowing into sewage treatment plants are difficult, if not impossible, to treat adequately. It is primarily for this reason that sewage sludge is so difficult to dispose of, since it very often contains large amounts of heavy metals and other toxic industrial wastes.

One aspect of sewage treatment neglected up to now, primarily because the cost are so overwhelming, is the treatment of storm runoff. Unfortunately the solution is not as straight forward as simply increasing the capacity of existing plants to handle the heavy loads associated with storms, or even to add treatment to storm drainage systems when they exist separately. Much of the urban and rural runoff does not go through conventional pipe systems, so additional systems would have to be built it all runoff is to be treated. Storm drainage washes urban streets clean. All material deposited on the streets, including crankcase drippings, rubber worn from auto tires, and bird, dog, and cat droppings are washed to sea. Modern studies have indicated that this runoff is a very significant source of coliforms and petroleum, to name just two pollutants of some concern to man. How to handle these nonpoint sources is a task presently facing marine environment managers and one that appears to have no inexpensive or simple resolution.

With most large urban areas disposal of the solid residue from sewage treatment plants is a solid waste disposal problem of the first magnitude. Ocean dumping in the near-shore coastal regime has been utilized for many years and, to a certain extent, will probably continue to be. Either the sludge must be treated more thoroughly before it is dumped or new deep sea dumping araas must be found. If new treatment or disposal techniques are not followed, there may be major changes in the coastal environment.

Agricultural Sources

The largest single class of nonindustrial polluters are farms. Agricultural pollutants include commerclal fertilizers, animal wastes, pesticides, herbicides, and sediments. In many cases the agricultural contribution of all these pollutants is greater than any other single source. The pollution can be stopped, and there have been cases in the past where particularly bad problems have been solved. An excellent example of this is the case of the duck farms on long Island. Long Island duck is a delicacy that Americans have enjoyed for many years so that the Island has developed a very large duck industry. For years the waste products from these ducks had simply washed into Long Island Sound and the incremental effect on Long Island Sound was getting more alarming each year. The sound was becoming completely overgrown with undesirable plants from the excessive nutrients, and all of the local fisheries were suffering very badiy. A concerted effort was made to clean up the duck farms by venting direct runoff from the farms and collecting the duck faces. This effort was extremely successful and Long Island sound fisheries are being steadily rejuvenated.

Recreational Activities

Usually when we think of marine recreation we think of a nonpolluted area since recreation is essential limited by pollution. We very rarely think of recreation in terms of producing pollution, but there is a significant amount of pollution produced by recreational activities. In shallow water motor boats stir up the sediment on the bottom, a condition which often persists for long periods of time. This increase in turbidity markedley affects the natural plant growth and probably has something last few years. In addition, power boats produce wakes, especially when operating at higher speeds, which tend to accelerate the rate of shore line erosion. This is especially true in narrow rivers and estuaries. The aspect of motor boating that has many investigators most concerned is the discharge of petroleum products into the environment. There are some figures indicating that recreational boats add as much petroleum and petroleum waste products to the environment as all other sources combined.

Even fishing sometimes adds to the pollution problem. Many fisherman, if they catch a fish of an undesirable type, will simply throw it back. The fish, as often as not, has been mortally wounded and will die. If the area is heavily fished, these dead organisms will have a significant impact on the environment as they got. As an aside, it should be noted that over-fishing is just as effective in decimatlng a fish population as any toxic pollu tant.

Construction

The last source of pollutants listed in Table 4.3 is construction. By then done on land contiguous with the sea, such as port facilitles. Implied here is both the actual construction of the structure and the associated activities that go along with construction. There must be all sort of support equipment, but most important, there must be all sort of support equipment, but most important, there must be support people. Since, in general, the amount of pollution is directly related to numbers of people, any large construction effort will bring with in the usual people-waste products. The effect of a new physical structure where one had not previously been is not too well known, bot one thing is sure the environment will never be the same as it was before. Some of these changes may be beneficial, but no matter how beneficial there are always going to be some members of society who real to any change by claimbing a degradation of the environment. Any marine construction project must be judged on the basis of the benefits to be derived by society as a whole rather than solely to those accruing to some small group.

Sources and Quantities of Marine Oil Pollution

The firsr step in assessing the threat arising from ships and offshore production is to see it in perspective against the other the apparently less emotive sources of oil. In 1978 Cowell updated earlier US National Research Council data (Table sources of oil in the marine environment. Comparison with the earlier 1973 US data (Table 4.3).

TABLE 4.3

Estimated Annual Inputs of Oil to the Oceans, 1978

Source	*Million tonnes*
Load-on-top tankers	0.11
Non-load-on-top tankers	0.50
Bilges and bunkering	0.12
Terminal operations	0.001
Dry docking	0.25
Tankery accidents	0.30
Non-tanker accidents	0.10
Total	1.38
Off shore oil production	0.06
Coastal oil refineries	0.06
Industrial waste	0.15
Municipal waste	0.30
Urban runoff	0.40
River runoff	0.40
Natural seeps	0.60
Atmospheric rainout	0.60
Total	3.57
Overall total	4.95

TABLE 4.4

Estimated Annual Input of Oil to the Oceans from Maritime Transportation Activities

Sources	*Million tonnes*
Load-on-top tankers	0.31
Non-load-on-top tankers	0.77
Bilges and bunkering	0.50
Terminal operations	0.003
Dry docking	0.25
Tanker accidents	0.20
Non-tanker accidents	0.10
Total	2.133

Shows that considerable improvements were made in reducing ship source pollution in the intervening period. The Intergovernmental Maritime Organisation, IMO (formerly IMCO) is currently engaged in another review which is expected to show further improvements in the period up to 1982. However, in terms of the perspective which is to be established it must be concluded that land-based sources contribute more to marine pollution than do ships almost three times as much that the contribution from offshore oil productlon is comparatively very small, that accidents contribute about 15% to total marine source pollution and only about 5% of the total oil input to the sea.

Such surveys provide vely useful information on the relative amounts from various sources, some of which otherwise receive little or no publicity, and helps in this way to provide a better perspective. As we have seen, they also provide a useful record of improvements when this has occurred. On the other hand, global figures in themselves do not give a direct estimate of possible effects. Thus if we take atmospheric rainout as possibly the best example of a uniform input, its impact is likely to be less noticeable than localised discharge through rivers. Again, the contribution of hydrocarbons from a river may be negligible as a contribution to global figures but quite important in a may be expected to have a greater effeet of hydrocarbon burden in a river may be expected to have a greater effect in the river itself then in the sea to which it discharges. Of course, as stated earlier, it will readily be assumed that massive releases of oil will have a much greater effect of hydrocarbon burden in a river may be expected to have a greater effect in the river itself than in the sea to which it discharges. Of course, as stated earlier, it will readily be assumtd that massive releases of oil will have a much greater effect than low-concentration operational discharges. Thus global figures are all very well, but in order to assess actual impact in a given location, one needs to consider on the one hand the presence or absence of continues oil layers on the sea surface, and on the other, the concentrations of hydrocarbons in the water column itself.

5

The Effects of Marine Pollution

Effects of Oil from Various Sources

Clearly the opportunities to study the effects of oil presented by continous natural seepage, refinery effluent, oil rig discharges, etc., on the one hand, and the more massive short-term injections of oil arising from oil arising from oil rig blowouts and tanker accidents on the other, are different, and differences exist even within these two broad classes. It may therefore by though that results obtained in one case may not be applicable in the others. It is thus worthwhile to consider types differences and to assess the extent to which results obtained at the various sites and incidents may be of universal application.

The first point to note in this endeavour is that oil does not dissolve in water. It floats on the sea surface as a thin layer when spilled or otherwise discharged because it is less dense than water and insoluble in it. This thin layer tends to break into droplets by wave action and these droplets become dispersed in the volume of sea water beneath the slick. Photochemical and biological oxidation of the sicks and of the dispersed oil droplets takes place producing oxygenated derivatives of the original oil components and these may form true solutions in water.

Thus the area of sea covered by the surface slick is proportional to the magnitude of the spillage, but the concerntrations in the sea arise from the slow dispersion of droplets of oxygented derivatives. Sea water concentrations are therefore a function of mass transfer rates from slick to water and not a function of the quantity spilled. Sea water concentrations are in fact independent of the quantity spilled, provided a surface layer has formed above the sea water volume in question. If more or less oil is spilled or otherwise introduced to the sea the result is more or less sea affected rathes than that a given volume is affected to a greater or lesser extent.

Oil concentrations are therefore controlled by the in solubility of the oil and mass transfer rates from surface slicks to the underlying sea. In the absence of detailed knowledge of mass transfer rates it is not possible to calculate the resulting concentrations, but upper limits can easily be established. Thus if the slick thickness to which the oil spreads and from which it subsequently disperses to the water is 0.1 mm, then the maximnm concentration which can achieved if the oil were instantaneously dispersed uniformly in the top metre of sea would be 100 ppm. Concentrations over other depth ranges and for other thicknesses are of course pro data.

It must be concluded therefore that is we leave aside for the time being the possible environmental effects of continuous oil slicks on the sea surface which occur when the capacity of the aqueous phase for oil is exceeded, we can discuss the other oil concentration-related aspects in the same manner whether a surface slick is present or not and whether the oil in question acrose from a natural seep, a blowout, cargo tank reputure or operational discharge from ship, oil rig or refinery. Generally speaking, we have limited our discussions to those materials introduced into the marine environment that are the direct result of man's activities, and with a few minor exceptions we shall continue to limit our discussions of pollution to those activities of man and not consider the deletrious effects of natural occurences.

Pollutant Types

In this chapter we shall attempt to get some idea as to what pollution does and why we consider it to be so undesirable. There are three basic type of pollutants : the pathogenic, the aesthetic, and the ecomorphic.

Pathogenic pollutants are those which cause disease. This disease may be fatal if the pollutant is a lethal poison.

Aesthetic pollutants are those pollutants causing a change in the environment displeasing to the eye, ear, or nose of man.

Ecomorphic pollutants, on the other hand, are those pollutants which produce a change in the physical characteristics of the enviroment in such a way that there may be drastic changes in the structure or composition of the biosphere.

Obviously, these three types of pollutants are not of equal import.

Pathogenic pollutants are certainly much more serious than the other two; however, ecomorphic pollutants are often an indicator of more serious types of polltion to follow. Furthermore, since pollution is man-produced and the effects are suffered by man, aesthetic problems are certainly of interest. Nevertheless in any management situation when trade-offs are required, it will certainly be necessary to rank different types of pollutants so that society can determine how it would like to spend is limited funds of time, effort, and money.

Acuate Effects

Let us look first at the pathogenic pollutants since these are obviously the most important. The effects of pathogenic pollutants are either acute or chronic. Acute effects are those which occur in a relatively short perlod of time while chronic effects may take time to be noticed, as in the case of carcinogenic pollutants, or the effect may be noticed immediately but continued for a very long period of time,

The accute effects are the easiest to determine because of the short time between administration and affiction. The easiest way of measuring acute effect is by feeding the pallutant in question to test organisms, such as since or selected fish, and observing the dosage required to will 50% of the organisms involved. This is usually done by feeding a pollution of test organisms increasing amounts of the pollutant, and for each dosage the number of individuals that succumb is noted. When these data are plotted, an S— shaped curve results, such as shown in Graph – 3.1 wherein dosage versus number of mortalities is plotted. From this curve it may be seen that there are a small number of individuals that require an exteremely large does befor they are killed while some are killed with a relatively small dose. By plotting this type of curve, it is leasy to locate the dose for which half the individuals die. This dosage is called the LD50, and it is this LD 50 which is usually used to compare the relative toxicity of one pollutant with another.

Another way of examining acute effect is to observe the effect of a given pollutant concentration on organisms over a somewhat longer period of time, noting how long it takes for given dosage to produce mortalities. This say be done by giving a predetermined concentration of the pollutant to the test animals and observing how long it takes to kill half of them. When data from an experiment such as this are plotted, a curve similar to that shown in graph 3.2 results. As may be seen, the curve is a hyperbola with the horizantal asymptotic suggesting a threshold concentration. In other words, below this asymptotic value there is no apparant effect, since at this concentration an finite amount of time is required for mortality.

The vertical asymptote, on the other hand, appears to be a saturation level. At this level any increase in the concentration will not produce any further decrease in the amount of time rquired for fatality. Evidently there is a finite time required for the pathogen to do its work, so that no matter how high the concentration, the time required to kill will not go below this amount.

Charonic Effects

With the asympototic values, suggests another concept : the threshold value. There appears to be a dose size for each pathogen below which the pollutant has no effect. The concern with threshold values for various pollutants is one aspect of the study of chronic effects. Chronic effects are the most difficult to measure because of the time involved; in some cases cancers have developed as long as 25 years after initial exposure to the carcinogenic agent. Neverthless, measurements have been made and for many materials threshold value seems to describe the data reasonably well.

Most experiments need some measure of the effect on the organisms other than death, so that many different measures are used. These are : deformity in the growth of organisms, damage to particular organs, change in heartbeat or breathing rate, genetic damage to individuals, change in the rate of increase of a population, life expectancy of individuals within a particular population, and fecundity of females with the population. Unfortunately, and index may be very descriptive of the effect of a pollutant on a particular species, but it may be completely ineffective in describing what happens when this pollutant comes in contact with other species.

A typical experiment using one of these measures would involve the variation in pathogen concentration while noting the variation in the heartbeat or some other measure. When these data are plotted the result is very often a straight line as shown in graph 3.3. This linear relation - ship between effect and concentration may be extrapolated back to determine the concentration for zero effect. When this is done the line will cross the axis at a concentration from zero. This is called the threshold value.

A great deal of caution must be used in interpreting these data. Some pathogens apparently have no threshold value associated with them, and it is always risky business to extrapolate a straight line. The actual manner in which the organisms reacts to the stimulus might very well be nonlinear at lower dosages. In addition some chronic effects may be so suitable that two or three generations of the organisms might be required to observe any change.

Synergism

Another complication in the examination and quantification of pathogenic pollutants is the phenomenon of synergism. A synergistic effect occurs when the combined effect of two or more materials acting together is greater than would be expected from the simple sum of the individual effects. Temperature, for example, is a very strong synergistic parameter, generally enhancing most pollutant effects as temperature is increased. The same is true of salinity and dissolved oxygen. Some pollutants, on the other hand, tend to decrease the effects of others, as might be in the case of a strong acid and a strong base present at the same time. Other pollutants may cause strong pathogens to be precipitated out of the water column or to be collected on sediments, so that in either case they end up on the bottom. Thus it is extremely important in the analysis of any pollutant to be aware of the other materials present and their synergistic tendencies.

Within the marine biosphere many organisms are affected by various pollutants. Whether or not a particular organism is affected by any given pollutants will depend on any variable.

For example, many polluants are found only in the water column while others, such as some of the pesticides and heavy metals, are adsorbed onto suspended sediments and usually find their way to the bottom within a relatively short period of time. Consequently, these latter types would tend to affect those organisms living on the bottom or feeding from bottom organisms more then they would affect the organisms living within the water column, such as free swimming fish.

Also of import in determining the effectiveness of a particular pollutant on living organisms is its relative solubility in water and oil. Pollutants more soluble in oil will tend to find their way to organisms that have a larger content of oil in their body tissues. This is particularly true of some of the pesticides which are more soluble in oil than water. The individual habits of marine organisms also affect their susceptibility to a particular polluant. Feeding habits with respect to time of day, portion of water column for aged, type of material ingested, and the method of digestion utilized all determine to a great extent the types of pollutante the organism will be exposed to. Similarly spawning habits determine the type of area and time of year in which a species is particularly sensitive to subtle changes in the environment. These changes affect not only the parents but also the offspring, and may be even their progency.

Other habits not having to do with spawning also help to determine whether an organism will be exposed to particular pollutants. Wheather the organism is sensitive to light or sound, for example, will often determine whether it is attracted to a particular out-fall. Thus we find that a pure and simple cause and effect relationship between a pollutant and an organism is not enough to determine completely the actual response of the organism in the real world. Laboratory results might be completely refused in the field simply because the organism does not respond to extraneous characteristics of the environment under natural conditions in the same manner in which it did in the laboratory.

Pathways to Man

Once some of the pollutant has been ingested by marine organisms, the major concern of man is the possibility of this pollutant appearing on his dinner table and causing a pathogenic response. Obviously if a fish ingests a pollutant and a human eats that fish, then that person will have ingested a does of that pollutant and there will probably be some danger. The question is, "How much ?" In order to arrive at an approximation of the actual amount of undesired material finding its wax into the reader's stomach, one must follow the pollutant through a number of steps.

Most organisms living in the sea tend to concentrate materials existing in the sea to much greater values that they are in the ocean itself. For example, a diatom, a small form of marine algae having a silicate frustule, has a body concentration of silicon about 40 thousand times as great as the oceanic waters from which the organism derives all of its material. Thus the diatom concentrates silicon very effectively so that if we eat diatoms, a large portion of our diet would be glassy. Similarly, other organisms, including fish, will concentrate other materials even if these do not naturally occur in the environment. But this amplification or concentration does not stop with one step. We must continually keep in mind the fact that an organism does not exist by itself in the marine environment. Any organism is dependent upon many other organisms for its existance. An edible fish, for example, might very well subsist on smaller fish which, in turn, might subsist on small zooplankton, which, in turn, may subsist on phytoplankton. There may be 5 to 10 individual links in a food chain leading to man, and there is the distinct possibility that for each one of these links a concentration of the pollutant occurs. Thus the total pathway to man for the pollutant might be a rather tortuous one, but it might result in a very high concentration of the pollutant material in the fish. This in itself may be of no concern to the individual unless he ingests the fish and if so, how often and how much he consumes. It is not enough simply to know that there is some pollutant present in marine organisms : one also should know how much is present, and in addition two other facts are required. This first is the accepted maximum level of ingestion of the pollutant before harm results, and the second is the amount of fish that can be eaten before this level is reached. In this way it might very well be possible to have a particular kind of fish one or two times a year with perfect safety, while if it is eaten once a day, it might very well have a toxic effect.

Ecomorphic Pollutants

There are many different types of pollutants that may be classified as ecomorphic, while some pollutants fall into all three of the classes stipulated above and, many fall into at least two. Sediment is a pollutant whose effect is primarily that of changing the envii onment since it is not pathogenic and very often is not aesthetically displeasing, although it can be. As it settles to the bottom, it will tend to bury the organisms that live on the bottom, such as cysters and clams, and eventually smother them. Sediment also tends to fill in marsh areas, killing the marsh grass, and completely changing the habitat. Since marsh areas are breeding grounds for small fish and an important ecological link in most of the oceanic life, any destructive process such as this is bound to markedly change the marine biological environment. On the other hand, in some cases where man's activities have produced large amounts of erosion and sediment has been brought down by rivers into estuaries, some estuarine areas have been filled enough to support marsh grasses. In some cases excess erosion can produce marsh lands rather than desrroy them. Whenever there is a depth change in an estuarine or coastal area, the effects are many. They range from changing the biological environment so that larger fish will no longer live in the shol areas to affecting the total circulation pattern of the area. But suffice it to say that changing depth in many cases does change the manner in which salt and fresh water mix in the coastal area and also the amount of flushing present in a particular region. When the sediment is in suspension it also has an effect on the eco-system, the most obvious aspect being a change in transparency. By making the water more opaque, light will not penetrate as deeply as before so that the thickness of the layer of water in which plants grow will be decreased. If the water is fairly shallow to begin with, this decrease in transparency may very well result in the inability of rooted plants to grow and some marsh lands may be destroyed. The effect of sediment, then is two-fold : changing both bottom and water properties. Both of these effects tend to change the physical characteristics of the ecosystem.

Another ecomorphic pollutant is oil, although oil sometimes produces toxic effects. The result of oil coating bird feathers is a well known physical effect. The oil does not poison birds; it sampIy makes it impossible for them to fly, and consequently many of them die. A film of oil on the surface will also decrease the amount of sunlight entering the water and, similarly, will limit the exchange of oxygen from the atmosphere. In addition to the aesthetic and pathogenic effects of oil, there are thus also ecomporphic effects.

The toxic effects of various nitrogen compounds are well known but fertilizers and other nutrients washed into the sea have a nontoxic effect on marine waters. These materials will do just what they are designed to do : make plants grow, whether these plants be terrestial or aquatic plants.

The toxic effects of various nitrogen compounds are well known but fertilizers and other nutrients washed into the sea have a nontoxic effect on marine waters. These materials will do just what they are designed to dot : make plants grow, whether these plants be terrestial or aquatic plants.

Those plants on the bottom of the blanket will tie, due to lack of light, and those roting plants will utilize oxygen in their decay processes. Even though there are more plants than before, producing more oxygen in the process of photosynthesis, so many of them are dying and decaying the result is to decrease the dissolved oxygen. This phenomenon it called "Eutrophication."

Another ecomorphic pollutant that seems to be receiving a lot of attention lately is heat. Usually supplied to the marine environment form electrical power plants or other industrial sources, this heat will increase the water temperature and may result in different kinds of damage to marine organisms Since most mutations are caused to thermal activity under normal conditions, the possibility of genetic damage is real. It is estimated that about 90% of the mutations occuring normally are thermally caused, while only about 10% are caused by radiation.

Aesthetic Pollutants

The last type of pollutant mentioned above was aesthetic pollutants. Aesthetic pollutants are those which offend the human senses and as such are considered by many to be unimportant. In many environmental problem areas, though, the aesthetic considerations often receive more attention by environmentally oriented citizens than some of the pathogenic pollutants. This is simply because the aesthetic pollutants are visible and what can be seen, smelled, or heard appears much more bothersome than that which is hidden, even though the hidden pollutant might be much more dangerous to life. Consequently, any scheme for controlling marine pollution must include some consideration of the aesthetic pollutants if it is to succeed. An excellent strategy seems to be to focus on the aesthetic pollutants and use them as a machanism to gather momentum to clean up the rest of the pollution problems.

Power transmission cable has caused more than one power company grief because of the environmental consideration given the local citizens who are concerned about the appearance of power cables running across the countryside. Oil wells, especially the offshore variety visible from resort areas, are of great concern to most environmentalists. The same thing is true of equipment required for dredging operations and the spoil areas resulting from these operations. To some people, especially those living in relatively pristine environments near the water, boats can also be an aesthetic pollutant, especially those that cause waves and noise. Effluents that cause the colour of the sea to change to increase the amount of suspended sediments also may be considered aesthetic pollutants. It simply is not as pleasant to go swimming in water that is cloudy of contains colouring material different from what one would expect in a normal, natural body of water.

In essence, any change from the pristine environment appears to many to be aesthetic pollution. Obviously we are living in an unreal world if we think the marine environment can be maintained in an unspoiled form. It should be borne in mind that many complaints about aesthetic pollution come from individuals who would father live in the primeval environment not realizing that it would not be available to them unless the commercial world about them supported it. There appears to be a dichotomy wherein of try to maintain the unspoiled environment in certain areas while letting others become over utilized. Nevertheless, there is a growing movement to include in the cost of every project a relatively small sum to improve its aesthetic qualities. This is, of course, exactly the same philosophy that is applied to the control of other forms of pollution. Additional money is spent in a chemical process, for example, to control the pollution-producing properties of the effluent since society believes that this additional sum of money is desirable expenditure. It may similarly be maintained that the expenditure for aesthetic pollution control is desirable as it also will tend to increase the quality of life.

This paragraph briefly those portions of these studies that are relevant to determining the effects of oil on marine wetlands. Also, the literature and out personal experiences with oiled marine wetlands are synthesized to allow an evaluation of methods or protection, cleanup, and restoration attempts that have been carried out in marine wetlands. This section accomplishes there two objectives by :

– Providing a brief review of the effects of all spills and related cleanup activities on salt marshes and mangrove ecosystems

– Reviewing methods of protecting marine wetlands from being oiled.

—Reviewing successful means of cleaning marine wetlands following oil spills.

—Reviewing and presenting techniques that have proven successful in restoring marine wetlands damaged by oil spills and/or cleanup operations.

—Establishing a set of criteria and discussing guidelines for decisions on means of protecting susceptible areas, and for cleaning and restoring oiled marine wetlands.

—The differences in growth patterns and life cycles are essential elements in consideration of methods of cleanup and restoration of marine wetlands.

—It should be noted that salt marsh and mangrave vegetation occur together in some parts of the world, *e.g.*, souther Brazil, southeast Australia. For the purpose of this discussion, we need to identify two terms.

—Recovery : return of a site to dominance by native organisms that are within the natural range of limits for structure and function in unprotected examples of the ecosystem within the local geographic area.

—Restoration : man's efforts to initiate and/or enhance the recovery process.

EFFECTS OF OIL SPILLS ON MARSHES AND MANGROVES

1. Oil Impacts to Marshes

Oil impacts to marshes will very with a number of factors including the amount of oil, type and magnitude of cleanup activities, type of oil, physical and biological structure of the marsh, latitude, and season. Subsequent persistence of damages and recovery of the system also depend on numerous physical, chemical, and biotic factors including weathering rate and degree of removal or retention of oil, availability of propagules (seeds or vegetative), successional processes, sediment erosion/acceration, and restrorative activities by man.

Plants can be affected in several ways. Physical smothering by oil can lead to reduced transpiration, respiration, and photosynthesis. Absorption of toxic oil fractions through the leaves or roots may cause poisoning of the plant by disrupting cell membrances and cellular organelles. Some species such as *juncusmaritimus*, *is gerarii*, and Spartina anglica exhibit epidermal or cellular resistance to oils.

There is a considerable range of sensitivity to oil. Some species are resistant even to repeated spills (*e.g.*, salicornea sp. Many of the more resistant species are also pernnials with large root systems that enable them to grow back following oil damage to aerial portions.

Oils vary in their toxicity, according to the content of low-boiling compounds, unsaturated compounds, and aromatics. In general, the higher the concentration of these constituents, the more toxic the oil. It is self evident that the amount of oil and frequency of oiling will effect the degree of damage, but it is less obvious that visocity of the oil is important. With light oil, there is a physical limit to the amount that will "stick" to a shore, with subsequent tides redistributing oils. In contrast, the viscosity of heavy oils often allows retention of large volumes and many cause mortality not through toxicity but through smothering. Heavy oils also tend to be more persistent and to extend the durtation of damage, thus slowing recovery.

Since and sediment structure of the marsh considerably affect the degree of damage and potentials for recovery. In the United States, Europe, and elsewhere marshes may be narrow fringing bands along the high water mark, especially in areas where tides are small, or marshes may be broad vegetational belts (occasionally many hundreds of meters wide) in estuaries or on sheltered coasts, especially where tidal ranges are large. Extensive marshes may not be completely covered even to massive spills, as oil will tend to affect the sides of the creeks and drainage channels first and then progress into the marshes plateau. Where vegetation is tall and dense (*e.g.*, in a spartinetum of juncetum), considerable volumes of all may be completely oiled, and after severe damage, there may be no source of propagules for recovery. In such areas, restorative action may be the only means of marsh reestablishment in the short term.

Sediment characteristics, including particle size distribution and drainage patterns, considerably affect potential for oil retention. Marshes in North America and Europe can be found in sediments ranging from medium grainted sands to very fine silts where more than 95% of sediment particles are less than 63 in diameter. Sands tend to be more freely draining and more easily penetrated by oils as shoots can occur. If oil penetrates anaerobic sediments weathering is reduced or stops, and the oil may be retained in unchanged form for considerable periods of time, reducing or preventing plant regrowth. However, where oil is weathered before or after incorporation, even very high levels may not prevent plant regrowth. Growth in salicornia sp., *suaeda maritima, Aster tripolium and Spartina anglica* has been reported run areas where levels of total aliphatic hydrocarbons of up to 5,875 ug/g were found.

Seasonal changes in the marsh may considerably affect the extent of oil damage. Oiling before or during flowering can cause reduced flowering and seed production. This may delay flowering and seed production (Dicks, unpublished data). During winter months may species die back and oil may affect only dead and decaying vegetation; however, in spring and summer growth, new shoots and germinating seedflings are particularly vulnerable.

In some cases, a major problem following oil damage to vegetation has been loss of sediment stability followed by erosion (*e.g.*, Isle Grande, France following the Amoco Cadiz oil spill). Where extensive rhizomatous root mats ramify the sediments or where vegetation cover is continuous (*e.g.*, in denise Spartina Stands), sediments may remain stable even when vegetation has been killed. In low marsh colonized mainly by annual species (*e.g.*, Salicornica) or where vegetation is sparse, root mats may be insufficient to prevent erosion. Where erosion occurs, lowering of marsh level may prevent reestablishment of vegetation Erosion may also follow damage to creek systems after cleanup activities (*e.g.*, during the Amoco Cadiz spill that affected the Isle Grande marshes. The importance of slat marshes in prevention of coastline erosion is well established and may be or prime importance in some areas.

Because of the preceding considerations, basin forest may have variable characteristics. Generally, however, basin forests are well developed with canopy heights that may reach 15-20 m.

Riverine forests : This forest type develops along the edges of estuaries, often as far as the inland extent of the saline intrusion. It is best developed, however, in the lower course of the estuary where water flows are moderate to high and high nutrient inputs prevail. This combination of adequate freshwater and nutrient inputs allows the development luxuriant stands.

On the periphery of the forest, the dominant species is the Rhizophora mangrove. This is an area where there is greater kinetic energy by due to the combination of river flow and tidal motion. The complex root system of Rhizophora, with its extraordinarily developed adventitious ("stilt") roots, allows the establishment of large trees on very unstable, soft soils.

In the inner forest, mixed stands of Laguncularia and Avicennia occur. Rieverine forests are highly productive with litter fall rates in excess of 4 g/m/day. Canopy heights reach 20 m in the best-developed forests.

Fringe forests ; This type occurs along the seaward edge of forests lining protected shorelines. There is usually a strong horizontal gradient in tropography as well as a singificant gradient in turbulence and tidal amplitude. Energy derived from the tides and waves decays rapidly inland where tidal flooding is further reduced by the rise in the mangrove floor. The reduced flusing inland results in the establishment of a phy-siochemical gradient in water quality, toward the outer edge of the fringe, where greater energy levels prevail, the large, heavy seedlings of Rhizophora become established. Inland this way and tidal energy dissipates, and in the higher, less flushed parts of the fringe, Avicennia becomes the dominant species.

Since frings are exposed, they are subjected to periodic destruction buy storms, waves, or scouring by strong current as. During storms large amounts of debris may be deposited in the outer fringe, reducing circulation to the inner fringe and the basins inland.

Overwash forests : These forests are formed on small island or projections from land masses (peninsulas) they are characteri-zed by intense flushing by daily tides. The high flushing rates do not allow the formation of strong salinity gradients nor the accumulation and aggradation of the soil or of nutrients factors that usually lead to a succession of species toward the interior. True overwash forests are thus monospecific (cominated by rhizophora).

The amount of flushing and nutrient availability are critical factors that determine the structure and the rate of overwash forests. They, overwash islands in coastal oligotrophic waters may not be as developed as those inside coastal lagoons where higher nutrient accumulation is possible. excessive flushing leads to erosion and loss of the forest whereas extremely low flushing rates lead to accumulation of debris and vertical aggradation inside the forest with reduced flushing rates toward the core of the island. These islands thus evolve into frings and basin forests. Cintron et al. have described the formation, aging, and decay of these islands is southwest Puerto Rico.

Dwarf forests Dwarf forest are found in marginal environ-ments where their structural development is limited by edaphic factors, probably the unavailability of nutrients. Mature trees in these forests are usually less than 3 m tall. Salinity is not the limiting factor. Although the vegetation is limited in heigh, leaf size is not reduced as usually happens when mangroves are under the influence of a chronic stresson. This type of forest is different from those that may be considered scrub forests and that develop under the influence of chronic stressor, such as high salinity or cold stress. The dominant species in Dwarf forest in Florida and Puerto Rico is Rhizophora.

Table 5.1. List 14 oil spills. worldwide, where some documentation of impact to mangroves has been observed and reported. Most of the earlier reports are anecdotal with little or no quantification as to the levels of oil contamination; the actual types of oil stranded in the forests; the areal extent of mangroves oiled, and actual numbers, sizes, or areal coverage of mangroves killed or stressed by the oil spill. In addition, the species of mangroves involved was often not mentioned. In addition to impacts to the trees themselves, the funal component of the ecosystem is usually treated by noting dead or stressed animals at the time of the spill, or attempting to quantify losses or changes by one-shot sampling. In particular, the sampling of infauna, in many of these cases, has not taken into account the normal seasonal variations in infnnal species and numbers. All these problems may lead to widely different observations of the "impact" of a spill by different investigators.

Due to the fact that floating oil is transported by waves and currents and strands on shorelines, low-wave energy ecosystems such as mangroves forests are routinely sites where oil accumulates after a spill. In addition, the inaccessibility of most mangrove forests makes oil removal very difficult, if not impossible, and the fine-grained and peaty anaerobic sediments characteristic of mangrove forests may reduce the rate of micorbial breakdown of oil.

These factors, plus the burrowing activities of crustaceans characteriestic of mangrove forests, can lead to persistent, high

TABLE 5.1

Comparrison of Oil Spills Impacting Mangroves

Source of spill and date	*Type of oil*	*Amount of oil*	*Mangrove species effected*	*Location*	*Impact on Mangroves*
1	2	3	4	5	6
Argea prima vessel 26 July 1968	Crude	10,000 tons	Unidentified	Guanica, puer to Rico	"This habitat was virtually destroyed
White water, vessel 13 Dec. 1968.	Diesel oil & Buncker C	20,000 barrels	Rhizaphora mangle Avicennia sp.	Galeta island panama	Death of young mangroves, loss of sessile animals and algae on prop on prop roots (loss still visible 66 months after spill)

(Contd.)

1	2	3	4	5	6
Pipeline break 1970.	Light crude	100,000 barrels	Unidedtified	Tarut Bay, Saudi Arabia	Defoliation, but many survived
Zoe Colcotronics 18 Aug. 1973.	Venezulan crude	37,000 barrels	Rhizophora mangle Avicennia Germinas	Cabo Rojo, puerto Rico	Death of adult trees (red and black) over an area of 1.0.2.7 hectares within 3 years
Santa Augusta Vessel 1971.	Crude	12.5 million liters	Rhizophora mangle	St. Croix, U.S. Virgin	5 hectares completely destroyed little or no recolonization after 7 years
Funiwa 5 Off-shore oil well, 17 Jan. 1980 to 1 Feb. 1980.	Crude	8.4 million gallons	Unidentified	Nigeria	338.6 hectares of mangroves killed some recovery in process
Peck slip large 19 Dec. 1978	Buncker C	440,000 to 460,000 barrels	Rhizophora	Between Punta San Agustin and Yabucoa Puerto Rico	"Significantly affected mangrove, crab snail, and eqiphyte populations,"

TABLE 5.2

Compartison of Oil Spill Impacting Mangroves

Source of spill and date	*Type of oil*	*Amount of oil*	*Mangrove species effected*	*Location*	*Impact on mangroves*
1	2	3	4	5	6
Sova Muru, vessel, 6 Jan. 1975.	Arabian light, Berri, and Murban crude.	54,000 barrels	Sibberatua sp. Rhizophora sp.	Indonesia	Some dead trees (both species unqantified areas of greatest impact in sheltered bays, low numbers of crabs and snails associated with elevated oil in sediments.

(*Contd.*)

1	2	3	4	5	6
Pipeline rupture 13 Oct 1976.	Crude	377 barrels	Avicennia germinans	Corpus Christi, Taxes	Mangroves burned to remove oil died; uncleaned mangroves recovery after minor defolition.
Unidentified vessel March 1977.	Venezuelan crude	1,000 barrels	Rhizophora mangle	Guayanilla Bay, Puerto Rico	Damage to mangrove root community; trees survived
St. Peter vessel Feb. 1976.	Crude	243,442 barrels	Rhizophora	Colombia/ Ecuador	No "noticeable long-term biological effects.". temporary decline in fishery harvests and calm harvesting
Garbos, 18 July 1975.	Crude oil & water emulsion	1,500-3,000	Rhizophora Avicennia germinans	Florida Keys,	Death of young red mangrove seedings and some Dwarif black mangroves

Howard Star, vessel, 5 Oct. 1978.	20% diesel 80% Bunker C	40,000 gallons	Rhizoophora mangle Avicennia germinans	Tampa, FL.	Death of all three species of mangroves, death of mollusks and polychaetes; root abnormalities.
World Encouragement, vessel, 10 Sept. 1979.	Light Arabian crude	29,060 gallons	Avicennia marina	Botany Bay N.S.W. Austrilia	Death of scattered mangroves 1-2 years after spill.

levels of oil contamination not only on the soil's surface but also deep in the sediments in the mangrove root core, and mangroves can be killed.

Table 5.2 lists generalized responses of mangroves to oil spills in two general categories – acute and chronic exposure would be short term (1.4 weeks) and may and with no further impact if the oil is removed either mechanically or by natural wave and current activity.

TABLE 5.3

Generalized Responees of Mangrove Forests to Oil Spills

Stage	*Observed Impact*
0-15 days	Deaths of birds, turles, fish, and invertebrates
15-30 days	Defoliation and death of small [< 1 m] mangroves-loss of aerial roots
30 days-1 year	Defoliation and death of medium [< 3 m] mangroves-tissue damage to aerial roots
1-5 years	Death of large [< 3 m] mangroves, loss of oild aerial roots and regrowth of new ones (sometimes deformed) Recolonization of oil damages areas by new seedlings
1-10 years	Reduction in litter fall, reduced reproduction, and reduced survial of seedlings Death or reduced growth of young trees colonizing spill site ? Increased insect damage ?
10-50 years	Complete recovery

6

Marine Oil Pollution

Introduction

Pollutants originating from domestic and industrial sources and from agricultural operations due to high inputs of heavy metals, hydrocarbons (crude oil), pesticides fungicides, insecticides have spread to coastal areas through rivers run off, via the atmosphere, direct discharges or dumping into the sea where the most of the active primary and secondary production direct, are being polluted, casusing serious damage to acquatic eco-systems.

Oill Spils

Oil spilt on ocean waters kills birds, fouls beaches, and poisons marine life. Hasan Jawaid Khan gives an account of these deadly oil spills, the damage they bring about and the ways by which an oil slick is contained tense of thousand of sea birds coated with oil shivering and dying on the beaches. At least a thousand sea otters succumbing in the oil with their livers and kidneys fatally impaired. And an unknown number of seals, whales and porpoises poisoned. Even before the tragic images of the deadly oil spill on the Alaskan coast could fade from memory, the specture of an oil spill is back again to haunt us-only this time it is much too bigger The enormous oil slick in the Gulf region, 30 times more than the Alaskan episode, threatens to set into motion an unprecedented ecological disaster that may take decades to fix.

Ironically, the oil that drivers millions of vehicles round the world. sometimes drives countless marine animals to a most cruel death, crude oil when refined drives automobiles and airplanes, runs factories and farm equipments, provides gas for heating and cooking and is a source for making drugs, cosmetics and fertilizers. But when crude oii spills on to ocean waters it spells death for marine animals and disaster for the ocean ecology.

There has always been a danger of major oil spills accurring near a coastal area with supertankers being increasingly used to carry industrial and heating oils. Several of these huge ships have been grounded and cracked open by the seas, their vast cargoes spilling out heavy oil into the oceans where currents can carry it many miles before it disperses and gradually sinks to the floor. Sometimes the currents carry the oil toward land where it fouls beaches and kills marine life.

The world first woke up to the disastrous consequences of an oil spill when on 18 March 1967 a Liberian tanker. Terry Canyon, ran a ground on the southwest cast of Great Britain, near the entrance to the English Channel, spilling 60,000 tons crude oil into the sea. Oil splittered on to 160 kilometers of coastline killing countless number of fish and birds: Two years later, in January 1969 occurred the second major oil spill off the coast of Santa Barbara in the United States when an offshore oil well below out resulting in the discharge of oil at the rate of 1,000 gallons per hour causing extensive damage to the coast.

In 1978, in the much publicized Amoco Cadiz disaster 68 million gallons of oil was dumped all along the French coast. And then on March 24, 1989 the supertanker Exxon Valdez belonging to the Exxon corporation, the largest petroleum company in the world, plied on to a reef off the coasts of Alaska. Through five gashed in its hull the 30,000 ton super tanker spilled over 11 million gallons of oil into the clean water of Alaska's Prince William Sound. As the oil hit 1,930 kilometers of shoreline. 100,000 seabirds died including 150 rare species of baldeagles. An unknown number of dead seals sank to the bottom of the ocean. And at least 1,000 sea otters perished. Even a few deer and a couple of bears that fed near the soreline were found dead.

Closer home, Indian coasts have also been withness to a few tanker disasters, none too serious thought. In July 1973, 3,000 tons of oil washed on to the Gujarat coast when an oil tanker, cosmos pioneer, ran around. In 1974 an American oil tanker Transhuron colided with one of the atolls of the Lacadives spilling 5,000 tons of special furnance oil causing extensive damage to marine life. Similary destruction was witnessed when the oil tanker Lajpat spilled thousands of tons of oil along the Bombay coast. The last time an oil spill threatened the India coast was in June 1989 when a Maltese tanker M.T. Puppy collided with a British vessel. The Maltese tanker spilled over 5,500 tons of furnance oil into the open seas off Bombay. At that time the fear of contamination of fish brought the fish industry to virtual halt at people stopped buying fish for fear it might cause cancer.

But not all the petroleum that gets into the marine environment is through oil spills. Natural seeps have been discharging petroleum into the marine environment for millions of years in amounts substantially greater than those resulting from present offshore production activities. More than 200 submarine oil seeps have been identified worldwid. An assessment of petroleum pollution of the world's oceans by the national Academty of Sciences, Washington, estimated that between 1.7 and 8.8 million metric tons of oil enter the oceans annually. Oil spills are by far the major contributors to this pollution. While other categories of pollution have shown a fifty per cent decrease, oil spills have been on the rise.

But what is it that makes crude oil shore so deadly ? Crude oil is rarely used in the form of product at the offshore wells but it is converted in refineries into a wide range of products such as gasoline, kerosene, diesel fuel, jet fuel, domestic and industrial fuel oils and petrochemicals feedstocks. Until the oil is refined it contains potentially dangenous components.

Crude oil is primarily made up of compounds of carbon and hydrogen called hydrocarbons. These hydrocarbons may be paraffins parafin oil is used as a fuel in heaters and lamps cycloparaffins (naphthenes) and aromatic compounds in varying proportions. Crudes founds in easter and aidwestern sections of the United states are predominantly paraffinic, while those found along the Gulf coast are usually naphthnic.

Crude oil also contains varying amounts of sulphur compounds, a small amount of nitrogen and very little oxygen or olefins which are unsaturated hydrocarbons. Nickel and vanadium are present in all crudes in high concentration. Iron may be found in inorganic form as a result of corrosion of pipes and containers used to produce and transport oil.

Paraffins like methane and ethane are asphyxiants, that is, cause suffocation. Some paraffins are central nervous system depressants. Liquid paraffins can remove oil from exposed skin and cause dermatitis or pheumonia in lung tissue. However, these are the least toxic of the hydrocarbons. The effects of cycloparaffins are much like those of the paraffins except that unsaturated cycloparaffins are more noious than the saturated ones, breathing high concentrations of their vapour can result in Irritation and anaesthesia, the most toxic of the hydrocarbons are the aromatic hydrocarbons. Inhalation of the vapour can cause acute intoxication. Benzone is particularly toxic and long-term expossure can cause naemia and leukopenia even at low conecntrations.

Sulphur compounds present in crude oil can also be toxic. Carbonyl sulfide is dangerously poisonous. It is lethal to rats at 2900 ppm (parts per million). The mechanism of toxic action appears to involve its breakdown to hydrogen sulfide. If acts principally on the central nervous system, with death resulting mainly from respiratory paralysis. Sulphur in the form of aromatic thiophenes, benzothiophenes, can be moderately toxic. These damage the livers and kidneys. Certain sulphur compounds like sercaptan can also be lethal.

Although the long-term effects of an oil spill are not so well known, the Alaskan oil spill provided an opportunity to study the short-term effects. As the 11 million gallons of oil spilled by the Exxon Valdex hit the shores, seabirds started shivering and dying The oil had broken down the natural insulating oils and waxes which shield the birds from water. As a result hypothermia (abnormally low body temperature) set in and the birds started dying. About 150 rare species of bald eagles also became victims when they ingested oil, scaven giving on oily seabird carcasses. Cleaning away the oil from the birds has not been very successful as it causes a severe strain on the birds. However, the British Wildlife Rescue Association has designed wool sweaters which absorb oil from the stricken birds. The sweaters have already been used to clean birds in the North sea and were found to be more effectively than cleaningwith detergents.

About 1,000 sea others died after their far became saturated with oil and provided no insulation. Others developed respiratory ailments as volatile components of the oil weakened membrances in their lungs. Some suffered liver and kidney damage caused by ingesting oil while cleaning their coasts.

Firstly were found to be the least affected. When fish from the oil spillage sites were tested no hydrocarbons were found in their flesh. The fish are efficient at converting hydrocarbons they ingest into metabolities which are then evcreted from the liver to the gall bladder. Moreover, because of their mobility the fish escape large-scale contaminated as they are able to avoid heavily contaminated areas.

When oil spills on to ocean waters it spreads rapidly over the surface. The force of gravity causes the lighter oil to seek a constant level by spreading horizontally on the heavier water.

The movement of the oil is caused by the cobined action of wind, surface currents waves and tides. Oil on water normally moves at about 1/30th of the wind speed. With large amounts of oil, as with accidental spills, the oil drift is largely independent of spill volume, spreading, or weathering. Since the thick portion of the slick drifts faster than the thin portion a heavy oil accumulation forms the leading edge of an advancing slick.

As the oil spreads it comes under the influence of several weathering processes that ultimately break down a spill with time. The first of these is evaporation which is dominant soon after oil is released. Evaporation is determined by wind velocity, nature of the roughness, and temperature. Almost 50 per cent of oil is lost through evaporation during an oil slik's lifetime. Some of the light, low-bowling hydrocarbons, such as benzene, toluence, and xylene are lost through evaporation. Their removal decreases toxicity of the oil to marine life. Muce of the oil that evaporates is photooxized in the atmosphere and some of it may return to the seas as atmospheric fallout.

A very small fraction of the oil dissolves in the water in the early stages of an oil spill. Lower-molecular-weight compounds tend to be the most soluble. However, this process is very insignificant. Natural dispersion also removes some oil from the water. In this process, small droplets of oil which are larger than dissolved molecules, are incorporated into the water in the form of dilute oil-in-water suspension. Crude oil contains trace amounts of altrogen, sulfur, and oxygen-bearing compounds which can act as natural surfactants. These surfactants reduce the oil-water interfacial tension allowing the oil to break up and to disperse into droplets more readily.

A part of the oil is also broken down by micobial degradation. Microorganisms present in the water have a great capacity to utilize hydrocarbons present in the oil as in energy source. This process especially speeds up when she oil disperses. Some organisms may also ingest dispersed oil droplets and subsequently deposite them as fecal pollets.

Emulsification is yet another weathering process in which water is incorporated into the floating oil forming a water-in-oil emulsion. Such emulsions, which may contain from 20 to 80 per cent water, are often very viscous and referred to as "mousse" once mousse formation starts, cleanup operation run into difficulties as it is almost impossible to pump. Ultimately the mouse is broken up by wind and wave action into tar balls that may wash ashore.

However, breaking up of an oil spiil takes time. And the longer the oil continues to float on water the more damage it does to the marine environment therefore, cleaning uo an oil spill fast asumes prime importance. An oil spill can be cleaned up by mechanical removal of the oil, by the use of chemical and microbial surfactants, by using absorbants, or by burning the oil slick.

Spills can be dealt with more easily if they are confined to a small area on the water surface. For this, mechanical booms or barriers are spread around on oil slick to check its progress and prevent it form hitting the shoreline. But sometimes high waves may splash the oil over the booms. The oil may even pass below the booms once it has piled against the barrier. So after the oil has been contained by the booms it is sucked up from the surfabe of the sea by vessel known as skimmers. Skimmers now available generally fall into one of two categories. The first, mechanical surface skimmers, remove the top layers of the water and oil from the surface but they are not very effective if there are high waves. They gulp large amounts of water unless some provision is made to allow the weir suction port to follow the water surface. A second type of skimmer operates on the principle of selective wetting of a surface by oil rather than by water. Rotating metal disk or conveyor belts dip into the water, a surface layer of oil removed.

The spilled oil can also be treated with dispersants. These chemicals are sprayed from aircrafts or ships. Dispersants cause the oil to spread further and disperse in a manner similar to the way soap removes oil from one's hands allowing the oil to be emulsified and washed away with water. A dispersant contains a surfactant, a solvent, and a stablizer. The solvent usually comprises the bulk of the sispersant and enables the surface-active agent or surfactant to mix with, and penetrate into the oil slick and form an emulsion. The stabilizer fixes the emulsion and prevents it from coalescing once it is formed. Dispersion increase the slick surface area and allows a rapid increase in the rate or microbial decomposition. But although dispersants are effective in diffusing a slick, these chemicals are toxic to marine life. And, since the emulsified out droplets sink into the water body, oil stays in the waters with its toxic components such as benzene aad toluence entering the food chain with disastrous longterm effects.

Absorbents are also used to facilitate the cleaning up of oil spilts. When they are applied to the slick, they abosrb the oil and prevent it from spreading, and when the absorbent material is removed from the water, the oil is removed. Natural materials such as peat moss, straw, sawdust, and pine bark can be used. Synthetic absorbents include polyethylene, polystyrene, polypropylene, and polyurethane. Of all synthetic absorbents, polyurethane is the most promising.

Burning oil slicks on the open seas has generally been less successful because the more volatile light fractions evaporate quickly from the oil slick. Also, the water removes heat faster than it can be created to support the combustion. But burning oil slicks also leads to extensive air pollution.

By far the safest way of treating an oil slick is by using biological agents for degrading oil. These microbial surfactants are sprayed from the air. They mix with the oil, emulsify it and disperse it throughout the water body so thinly that it no longer remains hazardous.

However, not every cleau-up method can clear up all oil spills. Clean-up methods are chosen on a case by methods are chosen on a case-by-case basis. But whatever the method, it is important that the efforts are mounted as soons as the oil spills is discovered. For the longer it takes for the cleaning up to start, the more distance the oil travels. And as the oil charts its destructive course it fouls beaches, kills marine animals and contaminates the food chain.

Gulf Oil Slick Making History

According to H.J.K, the massive oil slick in the Gulf is making history. With the total spillage of oil in the Gulf waters now standing at more than 330 million gallons, it is already 30 times more than the quantity spilled by the Exxon Valdez on the shores of Alasks. The oil slick that now stretches over an area more than 80 km long and 20 km wide is moving south at a speed of 20 km a day. Having already hit the Saudi shores, affecting birds and marine life, the slick is now threatening the shores of Bahrain, Gatar and the United Arab Emirates. Apart from killing sarine life the oil also theatens to disrupt the deslination plants on the western coast of the Gulf that provide nearly half the wates to Arabian states.

The enormous oil slick will disrupt the already fragile cosystem of the region. According to the world conservation Monitoring Centre in Cambridge, between 1 million and 2 million birds will die as a result of the gulf oil spillage. Some speies may never recover. Cormorants coates with oil have already started dying on the Saudi beaches. Dolphins may escape contamination as they seem to be able to sense a spill and streer clear of it. The dugong or sea-cows will be affected with their food supply of sea or grass getting contaminated. The three already endangered species of turtles the green, leatherback and hawks bill may be seriously affected. Coral reefs housing a diverse variety of fish may be destroyed. The oil is likely to affect the mangroves of Iran and a number of valuable shrimp fisheries.

No immediate threat to the Indian coastline is perceived so far according to oil experts. The oil spilt from the Al-Ahmadi terminal is export quality Kuwaiti crude, extremely light and fluid. Hence, much of it would evaporate. In the first 24 hours, 35 per cent of the crude is likely to evaporate and in the next 10 days about 45 per cent. Even if some of the oil manages to find its way out of the Gulf, much of it would be broken up by the rough tropical waters of the Arabian Sea. Due to burning of the oil in the Gulf and attempts for its removal, a very small quanity of tar balls may eventually hit the Indian coast. These tar palls can just be collected and set on fire.

Gulf Spill : No Threat to India

Biman Basu made survey on Gulf oil spill and he pointed out that the oil spill in the Gulf is the largest so far, spreading over 700 sq km, it does not pose any pollution threat to Indian waters. According to Dr. Peter.

"This is not so much environmental terrorism as an environmental crime." said Worldwatch founder Les Brown, "We need a code of ethics like the Geneva Convention (governing treatment of prisoner of war) for the environmental field. The Gulf could die in a matter of months,"

Ancient warriors knew how to use the environment as a weapon. Corpses were catapulted into besieged cities to spread disease; water supplies were diverted to cause drough or floods; wells were poisoned. The Romans spread salt on the fields of Carthage to deny food to their enemies; Russian troops defeated Napoleon's army by torching the earth as they retreated, destroying all crops animals and human dwellings.

Prime Minister Winston Churchill planned to spread burning oil on Britain's beaches to block any German invasion in the Second World War. In the same war the Dutch opened up their sea dikes to flood their own land in a bid to stop the advancing Nazi troops.

The U.S. Forces in Vietnam also practised environmental warfare when they sprayed Agent Orange to defoliate vaste stretches of forest land deprive Viet Cong guerillas of protective cover. The spraying destoryed large number of animals that lived in the forests, polluted waterways with the reputedly, cancer-causing chemical dioxin, and Vietnamese exposed to defoliated areas reported increased rates of miscarriages and birth deformities. Heydemann, Science Counsellor in the US Embassy in New Delhi, the oil may not come out of the Gulf for years because of the current patterns in the region. By that time most of it would have been disintegrated by natural bacteria. But the slick will cause irreparable damage to the rich marine ecosystem of the Gulf.

The Environment as a Weapon

Ben Barber studied that the gaint oil slick released into the waters of the Gulf during the war has beed denounced as "environmental terrorism" which along with deliberately set oil well and refinery fires, could alter the region's ecology for the years to come.

Yet, since Biblical times, armies have destoryed the environment to deny and enemy food, water or shelter. "The phenomenon is not new there have been efforts to degrade the environment as part of war fare for sometimr." said Mr. Chris Flavin an analyst with the Washington-based environmental think-tank, Worldwatch institute. But modern technology has upped the ante." he added "There's a much greater impact."

The estimated 460 million gallons of oil released in to the shallow waters of the Gulf is by for the world's greatest oil spill. Spreading south from off the Kuwaiti and Saudi coasts towards Bahrain and Gatar, it threatens millions of sea birds and marine life forms, including the rare dugong or sea cow, the mammal that supposedly gave rise to the legend of the mermaid.

Since the war ended in 1975, low-value bamboo and grasses have invaded defoliated areas, preventing the regrowth of valuable hardwood forests.

The U.S. also seeded clouds over Asia to try to alter Vietnam's rainfall and make supply trains to muddy to use, said Prof. George Rathjens of the Massachusetts Institute of Technology. A political science teacher who has specialised in nuclear weapons and environmental issues, he said some modern military planners have proposed cloud seeding to divert rainfall from an enemy's crops.

In addition to the releases of oil into the Gulf, several Kuwaiti oil refinerises were set on fire in what may have been an attempt to raise a smoke shield against attacking aircraft. Some scientists have warned that such huge fires could block out sufficients sunlight to disrupt monsoon rains as far away as South Asia. The worst-case scenario warned that massive famine could result.

Prof. Rathjens, however said it is unlikely the fires would result in the phenomenon known as "Nuclear Winter" the predicated effect on the planet of an atomic war.

Biodegradation of Crude Oil in a Marine Environment

Ballerini-D and J.P. Vandecasteele studied the aims essentially at quantifying the processes of microbial degradation of crude oil in optimal conditions compatible with a marine environment. Our purpose, specifically, was to determine the porportion of crude which could undergo biological degradation, and to improve our knowledge of the biodegradation kinetics of the various hydrocarbon families which constitute a crude oil.

This work was performed in laboratory reactors where various physiochemical parameters such as pH. temperature, stirring speed and air flow rate were strictly controlled. The study was conducted first in batch then in continuous cultures,

The compositon of the mineral medium used for the culture is shown in Table 6.1. This composition was chosen by taking the average composition of the Atlantic Ocean as a basis (1) and enriching it in nitrogen, phosphorus and iron. The concentrations of these three elements were respectively raised from 0.5 to 235 mg/L for nitrogen, from 0.007 to 26.7 mg/L for phosphorus and from 0/001 to 0.4 mg/L for iron and the pH of this medium was adjusted to 8.1 the average pH of seawater.

TABLE 6.1

Mineral Medium

Salts	*Concentration (g/L)*
Sodium Chloride	23.9
Meginesium Chloride	10.8
Calcium Chloride	1.15
Pottasium Chloride	0.74
Sodium Sulphate	0.40
Sodium Sulphate	0.023
Sodium Bromide	0.117
Sodium Fluoride	0.002
Sodium Bicorbonate	0.196
Silican Dioxide	0.022
Sodium Oxide	0.022
Ferrous Sulphate	0.002
Amonium Chloride	0.9
Pottasium Hydrogen Phosphate	0.15

In order to approximate the conditions existing at sea, where evaporation is not negligible (2) we mainly used crude oil which had been topped at 240 degree C. In the present case, we used a residue of an Arabian light crude, obtained by distillation under reduced pressure, in which all the fractions distilling below 240 degree C had been removed.

TABLE 6.2

N-Alkanes Composition of Saturated Hydrocarbons

C-Number	*Arabian Light 240+*	*C-Number*	*Arabian Light 240+*
15	3.44	26	3.75
16	7.72	27	3.18
17	10.13	28	2.54
18	10.42	29	2.05
19	9.73	30	1.85
20	9.10	31	1.47
21	8.23	32	1.20
22	7.03	33	1.01
23	6.12	34	0.76
24	5.37	35	0.52

Table 6.2 shows that in the alkane distrubution of Arabian light crude oil topped at 240 degree C n-paraffins of chain length below C14 have been completely removed. In oil spills at sea, all compounds with a number of carbons below 15 disappear after a residence time of about 10 days.

The reactor used in our studies is glass cylinder equipped with two stainless steel end plates. Its total volume is approximately 3 liters. Stirring is achieved with a simple 4-bladed turbine, the speed of which is adjusted between 600 and 800 rpm. The reactor is epuipped with automatic pH of the culture is maintained at 8.1 by addition of 1N sodium hydroxide, the temperature is kept at 20 degree C= 0.2 degree C and the air flow rate is maintained at a value of 1 liter air/L of medium/hr. Experiments are condncted in nonsterile conditions.

The analytical methodology utilized to follow the processes of crude oil degradation is also summarized. Gaseous elluent from the fermentor first goes through a flask containing carbon tetrachloride where the hydro carbon vapors are trapped, then in a second flask containing a known amount of IN potassium hydroxide, which traps carbon dioxide. Hydrocarbons are then determined by infrared spectrophotometry and the carbon dioxide is determined by titration.

Separation of asphalotenes is first performed on the hydrocarbon residue. Asphaltenes are precipitated by boiling with heptane under reflux for 1 hour. Insoluble materials are then separated by filtration, rinsed with hot heptane, then dried and weighted.

On the residue obtaine evaporation, separation of the three main classes of compounds of crude oil, saturated hydrocarbons, aromatic hydrocarbons and resins is performed either by thin layer chromatography on silica gel or by liquid chromatography on a silica gel column using cyclohexane as the elution solvent.

The sum of the weights of the four fractions recovered in this procedure always represents 90 to 100% of the initial weight of the total oil sample. On the saturated and aromatic fractions, more detailed analyses using gas chromatography and mass spectrometry are then performed.

The isolation and selection of the strains of microorganisms used were performed starting from marine silt and sand samples collected at places hit by crude oil spills.

The first enrichment cultures were performed by successive transfers in liquied medium to which 2 g/L of crude had been added, first in shaken flasks and, soon afterward, in laboratory fermentors in order to obtain perfectly defined culture conditions.

In the course of these successive batch cultures we observed a very important decrease of the lag phase and an improvement of the final biodegradation performance. A large improvement of the dispersion of the hydrocarbon phase in the mineral medium was imultaneously observed. A very fine emulsion of the organic phase in the aqueous phase was thus obtained, leading to a marked increase of the reactional area.

The bacterial association present in our selected cultures consists of four dominant bacterial genera : Pseudomonas, Moraxella, Acinetobacter and Flavobacterium. During a batch culture we studied the changes in the bacterial flora. Although at the beginning the dominant strains belonged mainly to the genus Moraxella, the Pseudomonas strains predominated later on, as oil biodegradation advanced.

The biodegradation process during the batch cultures can be illustrated by following the changes of various parameters. For example, we have represented biomass and carbon dioxide production, the latter in both the aqueous and gaseous phases. Total production of Carbon dioxide follows an evolutaion quite comparable to that of biomass production. At the end of the culture, whereas hydrocarbon consumption reaches 2 g/L the total amount of carbon dioxide produced is 1.45 g/L and that of biomass is 1.4 g/L. The changes in time of dissolved oxygen concentration in the medium, as well as consumption of ammonia nitrogen and hydrocarbons are shown in figure 6. The amount of hydrocarbons lost by evaporation is quite negligible as it is measure on a 48 hour period and is always below 10 mg. A perfect correspondence between the evolution of the consumption of ammonia nitrogen and hydrocarbon can be again noted.

In addition, during the acceleration period of the biodegradation process, a very distinct decrease in the oxygen dissolved in the medium occurs. Actually, dissolved oxygen concentration even becomes a limiting factor since values of 5% of the saturation level are read. Later, as the velocity of the

TABLE 6.3

Analytical Methodology

Dissolved oxygen		*Fermenter*	*Exhaust gas*	*Residual Oxygen* *CO2* *Hydrocarbons*
Liquid sample Centrifugation + Filtration		Liquid sample Extraction		Liquid sample Biuret method
Aqueous phase CO2 Residual		Hydrocarbon phase Evaporation		Proteins Biomass Cells Washing and drying Dry weight of cells
Org. Carbon	Res. Nitrogen Biomass	Res. Hydrocarbons		

TABLE 6.4

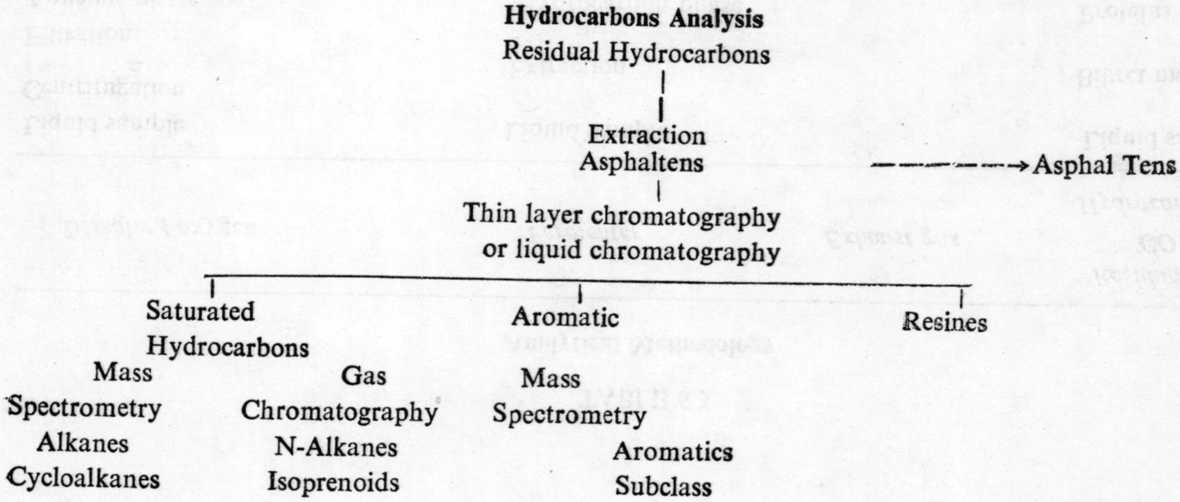

Hydrocarbons Analysis

Residual Hydrocarbons

Extraction

Asphaltens → Asphal Tens

Thin layer chromatography
or liquid chromatography

Saturated Hydrocarbons

- Mass Spectrometry
  - Alkanes
  - Cycloalkanes
- Gas Chromatography
  - N-Alkanes
  - Isoprenoids

Aromatic

- Mass Spectrometry
  - Aromatics Subclass

Resines

TABLE 6.5

Degradation of Hydrocarbons

	Start of batch		*End of the batch*		*Hydrocarbons consumed*	
	[*g*/*L*]	%	[*g*/*L*]	%	[*g*/*L*]	%
Total Hydrocarbons	2.65	—	1.57	—	1.08	41
Saturated Hydrocarbons	1.17	44.2	0.39	24.9	0.78	67
Aromatics	1.00	37.5	0.73	46.5	0.27	27
Resins	0.42	15.9	0.39	24.2	0.03	7
Asphaltenes	0.06	2.4	0.06	4.4	0.00	0

bio-degradation process decreases, the concentration of oxygen dissolved in the medium increases again, but without reaching the saturation value.

TABLE 6.6

Degradation of Saturated Hydrocarbons

Hydrocarbons	*Start of batch* [*mg*/*L*]	*End of the batch* [*mg*/*L*]	*Hydrocarbons consumed* [*mg*/*L*]	%
Saturated Hydrocarbons	1170	390	780	67
Alkanes	739	82	657	88.9
1- ring	99	51	44	44.4
2–ring	136	89	47	34.5
3–ring	92	79	13	14.1
4–ring	55	50	(5)	—
5–ring	27	24	(3)	—
6–ring	22	15	(7)	—

TABLE 6.7

Degradation of Aromatic Hydrocarbons

Hydrocarbons	*Start of batch* [*mg*/*L*]	*End of the batch* [*mg*/*L*]	*Hydrocarbons consumed* [*mg*/*L*]	%
Monoaromatics	268	138	130	48.5
Diaromatics	251	168	83	33.0
Other compounds	481	424	57	11.8

TABLE 6.8

Degradation of Monoramations

Hydrocarbons	*Start of batch* [*mg*/*L*]	*End of the batch* [*mg*/*L*]	*Hydrocarbons consumed* [*mg*/*L*]	%
Alkylbenzenes	113.4	36.6	76.8	67.7
Benzocyclo Paraffins	100.0	53.8	46.2	46.2
Benzodicyclo Paraffins	54.9	47.4	7.5	13.7

TABLE 6.9

Degradation of Diaromatic

Hydrocarbons	*Start of batch* [*mg*/*L*]	*End of the batch* [*mg*/*L*]	*Hydrocarbons consumed* [*mg*/*L*]	%
Naphthalenes	98.3	49.1	49.2	50.0
Acenaphtenes	81.4	60.4	21.0	25.8
Fluorenes	71.0	58.3	12.7	17.9

The results of mass spectrometric analysis of the saturated fraction are presented in Table 6.5. First they indicate that alkanes are the main target of biodegradation since 88.9% have disappeared at the end of the culture. This allows us to conclude that, in addition to *n*-alkanes and isoprenoids which represent only 14.8% of the saturated fraction, the great majority of isoalkanes is consumed by microorganisms. Among naphthenic compounds, 1-ring and 2-ring naphthenes are the main targets of biodegradation, with respective percentages of biodegradation reaching 44 and 47%.

For the aromatic fraction results presented in Table 6.5 indicate that the microbial action is particularly evident at the level of mono—and diaromatic compounds. At the end of the culture all mono and diaromatic compounds with a carbon number below 16 have disappeared. Among monoaromatic compounds, it can be seen in Table 6.6 that the compounds most susceptible to microbial action are alkylbenzenes, 67.7% of which have disappeared at the end of the culture, and benzocycloparaffins, 46.2% of which have been consumed during this experiment.

The results presented in Table 6.7 illustrate the microbial action on diaromatic compounds and, in particular, the effect of microbial attack on the residual content in naphthalene derivatives, 50% of which are consumed during the biodegradation process.

The primary purpose of this paragraph is to provide some guidelines for rehabilitating coral reef habitats that have been impacted by oil spills. The rehabilitation process in the final step of a spill response effort that also includes actions to contain, cleanup, assess damages, and miltigate damages from a spill. Because our ability to rehabilitate damaged coral refs is limited, this ordering of events also represents priorities for actions to be taken when a reef is threatened by oil pollution. In view of these priorities, the objectives of this chapter are threefold :

—To identify reef areas particularly sensitive to oil pollution incidents and to suggest means to minimize the threat of such incidents.

—To suggest techniques for assessing the impact of oil pollution incidents on coral reefs and their associated communities, and

—To provide guidelines for rehabilitating a reef after it has been impacted by oil pollution.

6. Carol Reefs and Petroleum Infrastructure

Coral reefs are structures created and maintained by the establishment and growth of populations of hermatypic corals and coralline algae. They may be comprised of wave resistant emergent of submerged reefal zones, or a combination of both. Geomorphically barrier and fringing reef protect the insullar and continental coastlines that they border from erosion. Reef rock that forms terrestrial substratum on islands and recently uplifted coastal margins is often the sole or major component of limestone. Geologically older reef formations are found far inland and may serve as porous, oil bearing strata.

Reefs typically provide habitat for a large variety of attached plants and epifauna, infauna mobile invertebrates, and fishes. The large numbers of economically important species they support make reefs locally important to commercial sport fisheries. The resultant high diversity and abundance of reef associates and the functional and spatial dominance of corals and coralline algae are the essential characteristics of coral reefs.

Coral reefs are circumglobal in the tropics and subtropics between the norther and souther hemispheric 18.5 degree climatic isotherms. A majority of coral species and the most diverse and prolific reefs occur in Indo-West Pacific seas. Tropical West Atlantic and Eastern Pacific reefs are generally less diverse in terms of caroals and reef associates, but are functionally quite as important.

In a recent interview of the impact of oil upon corals, Ray (1980) pointed out that extensive tanker traffic and oil-related activity occurs within the biogrographic zones occupied by coral reefs. Sufficient information exists to enable the production of detailed maps showing the location of coral reefs in relation to petroleum infrastructure. Such maps may be a useful aid in the identification of high risk areas. Two areas that have well developed reefs and much petroleum activity are given as examples in this discussion.

Biological Effects Actually Observed

Having now made the effort to consider from theoretical point of view the system which it is thought may give rise to biological effects, it is not time to consider whether these effects can actually be observed under the conditions which prevail in the marine environment.

1. Natural Fluctuation

The marine environment is, however, subject to a wide range of influences the effects of which may swamp any effects which may be due to pollution. This is the well-known signal/noise ratio problem commonly encountered in the physical sciences. On the other hand, if studies are conducted in the laboratory the results can be no more than indicators of what will happen in the real world because it is quite impossible to reproduce the marine environment in the laboratory. Thus on the one hand we have the problem that the data obtained in what may be well-regulated laboratory experiments, in which the pollution parameter may be isolated for study, do not give results necessarily applicable to the marine environment, and on the other we have real environment studies in which the pollution effects are not isolatable and are usually swamped by other more influential effects.

2. Correlation of Results Obtained in the Laboratory and at Sea

The review also covers results obtained by exposing organisms to oil in the laboratory. Here again there are difficulties. Often the concentrations used in order to observe an effect are higher than could possibly be experienced in the marine environment itself or are continued for greater periods of time.

Again, even when the concentrations are comparable, it is impossible to extrapolate to the real situation.

It is quite clear that one can measure in the laboratory lethal and sub-lethal effects on organisms exposed to dissolved oil components and disoersed droplets of oil in the water column. It is also clear that the concentrations of oil in the water column at real spills can be broadly comparable to those in the laboratory studies. In addition similar effects, both lethal and sub-lethal, on planktonic species can be observed at sea under real spills. When one attempts to evaluate the significance of those observations, however, in the only manner possible or meaningful, *viz.* by attempting to observe subsequent changes in fish populations, no such changes are discernible.

There are a number of quite reasonable explanations for this state of affairs Thus even if plankton populations were reduced significantly under oil slicks, phytoplankton is in continous production and the is rapidly restored as the oil alick moves on. Even if fish egg and larval stage numbers were similarly reduced it is fact that very few would have reached maturity anyway.

The losses caused by the oil merely cause losses which would otherwise have taken place naturally.

3. Larger Marine Organisms

The conclusions reached above regarding plankton in general do not of course rule out the possibility that larger marine organisms may be affected. When this possibility is considered, however, it is found that free-moving fish and crustacea are largely unaffected. Sedentary crestacea on the other hand may be subject to smothering with an oil layer deposited by the outgoing tide. Grazing molluscs and, of course, sea-weeds are liable to similar fate while filter-feeding molluscs can ingest oil in separating out food particles. Generally mortality is highest with fresh oil, weathered oil having little effect. In any case the effects are transient as regards populations and depuration occurs rapidly with filter feeders when exposed to clean water.

Some species are not sufficiently mobile to escape, do not possess shells by which to isolate themselves or have other protective coatings. Worms living in sandy or muddy beaches may be killed if oil components penetrate the substratum. Of course, oil will not penetrate across the water-table interface and so this will occur mainly in well-drained beaches.

4. Birds

With birds it can be concluded that soluble and sipersed oil components will have no effect and we have now reached a pure example of the effects of physical coating. There is no doubt that this form of pollution has a very serious effect at least on individual birds, but here again the Royal Commission has not been able to demonstrate conclusively that there is any threat to populations. There is, however, considerable cause for concern, particularly in relation to major spills close to a breeding colony onshore. It is obvious that oiled birds are one of the main vehicles of public awareness of oil pollution and arouse widespread feelings of pity and revulsion.

5. Large Mammals

There seems little possibility of affecting large marine mammals such as the cetaceans. Seals on the other hand may become oiled as they leave and re enter the sea and this could result in loss of insulation. It has been noted, however, that seal populations around the UK are generally stable and that grey seal numbers have been increasing dramatically for the past 50 years.

6. Humans

In the early 1970s attention was given to the possibility that polyaromatic hydrocarbons present in oil pollution might concentrate in the tissues of marine organisms and that those concentrations might increase up the food web to levels which could induce cancer in man Research results now available, however, indicate that in common with other petroleum-derived hydrocarbons these compounds are rapidly released when the organisms are exposed to clean water and it is extremely unlikely that they could accumulate in the manner orginally feared. It has also been shown that these compounds are in any case the inevitable products of the combustion of most types of organic material such as wood, garden rubbish and even tobacco, and as such are widely distributed in the environment. Furthermore they are present in many foods and it is therefore possible to show on the basis of dietary studies that the consumption of sea food would be unlikely to provide more than 2—3% of the normal intake. Recent research has also failed to establish a connection between this form of pollution and cancer in the marine animals themselves and it is extremely unlikely, to say the least, that ingestion of cancerous tissue from animals could cause cancer in man in any case.

Aims and Objective of Oil Spill Response

The aims and objective of oil spill response should therefore be to protect amenity, fishery and wildlife resources and the efforts expended should ideally have some relationship to the quantification of threat to those resources if nothing is done. If nothing is done to respond to an oil slick far enough at sea for it to disperse through natural forces before it reaches shore, then minimum impact on the environment will result since there will be no amenity loss, and no effect on inshore fisheries. The oil will disperse far at sea when its effect is least. The only possibility of quantifiable damage resulting would be if high concentrations of seabirds became affected.

If natural dispersion forces are unable to remove the oil from the sea surface before it reaches shore, then, in addition to seabirds, inshore fisheries, the flora and fauna of the inshore zone and amenity are at risk. In terms of quantified risk, therefore, there is no likely to be greater environmental impact than in the previous example. It is reasonable therefore to make greater efforts to respond in this case than in the previous one.

It should however, be realised that efforts should be made to deal with the oil in the lower-risk are, *i.e.*, at sea, before it reaches the comparatively high-risk area, *i.e.*, the inshore zone. If it is possible to prevent oil reaching the high-risk zone, minimum damage will result. If response occurs only when the oil has reached the high-risk zone then the damage will already have occured and one is then no longer preventing damage but only attempting to assist the area to recover from the damage it has already sustained.

It is therefore clearly preferable to deal with the oil in low-risk arteas before it reaches those of high risk. If this is impossible, then the aim should be to return the damaged areas to their original state as quickly as possible and the best way to assist in this will be to remove the oil as quickly as possible if natural processes are considered to be too slow.

1. Methods of Oil Spill Response

There are three possible responses to oil spills at sea.

- It can be decided to leave the oil to be dispersed by natural processes.
- The natural doispersion rate may be increased by the use of chemical.
- Attempts may be made to remove the oil from the sea surface by mechanical means.

The nil response option will be possible when no resources are threatened and natural dispersion rates are fast enough to remove the oil from the surface before any resource comes under threat. The use of chemical dispersants should be seen as a means to increase natural dispersion rates so that resources are less likely to come under threat. It is of course preferable to remove the oil completely from the environment, and so mechanical recovery devices are favoured provided they will work sufficiently to deal with the oil in the low–risk zones before it reaches those of high risk.

It is generally accepted that if recovery is not possible far at sea in a given situation, it may be preferable to remove the oil completely from the environment, and so mechanical recovery devices are favoured provided they will work sufficiently to deal with the oil in the low-risk zones before it reaches those of high risk.

It is generall accepted that if recovery is not possible far at sea in a given situation, it may be preferable to disperse the oil there and so prevent damage later in a high–risk sheltered zone than to wait and attempt to recover it when it has reached the high-risk sheltered zone. The latter option will not prevent damage. It will merely remove the oil after the damage is done. Such belted action will of course assist in the recovery of the area affected.

The Use of Dispersants

Clearly oil does not remain permanently on the sea surface. The pollutant may disperse into the water colum either completely or partially under the action of natural forces and or it may come shore. If the oil is spilled close to shore there is little opportunity for natural dispersion before the slicks reach shore. In such circumstances beach pollution seems inevitable. However, even in the Amoco Cadiz it has been estimated that some 50% of the spillage dispersed into the water column in the prevailing conditions of high natural agitation rather than stranding on the beaches.

With the advent of North Sea oil exploration and production, efforts were made to estimate the quantities likely to reach shore by considering natural disperison rates in relation to the speed of travel on wind and tide. It had been concluded that for Ekofisk oil only very small percentages of the original spillages have any chance of polluting beaches.

Thus although natural dispersion does take place, it cannot be relied upon in general to remove the pollutant from the sea surface before it reaches shore. The extent to which natural dispersior will assist is a function of oil type, quantity spilled and distance from shore of the spillage source.

It is important to recognise at this point that dispersants are simply as means of incrasing the natural dispersion rate so that sufficient before it reaches the showe. Certainly it is necessary to treat an in which this is an advantage. Thus the spreading phenomenon itself is form of dispersion. In fact it is two-dimensional dispersion and all that remains to be done is to add the third dimension, *i.e.*, to disperse the surface oil into the body of the sea.

Oil concentrations measured under chemically dispersed oil slicks and under the naturally dispersing Ekofish Bravo oil slicks were much lower than 100 ppm because the oil, of course, disperses, throughtout the sea water to even greater depths than 1m.

Further experiments on this topic have been carried out on Kuwait crude oil at experimentlly controlled thicknesses, with the fan-jet nozzle arrangement used for dispersant efficiency testing at sea. Here slicks up to 1 mm in thickness were produced in order to produce high initial concentrations in the water by use of appropriately enhanced dispersant discharge rates. Maximum possible concentration in the top metre on dispersal of a 1 mm thick slick would be 1000 ppm as opposed to the 100 ppm arising from the normal 0.1. mm thick case. The aim of these experiments was to study rates of dilution of the dispersed oil into the sea following treatment. Wind speeds on this occasion were 8 10 knots with sea state 2–3. With this degree of agitation, observed concentrations were low, suggesting rapid transportation of oil to greater depths by natural turbulence as shown in Table 6.1. When these reults are compared with the theoretical concentration of 1000 ppm. if all the oil remained uniformly dispersed in the top metre, there is a strong suggestion that intial concentrations in surface waters are reduced by dillution to greater depths.

The results of these chemical dispersion experiments in calm and slightly rougher conditions suggest that while initial concentrations might be higher than for natural dispersion, subsequent dilution is rapid, even for slick thicknesses ten times thicker than those normally treated. As a result the persistence of significant amounts of oil in the surface waters is likely to be of shorter duration if dispersants are used than if they are not.

TABLE 6.10

Chemical Dispersion of 1 mm Thick Slicks of Kuwait Oil

Time after discharge (min)	*Concentration of Kuwait crude oil (ppm) in upper metre of sea water*		
	Run 1	Run 2	Run 3
0	34.4	24.2	0.85
1	—	15.8	—
2	47.8	—	8.7
2.5	—	12.2	—
5	—	9.4	—
7	17.8	—	3.5
10	—	5.2	—
15	—	—	1.7
18	1.9	—	—
25	—	4.2	—
40	0.8	—	1.35
50	—	1.9	—
80	—	—	1.5
100	2.2	0.8	—

The question of the possible impact of dispersed oil on organisms has been taken further by McAuliffe and his co-workers, who have demonstrated that evaporation tends to ensure that the dispersed droplets do not include the toxic fractions of the crude oil.

Oil Recovery at Sea

Oil recovery at sea it is necessary to return to the earlier assessment of the problem. It will be recalled that the counter rate for a 1 m wide unit travelling at 1 m 0 2 tonnes/h. It is also a known fact that if a barrier having draught and free board a skimmer or a boom for example is moved across a water surface at speeds greater than 1 knot there is set up a flow of water beneath the barrier which is sufficient to carry with it any floating oil which is in front of the barrier : consequently the encounter rate in the oil recoervy context cannot be increased by increase in speed of travel in the manner appropriate to dispersent application. At first sight the only option is to increase encounter rate by increasing the width of the collection unit by the use of booms. Thus a boom array of width 2:0 m will increase encounter rate of 90 tonnes/h. Such an array, however, is extremely cumbersome in practice.

To remove oil pollution from the marine environment before it could reach sensitive inshore areas and beaches and from a realisation that, in spite of claims to the contrary, no significant quantities of oil had ever been recovered at sea. The objectives of the programme were to find out why performance was so low and how to improve it with due regard to cost-benefit concepts. To this end, available equipment was classified in terms of the nature of the skimming element, *e.g.* absorption belt, disc. ropel vortex chamber of weir/direct suction device. In similar manner booms were classified in terms of their identifiable design elements. Examples of each type of stimmer and boom were them acquires from evaluation at sea in the presence of oil.

As a result of these investigations it has been found that recovery equipment fairs to perform satisfactorily in waves for the following reasons :

- The inertial mass of the equipment is too great.
- The linear dimensions of rigid elements, or of the entire systems, are too great in relation to encountered warelengths.

This being so purpose-built vessels incoporating the skimming function in as a rigid integral element in their construction will be inoperative in waves. This conclusion means that great cost savings are immediately possible, since such vessels are extremely expensive to build end maintain and wou'd if chosen be required in large numbers in order to overcome the enormous logistic difficulties inherent in this concent.

Another system which can be reported on favourably is that developed by ORI/Star Offshore, known as the Force 7.4. This is a single-ship system and is based on the flexible absorption rope principle. Consequently it has excellent wave—following characteristics and should recover oil of viscosities allowing adhension to the rope at rates controlled only by encounter rate.

These two systems meet the identified requirements is different ways. They may differt, however, in encounter rate potential, the Springsweep system having a collection boom while the Force 7 does not. On the other hand the Force 7 may be capable of operating at a greater ship speed. It is believed that further evaluation of these systems can now be achieved only through operation at real spills. Decisions can then be taken on a cost-effectiveness footing in the light or considerations present to here.

The Eleni. V. incident involving a spill of heavy fuel oil which was solid at sea temperature, represented a particularly difficult case. The Antonia Gramsci incident, however, revealed that solid oil in the presence of ice presents even greater problems. In the end some 400 m of pure oil was recovered at sea (the actual recovery rate is not, available) and some 400-500 m3 was subsequently recovered from 300 km of coastline at a cost of 17,500 m3.

11. Results of Investigations on Remote - Sensing Techniques for Oil at Sea

It has been shown that oil slicks on water are detectable by observing reflected light in the near— U.V. visible and near— IR regions of the electromagnetic spectrum. In addition, slicks may be observed in the thermal IR region because of apparent differences in surface temperature as between oil and water.

In order to select the best wavelength windows for operation, however, it is necessary to consider the problem in greater detail. Apart from the surface - reflected raidance in which one is interest. There are two other background components contributing to the total radiance detected by a remote sensor. These are a volume - reflected component and a path radiance scattered by the intervening atmosphere into the sensor. This latter components depends on path length and at higher altitudes can be the predominant effect. In addition, the sources of the reflected radiance have to be considered, viz., the sky radiance which is reflected at the surface component and the so-called global radiance which is the sum of the sky and sum radiances and is received by the sensor as the volume and atmospheric path radianc.

Thermal radiance devies measure apparent temperature which arises from the physical or 'real' temperature and the thermal emissivity. The presence of an oil slick can cause changes in both parameters. In the case of physical temperature an oil slick could in principle produce the following effects :

--The layer could absorb solar radiation and become hotter than the underlying and surrounding sea.

—Oil close to spill source could retain heat and thus be better than the sea.

--Evaporation of volatile components could have a cooling effect on the oil relative to the sea.

—Oil could reduce evaporation of water and thus produce a warming effect relative to the sea surface where water would continue to evaporate.

-- Oil could restrict heat transfer between the atmosphere and the sea so that in warm weather the sea would be cooler under the oil and in cold weather it could be warmer than it would otherwise be.

—The movement of wind over the oil slick could warm it up by a mechanism of viscous dissipation of energy relative to the sea surface.

From the above list of possibilities it is clear that oil slicks at sea could be hotter than sea water or cooler, depending on the final outcome of a variety of processes individually giving rise to conflicting results, water. Oil is variously reported to have an emissivity 0.02 0.005 less than water, which may be expected to give a temperature contrast of 1-3 degee K.

12. Low Light Level Television

This equipment is well worth investigating as a remote—sensing tool for oil on water. If satisfactory performance can be demonstrated one immediately has a number of advantages, via low cost and ease of operation together with real-time display of the imagery. LLLTV can have a spectral response in the 250-1200 nm region of the spectrum depending on the characteristics of the tube used. Oil has a greater surface reflectance than water in this region and so it should be possible to see oil in contrast to the water.

Infrared

Some tank and wind tunnel studies have been carried out to investigate possible mechanisms to explain the difference in physical temperature between oil slicks and the surrounding and underlying water 5. In these experiments, thermocouples were places in the oil and in the water immediately below the surface at 1 mm depth and in the bulk water at a few centimetres depth. Control tanks containing only water were similarly equipped with thermocouples at 1 mm and at a few centimetres depth.

14. Line Scanners

Ultraviolet and infrared line scanners, have received considerable attention in a number of countries and the Daedalus system features prominently in this work. Canadian and US workers have evaluated the Daedalus 1230 dual-channel line scanner which is fitted with a UV detector sensitive in the 270-370 nm region and a thermal IR detector for the range 850-1250 nm and the Daedalus 1260 multi-spectral scanner in which the near-UV to near-IR region, 380-1100 nm, is divided into ten channels and there is in addition the usual thermal IR part at 850-1250 nm.

15. Ultraviolet

The UV imagery from the dual-channel unit gave good contrast for the thin regions of the slick. This device had a better performance than the multi-spectral scanner mainly because of the lower noise equivalent radiance value for the UV detector. This fact indicates that features other those such as detector sensitivity and noise levels will affect results and to some extent therefore the results obtained apply only to the system used.

16. Microwaves

Microwaves sensors are available with wavelengths in the range 0.1-100 cm and can operate either in the passvie mode, measuring difference in brightness temperature between oil and water at a given wavelength, or in the active mode as radars receiving a back scatter from the sea or oil surface.

17. Radar

Waves at sea are of two types, long wavelength, large amplitude gravity waves and small capillary waves, the latter being the first to be produced as wind speed increases from zero and which ultimately are super imposed on the larger gravity waves. Radar backscatter is mainly due to these capillary waves, but imaging radars can see gravity waves because of the increased concentrations of capillary waves on the downwind faces of gravity waves as comared to the upwind sides. This produces a periodicity in the radar backscatter of capillary waves even though the radar wavelength is very much smaller than that of the gravity waves. This is turn suggests that backscatter intensity will vary with viewing direction with respect to wind direction.

18. Microwave Radiometry

Microvave radiometry is a passive technique which selects changes in microwave brightness of the sea in the presence of oil slicks in a manner analogous to the infrared technique. It also offers the possibility of measuring oil slick thickness with the added advantage over infrared that it is independent of atmospheric water content *i.e.* fog or rain.

Calculations of microwave brightness of oil over water for a given frequency predict alternating maxima and minima as the oil thickness increases. By using two frequencies, ambiguities can be removed and thickness uniquely determined over a wipe range. Measured antenna temperature is the average of the brightness temperature over all directions weighted by the antenna response pattern. The total brightness temperature in any direction is due to the radiation emitted by the surface, the downward radiation of the sky reflected by the surface, and the emission and attenuation of the atmosphere between the surface and the radiometer.

The quantification of oil in effluent waters will be discussed. In both these situations the source of the oil is known and it is the quantity of hydrocarbons in the water which is being sought. In the aspect now under discussion it is the source of pollution which is to be established. This requires a different approach. Before discussing these different requirements, however, it may be worthwhile to recall who analysis may be necessary in this context. Aerial surveillance with standard photographic equipment is not in itself sufficient to establish that a named ship identified in a photograph, is actually responsible for discharging the oil which appears to emanate from that ship in the photographic evidence. In fact the best way to establish that the vessel is discharging oil is to sample the area which shows as an oil slick in the photographs and to characterise that sample by chemical means in such a way as to show that it is identical to a sample of the oil carried on board.

It is worth recalling also that this comparison between pollutant and putative source may be advisable even in the case of a shipping casualty where attribution of oil source might be thought obvious. This can rise when passing vessels take advantage of the widespread pollution arising from a casualty in a given area to discharge tank washings, bilges, etc. As a result some of the oil arriving on shore may be erroneously attributed to the casualty and the operational discharge offenders may escape detection.

19. Sampling of the Oil Carried on Board Ship

It has already been stated that the best way of establishing that a pollution sample orginted from a suspect ship is to compare the results of chemical analysis of the pollutant with that of the oil carried by the ship. In fact it is the only way. Such is the complexcity of individual oils and the wide variety of potential sources of distinct oils that it is quite impossible on the basis of a pollutant sample to state the source of that pollutant. Generally speaking, the best that can be done with an unreferenced sample is to say that it is a fresh crude oil, a weathered crude oil, a light or heavy fuel oil or tank washings. This is quite insufficient to associate it with a parlicular source.

This being so, it is necessary in a case of suspected operational discharge to sample all the oils on board including bunker fuel and lubricating oil. This may involve sampling all the tanks, though reference to the cargo manifest may help to reduce the amount of required sampling. Similarly in a shipping casualty it is useful to sample all oils on board since damage to the vessel can result in the release of an variety of oils.

20. Sampling from the Sea and Beaches

In collecting samples of liquid oil from the surface of the sea, scare is necessary to ensure that oil is indeed being collected and that the result is not simply a sample of dirty water in an oil contaminated container. Where the pollutant is a relatively thick layer of water-in-oil emulsion it is easier than if the pollutant is fresh oil present to about 0.1 mm thick or even less, but in all cases it is easier to collect water than oil. The use of a container with a bottom outlet and tap is helpful in collecting sufficient oil since with such a device water can be drained off and sampling repeated if necessary. A funnel can be used in this way, using the finger to release the water and retained the oil.

Alternatively where the oil layer is very thin or is in the form of many small isolated globules of oil or emulsion, it may be possible to use adsorption pads. These may be of Teflon, steel or polyurethane. The oil sticks to the pad when it is placed lightly on the oil-contaminated sea surface. The pad is then placed in a sealed airtight container for transport to the laboratory. Oil can be removed from the pad by use of a suitable solvent and this operation can be carried out either before transportation to the laboratory or after arrival there.

21. The Nature of the Oil Spill Response Problem in Inshore Waters and Beaches

Everything that has been said in the chapters on at-sea oil spill response holds also for inshore waters. However, there are a number of additional points of specific relevance to the inshore situation.

As oil approaches the shore, the efforts made to combat it either by dispersants or by mechanical recovery means will of necessity be conducted closer and closer to shore, and if these efforts are inadequate the oil will eventually strand on the shoreline. The extent to which the oil strands will depend on the extent to which it is treatable at sea and this in turn will depend on soil size, oil type and the proximity to shore of the original spillage.

So far, beach-cleaning costs per tonne are considred to be so high as to justify operations at sea. For the moment it will be assumed that if activities at sea were justified, they presumably still are close to shore. The next step is to consider dispersants and mechanical recovery separately with a view to establishing whether their ought to be an reasons for discontinuing activities commenced at sea simply because the oil is coming closer and closer to shore, and alternatively the extent to which it might actually be easier to carry out the desired operations now that the oil slicks may be reaching more sheltered waters.

22. Oil Recovery

In cases of oils which are not amenable to dispersants, only recovery is possible. As with dispersants, the establishment of water-in-oil emulsions with their increased viscosity will render the recovery of oil more difficult. On the other hand, the possibility of thicker layers brought about by the booming effect of the beach itself (the best boom available) may provide greater layer thicknesses and therefore the possiblity of increased encounter rates for oil recovery systems. In addition, unless the inshore waters are exposed to the full force of the weather the general sheltered nature of many inshore situations will assist in oil recovery operations. In general, therefore, provided there is enough sea room and depth of water for ship manoeures, the deep-sea equipment will be usable in sheltered inshore conditions.

However, in addition, because of the shallower water depths it may be convenient to more booms rather than to tow them. Moore of booms, being static of course, do not increase encounter rate but are used to protect speicified stretches of shoreline and/or to deflect moving oil to a selected recovery point. These techniques are specific to the inshore situation.

In general, mechanical recovery of oil and water in oil emulsions should be easier in sheltered waters than at sea. Indeed it may be better to view oil recovery as a sheltered water technique which may in certain circumstances by usable at sea rather than to present it as a sea going technique which can automatically be used in sheltered environments. Be that as it may, boom utilisation and oil recovery techniques in relation to the particular inshore situation.

Where sea room and depth of water limite such operations there is scope for smaller devices deployable from smaller vessel, *e.g*, the net system from inshore fishing boats. However, the use of small vessels is not without its difficulties. The logistic problem arising from lack of storage on board mitigates against the small vessel approach. Again, if the oil is already against a harbour wall or other coastal structure it may be simpler to deploy the oil recovery equipment directly from the land. There is little point in working from a small boat if one can work directly from the river bank or quay wall or shore. Recovered fluid is then already ashore and one step in the logistics of waterborne operations is immediately eliminated.

In considering how best to deal with oil once it has come ashore it is necessary to have regard to the type of beach material affected. Beach material is classified in terms of grain size.

Mud is the term used to descride grain sizes less then 0.05 mm. Mud beaches generally have a slope of less than 1 degree they develop in areas of low water velocity which permits the deposition and retention of such fine material. Such beaches are saturated with water at all times and because of the low drainage which this implies, the surface is usually covered with a thin layer of water. They have very low load-bearing capacity and are generally speaking of high biological value.

Sand beaches have a particle size range from 0.05 to 2.0 mm with beach slopes between 1 degree and 40 degree. Such beaches are generally more exposed than mud beaches and are subject to seasonal erosion and deposition cycles depending on the energy of the incoming waves. Drainage rates are higher than for mud but again permanent saturation and surface water layers may be encountered. Load-bearing capacity is higher than for muds, Sand beaches are of low biological value.

Gravel and pebble beaches are of particle size 2.0-50 mm and 50-256 mm respectively and tend to be narrower and steeper as the particle size increases from gravel to pebble. Snch beaches are again of low biological value.

Apart from these physical difference due to particle size, other parameters are relevant such as exposure of the beach in question, the onshore energy levels of the waves to which it is exposed and the accessibility of the beach from the point of deploying pollution response equipment.

23. Criteria for the Selection of Moorable Booms

It is important to distinguish the specific uses of booms. In the first place the booms may be used in a sweeping mode to concentrate oil towards a skimmer so as to increase the oil encounter rate of that skimmer. In the second place booms may be used to protect certain coastal resources from oil contamination or to deflect oil on to a nominated or sacrificial beach for recovery. In the former case the booms are deployed from ships and are used in a mobile mode. In the latter case they may be, therefore usad in a stationary mode. Of course many aspects of boom design are common to both applications, but it is as well to be aware of those aspects in which boom design is specific to one situation or the other. Some booms are usable in both the towards and moored conditions but others are not.

It will rarely be possible to deploy moored booms in such a way as to protect the very large lengths of open coastline which may be threatened by oil pollution in a major incident. The use of such booms must be selective. In addition, depending on time-scales, logistic problems, etc., it may be impossible to have such booms in place in the required time. However, in some cases it will be possible to consider these matters as part of an overall plan for cargo transfer in a safe haven. In such a case the deployment of any necessary booms will require to be completed in good time for the arrival of the casualty.

The selection of towed booms for use at sea has already been discussed in Section 3.4. It is now time to discuss criteria for the selection of morable booms for coastal protection. The objective is to reduce the range of possible boom designs which need to be considered and to identify those elements of boom design which need to be convested in a boom specification.

1. Boom Specification

If a stationary floating barrier is placed at right-angles to flowing water, the water must of necessity pass beneath the barrier. It is found that water passing in this way beneath the barrier. It is found that water passing in this way beneath floating booms carries oil with it if the flow rate normal to the boom is greater than 1 knot. It seems unlikely that performance can be raised significantly be attention to detailed boom design since the limit appears to be quite fundamental. What is certain,. however, is that it is quite possible to design a boom the performance of which will fall short of the limit for quite avoidable reasons. Boom design therefore is a matter of ensureing that the final product will.

- Attain the fundamental performace limit :
- Maintain this performance in waves and currents when moored in position.
- Be of adequate strength to withstand the loading forces involved.
- Be light enough to handle in deployment, use and recovery.
- Be of low enough bulk to facilitate storage and transportation.

Oil Recovery in Inshoore Waters

1. Encounter rate, 2. Reduced performance as viscosity increases, and 3. Reduced performance in waves. If these three problems cannot be solved to a satisfactory extent, some oil will come ashore.

The problems of oil recovery in sheltered waters and close to shore, in decks, harbours, etc., are rather different. To begin with, the urgency to remove the oil before it reaches shore is now gone. It although obviously the rate of removal relates to cost per tonne of oil removed and to that extent remains important. As it happens, however, the oil pressed against the shore or other beach structure may be in a much thicker layer and therefore allow very satisfactory recovery rates. Secondly, reduced performance because of increase in viscosity may not be so significant since, as stated above, the urgency may have gone but of course costs remain important. Thirdly, waves will be much reduced and in certain cirucmstances totally absent. However, whereas at sea one is content to sweep the thickest layers using booms and to leave the thinner regions, and while in sheltered waters booms may still be used to reduce the area over which the oil is spread so as to maintain an adequate thickness or recovery, there will be situations in which it will be essential to be able to collect oil which is present in only very thin layers and eventually to effect complete removal of oil from the water surfaces.

SKIMMERS FOR GENERAL INSHORE USE

1. Weir Skimmer (Slurp Skimmer)

Perhaps the most basic oil skimmer of all is that developed by Esso Research centre and known as the Self-Levelling Unit for Removing Pollution. of SLURP2. The SLURP, is a weir skimmer with no moving parts. It is of small size, 935 mm in width ann weighing 28 kg, and can operate in water depths as little as 25 cm.

The attitude of the floating skimmer and consequently the depth of the weir depend on the amount of libuid contained in the unit. Since high pump rates are appropriate for deep oil layers and low pump rates for shallow layers, the device is designed so that a high pump rate maintains a low loading and therefore a floating attitude which results in a deep weir position. Conversely a slow pump rate maintains a high fluid loading and consequently a floating attitude which provides a shallow weir position. Clearly, to achieve the best results the skimmer should be should be used with a variable-speed pump.

2. The Komara Miniskimmer

One of the commonest mniafestations of the principle of preferential adsorption is that of the adsorption disc which is the basis of the Komara Miniskimmer 3. This device is well worth a study in its own right but, being typical of a number of such devices employing disc, the results obtained can be of general application.

Disposal of Recovered Oil

Oil may be collected from water surfaces or from a variety of beaches comprising different types of solid material. So far in considering the problems of oil spill response we have considered the properties of spilled oil in relation to the means of response, viz, recovery or dispersants. It is now necessary, assuming that oil has been recovered, to consider its properties and levels and types of contamination from the point of view of temporary storage, transportation and final recycling or disposal.

Oil collected from water surfaces, even if originally of low viscosity, will have lost its more volatile fractions by evaporation and will almost certainly have formed water-in-oil emulsions by the time it is collected. As such it will be extremely viscous and, being non-Newtonian or thixotropic in properties, it will be virtually solid when allowed to stand in storage of any kind. The main contaminant is, however, water, so that if the emuslion can be broken there is a good chance that the oil fraction could be put to some use. Indeed if the recovered emulsion is to be handled through storage, transport, etc., it is essential that the emulsion be broken anyway.

Oil collected from the beach is another matter entirely. It may contain sand, single, pebbles, stones, sea wood and the whole range of potential beach debris either separately or together. Indeed because of the difficulty with graders and scrapers in skimming the desired thin layer, material collected from beaches tends to be oil contaminated in this form is to be reprocessed or otherwise put to useful purposes, it entire mass must be disposed of by some means or other.

If it is intended to reprocess recovered oils through a refinery it is important that they are not contaminated with dispersant. The identification by analytical means of dispersants in oil is difficult but under investigation at present. The best means of avoiding the problem, however, is to ensure that when the emulsion becomes established to the point where dispersants are no longer effective, their use should be immediately discontinued. If they did, the dispersant would be effective. When they do not simply wash off into the sea and become diluted to harmless levels.

There is some talk at present of intentionally gelling oils to render them more easily collectable in nets, *i.e.* without extrusion, if their properties are already such that other means of collection are precluded by high viscosity. Just how it is proposed to mix the gelling agent into such highly viscous materials under the conditions prevailing at sea is as yet quite unclear. However, what can be stated clearly is that such agents ought not to be of such a type as to give rise to problems with either final disposal or reprocessing.

Demulsification

It has been stated elsewhere that crude oils which spread on the sea surface after spillage form water-in-oil emulsions in which oil is the continous phase and the water is present as small droplets dispersed throughout the oil. Such emulsions are more viscous than the original oils and have non-Newtonian properties, *i.e.* they are thixotropic and their flow rates are a function of the stress applied. Thus under the influence of wave action they may have viscosity which permits pumping, but once in a storage tank they will increase in viscosity by standing still and be virtually impossible to remove from the tank when the time comes to do so.

General Problems of Oil-water Separation

A dispersion of two immiscible liquids is thermodynamically unstable, tending to reduce its free energy by reducing the interfacial area between the two phases by droplet coalescence. Droplet coalescence occurs to a limited extent between rising droplets, but eventually coalescence of droplets in the more densely packed region under the phase boundary and with in the growing continuous phase itself assumes more importance. Finally two separate continuous phases are formed, the separation having been achieved by gravity acting on components of differing denisty.

Emulsions by contrast are quasi-stable systems in which coalescence is inhibited, often by the presence of a third component, present usually at comparatively low concentration and which is adsorbed on the droplet surfaces. This component is known as an emulsifying agent or emulsifier. Naturally occurring emulsifiers give rise to water-in-oil emulsions.

Although dispersions tend to separate by gravity, they will not readily do so if the droplet size is so small that movement towards the continuous phase boundary is interfered with by Brownian movement within the continuous phase in which the droplet is located. The term 'secondary dispersion' is used to describe very small droplet size dispersions. These are responsible for persistent hazes in a number of industrial processes and require special techniques for separation.

7

Controling Marine Pollution

Environmental Effect of Oil and the Chemicals Used to Control I.T.

There are many factors, acting both individually and in combination, which govern the effect of oil on marine life. These will include the type and quantity of oil, the duration and quantity of pollution experienced by the organism, the state of the oil, *e.g* , fresh, weathered etc., the season, with respect to the annual cycle of the organism, and the habitat and the natural stresses to which the organism is subjected. Any or all of these can affect the organism in many different ways. The effect may be lethal or sub-lethal, in the latter it can disrupt physiological or behavioural activities and death may result due to interference with feeding of reproduction. The uptake of oil can result in tainting or possible carcinogenesis either of the organism contaminated or one higher up the food chain.

The visible and well-known effects are beach pollution and the death, due to oiling, of seabirds. It is not unreasonable to wonder, if not actually to fear, whether oil might nor adversely affect marine life and, in particular, harm fish the source of much food for man and his domestic animals either by reducing their numbers of rendering them unfit to ear.

Like all life, life in the sea depends upon solar radiation for its source of energy. Through photosynthesis, marine plants, of which by far the most important are the minute drifting organisms collectively know as phytoplankton, store this energy in a form which other organisms such as zooplankton and the fish which prey upon it can utilies, a simplified diagram showing the board outling of what is in reality a highly complex food web. It is helpful to realise that at each step the efficiency of conversion of frood into body weight is only about 10%. Nelson Smith estimates that man would require at least on kilogram of phytoplankton to gain one gram in weight. This is a useful statistic for it highlights the fact that direct effects on fish stocks eaten by man are of much greater economic importance than equivalent damage in terms of biomass lost, to the planktonic organisms on which the fish depend.

The food web diagram also highlights the fact that frsh, and other organisms well removed from the primary production stage represented by the phytoplankton, have by proxity, consumed relatively enormous quantities of organic materials some of which, although only present in small concentrations in phytoplankton, may collect at the higher tropic levels of the food web. The question of whether there is an accumulation of petroleum hydrocarbons compounds, if they represent a credible threat to the resource or the consnmer, and the other possible effects on marine life of oil and of chemicals and methods used to clean it up.

Plankton

At almost all major oil spills, lay men and ecologist alike express fears about possible harmful effects on plankton. Concern can usually be summarised under three headings :

- A layear of oil on the surface will, by occluding light, cause a serious drop in photosynthesis by phyroplankton.
- The oil layer will interfere with gaseout interchange at the sea surface and dissolved oxygen levels will thereby be lowered.

– Oil and dispersants will exert serious toxic effects on plankton.

How real are these effects and what is their ecological significance ? The first and second are the indirect consequences of meansurable physico/chemical phenomena and will be treated first.

1. Occulsion of Light

Ottway studied the light transmitting properties of 20 crude oils made up as 5% solutions in white sprit and shoed that different crude oils vary widely in this respect. Oils high in asphaltenes and sulphur were found to absorb most light and, for all oils, the absorption spectra exhibited maxima at the blue end of the spectrum (325 – 350 nm), indicating that the 44 same group of compounds is mainly responsible in all of the oils tested. A number of photosynthetic pigments found in phytoplankton also have absorption maxima at the blue end of the spectrum. Potentially, at least, their photosynthetic activity could be impeded by crude oils spilt at sea. It is important to remember the scale of the problem. A huge slick of black oil covering 2000 square miles of the North Sea actually covers less than 1% of its area. It is safe to conclude that occlusion of light by spilled oil, a phenomenon easily demonstrated in the laboratory, has no ecological significance for the plankton of the open area.

2. Effects on Dissolved Oxygen Levels

The solubility of oxygen in most hydrocarbon mixtures is similar to that in sea water. An oil slick is not, therefore, an impenetrable barrier to gaseous interchange. For a full discussion of this issue, the reader should consult Nelson Smith; suffice it to say that in a 2 day trial, Brown and Reid found that boild water, beneath a 17 mm layer of oil, absorbed 73% as much oxygen as the control. Confirmation that oil slicks do not interfere significantly with gaseous interchange at the surface of the open sea is provided, by an observation by the

Scripps Institution of Occeanography, on dissolved oxygen levels below a heavy oil slick in the Santa Barbara Channel. The oxygen saturation beneath the slick was 98.5% of that in water outside the slick area.

3. Toxic Effects

There is abundance evidence that freshly-spilled crude oils contain low boiling point substances which are actually to ic to the planktonic organisms. The most toxic of these are water soluble aromatic derivatives. Low molecular weight alkanes (10 carbon atoms or less) may induce narcosis in high concentrations but these are unlikely to result from a crude oil spill in the open sea. The aromatic solvents used in early emulsifiers were also found to be highly toxic to planktonic organisms at levels of less than one part per million. In latter formulations of equivalent dispersing power, the use of non-aromatic solvents has reduced toxicity by over two orders of magnitude.

Useful as loboratory assessments of toxicity can be for comparing the acute toxicity of oils and dispersant chemicals to small number of organisms they are rarely a reliable guide to effects on wild populations. In that such tests are necessarily short term they under estimate toxicity, but on the other hand, the toxicant concentrations used in laboratory experiments are rarely maintained for any length of time in the sea. Evoporate losses and the rapid dilution of residual, soluble compounds ensures that toxic effects are short-lasting, even for high toxicity, solvent emulsion of the aromatic type. Thus although highly localised short-term effects on plankton were observed following the massive use of high concentrations to disperse Torrey canyon oil. There was no evident that any planktonic species was significantly affected the population level. The Torey canyon experiance was quiete exceptional in the amount and toxicity of the materials used to disperse the oil, and even there it would seem that the rapid evoporation and dilution of the toxicity combined with the disperssed nature and rapid trunover of the plankton to minimise the ecological impact. For other major spillages, including the notorious Santaa Barbara blow-out the toxic effects on the planktonic tissue have proved to be virtually detectable. The plankton of milfold Haven was examined to see if the development of a major oil port had any effect. The report stated that changes which have occured are no greater than might have been produced by natural environment changes and population dynamics. Sanbourn suggests however that the effect on benthic larvae when they are in upper layer of the ocean may be more longer lasting as benethic animals require years to reach maturity and so the effect on the larvae may endour longer. The only planktonic species which may conceively be in any ecologically significant danger from the toxicants associated with crude oil or dispersants are those which form fairly localised aggregations. Arrow worms fish eggs, and larvae may come in to this catogory. The likelyhood of ecologically significant effects in such cases is examined in detail.

Finally, to keep our assessment of toxic effect on plankton in their true perspective it is helpful to consider the scale of plankton production of in the sea relative to the that of petroleum spilled. Fraser estimates annual world phytoplankton production to be about 150,000 million tons and that of zooplankton 15,000 million tons. By contrast estimates of annual losses of petroleum in the sea vary from 2.5 million to an improbable maximum of 10 million tons. Only a fraction of this petroleum is toxic to plankton and very little of this is ever likely to come into contact with planktonic organisms.

Fisheries

As was said earlier, the purpose of this chapter is to arrive at an assessment of the effects of oil pollution.' an environmental stress, for which man is largely responsible, on the biology of the sea. It is important, in this context, to consider the particular case of sea fisheries, a sector of the marine environment in which man already exerts a direct and measurable influence. The term, 'fisheries', has a variety of meanings, the widest embracing all exploited stocks of marine organisms from macro-algae to whales, and the narrowest exploited species of fish alone. In this chapter, the term is taken to mean the fish and shellfish of commerce.

Oil pollution is potential treat to these resources for three main resons :

--Pollution any directly harm fish and shellfish stocks.

—Pollutants adhering to, or accumulated by, fish and shellfish may render them unacceptable to the consumer.

—The presence of spilled oil may interfere physically with fishing operation.

Controlling Pollution

Now that the nature of pollution and some of the sources of this undesirable product of society have been considered, let us concern ourselves with some of the avenues open to us to accomplish some sort of control. The most obvious control strategy that can be used is to some how or other completely prevent the introduction of the pollutant into the environment. This can be done by not producing the pollutant or by restructuring the process so that the pollutant is no longer a byproduct. Let us consider a few major sources of pollutants and some possible methods of control in these particular cases.

The most obvious solution to the problem of maintenance redging is to cut off the sediment supply to the areas where sedimentation is a major problem. This can be done in a number of different ways. The most effective of all is to prevent upstream erosion, but at the same time this is perhaps the most difficult. The entire watershed must be policed very carefully to make sure that the natural landscape is change to such an extent that erosion no longer occurs. This means extensive terracing and replanting of areas that have been denuded for on reason or another. Of course, this also means that extreme measures must be taken in areas that have no natural cover, such as agricultural areas or areas where contruction is underway. A certain amount of this is being done and these are a number of legal requirements for persons engaged in construction or agricultural activities.

Another method of preventing sediment from reaching the undersired area is to provide settling ponds. If a stream is identified that carries a large sediment load, a pond and dam arrangement can be built so that the velocity of the stream is decreased to zero and the suspended sediment will have a chance to settle. The water is released after it has dropped the major portion of its load and is allowed to proceed downstream. The solution since the ponds will fill up rather rapidly, requiring either building of new ponds or dredging of some sort. Sometimes the sedimentation that occurs is channel area is a result of sediment loads that are introduced into the marine environment from nearby rather than those carried from far upstream. Thi occurs, for example, when a chennel is dredged with unstable sides so that the material just tends to slough into the deeper regions. This requires continual dredging as the removed sediment is almost immediately replaced by bottom material from the sides. One method of correcting this situation is by stablization of the bottom. Adding larger, more dense material such as gravel to the bottom is a technique utilized occasionally, although this is usually more expensive than dredging so that it is not done too often. Bottom stabilization, however, is a technique that is being used more and more to prevent the movement of bottom materials within relatively small contiguous areas.

Oil Pollution

Another problem that, to a certain extent, appears amenable to prevention at the source is that involving oil. Unfortunately, the sources of oil in the marine environment are extremely difficult to delieate. Many figures have been published and, in almost all cases, there is a significant disagreement as to the amount of oil discharge into the marine environment and the sources of the oil. There is no doubt, though, that a large portion of this amount originates on land as waste product. As would be expected, the major source of this is associated with the automobile. Some of this lost oil is dropped from leaks in cars and trucks, some is deliberately dumped as used crankcase oil, while some results from the deposition of unburned exhaust gases. From roads and streets this material is washed into the marine environment, usually without benefit of treatment. Even when passed through treatment plants, however, petroleum-rich effluents still provide problems as they are difficult to treat and they tend to make treatment for other pollutants less effective. All the experts agree that the greatest terrestial source of petroleum products in the ocean is used crankcase oil. Some go so far as to indicate that this source supplices more petroleum to the sea than any other source. This may be true because within the last decade or so the habits of American motorist have change markedly to the extent that a large portion of them now change their own oil, discarding the used oil in a manner that probably causes it to end up in storm sewers. The major reason for this probably is the almost complete disappearance of the used lubricating oil re-refining industry in recent years since it was not economically feasible to refined oil. However, with the modern continual increase in the price of new oil, the re-refining industry is having a rebirth so that a large portion of the oil previously thrown away will now be reused.

Another entirely different source of oil in the marine environment is that resulting from accidents that occur during shipping and transferring processes generally speaking. The more handling steps involved, the more accidents and associated losses can be expected. The figures as to how much is actually lost in handling accidents compared to that lost in normal ship procedures, such as pumping bilges, is not well known, but there is no doubt that a very large portion of the oil reaching the marine environment is the result of poor handling procedures in both the operation of vessel and the transfer of oil from one carrier to another. Better procedures are need, but perhaps even more than better procedures, structure enforcement of accepted safe procedures would go a long way to decreasing the amount of oil that enters the ocean each year.

When a tanker empties its load of oil, the dynamic characteristics of this vessel are markedly changed. Its weight is decreased about a thousand times and therefore it becomes extremely difficult to drive the ship, since it was designed to be driven with a full load. Therefore when most tankers do not have a load of oil, they will fill their tanks with water for ballast. When they return for a fresh carg of oil, they must pump this water from the tanks, releasing large amounts of oil as the residue left in the tanks is washed out. There have been many schemes suggested for decreasing the amount of oil that is wasted in the ballasting-unballasting process; however, it is not clear at this time how effective these processes are or how effectively any requirements can be enforced.

Modern supertankers are extremely large vessels and therefore have major structural weaknesses, so that occasionally they will break up in unusually heavy seas. They are simply not designed to be utilized under unusual storm conditions, so that there will continue to be losses of this type in rough weather. In passing, it should be mentioned that once oil is spilled at sea under large wave conditions there is no way for this oil to be retrieved. On the other hand, oil may be retrieved inharbor areas where the sea surface is relatively calm, but only when there are waves no higher than approximately one meter. The obvious way the only way to prevent oil from getting to the marine environment when a ship founders is to prevent the accident from occurring in the first place. Alternatively, once the accident has occurred the oil must be prevented from escaping from the ship. It is somewhat doubtful whether these solutions will ever be possible.

Recycling and Reclamation

If it is impossible for one reasons or another to prevent the introduction of a pollutant into the system, it may be possible at some place along the line to extract this pollutant and resue it. It should be kept in mind that although "consumer" is a commonly used word, there is no such thing as a consumer. The word tends to imply that material is being used up, while, in actuality, it is just borrowed for a while and returned. It may be in a somewhat different form or perhaps a somewhat different shape, but nevertheless it is still returned. We don't destroy any of this mass; we just change its form, so that the general concept of recycling or reclamation is extremely appealing, especially when we consider our larger solid forms of waste. If we could find some way to utilize all of these materials, we would solve a number of our problems especially those involved with space.

Sometimes, though, it is not necessarily desirable to solve a space problem sometimes the space problem works to our advantage. For example, it has been found that biological communities living in the sea require a certain amount of physical shelter. Some species just like to be alone, whereas in other cases the young of the species require places to hide to protect against predation. A marsh or wetlands area is a good breeding place because both of these conditions prevail. It has been found that in many cases these conditions can be created artificially by introducing large juck articles such as old automobiles or worn out ships to form effective artificial fishing reefs.

There are disadvantages to using waste products for this sort of activity. One is that in many cases these junk objects are transported to undesirable areas by dynamic oceanic forces,

Pollution is not controlled when automobile fenders and doors wash up on swimming beaches. When creating a fishing reef, steps must be taken to retain the integrity of these reefs for a long period of time. If proper attention is paid to the magnitude and nature of oceanic forces, artificial reefs can be made relatively permanent.

In actuality the whole recycling and reclamation business is predicated on cost. If it is economically feasib'e to recycle or reclaim material, it will be recycled or reclaimed. If it costs more money to use the recycled material than new material, then the material will not be recycled. It is difficult to imagine that certain materials, such as glass, will ever be recycled to any great extent because silicon is one of the most common elements in the earth's crust and it costs just about as much to make a new bottle as it does to recycle an old one. However, in the case of aluminium there is about a factor of five involved in recycling coast as opposed to manufacturing from scratch.

With the present state of the economy where things become more expensive from year to year, it appears that more items will find themselves on the list of materials to be recycled or reclaimed. Industrial processes will change as it becomes more feasible to extrat materials for the waste stream from a cost standpoint and, at the same time, industrial waste streams will become less and less polluted. Even in the area of multiple waste product use, such as the combination of water heat from either manufacturing or electrical power generation and waste nutrients from sewage treatment plants for the purposes of aquaculture, cost will always be the controlling factor.

It has been known for some time that evaluated temperatures and the artificial addition of nutrients will increase growth rates of many organisms markedly. The choice of which organism to grow is involved not only with which would be best to grow, but also which there is a market for. Setting up an aquaculture system involves picking organisms which respond favourably to the environment, developing a system by which the optimum growth rate can be produced, developing a marketing system so that the end product will be sold at the maximum possible price, and assuring the continuing existence of market for everything produced. Not only is science included but also sociology and economics must be considered, and it is probably in these latter two areas that the major difficulties reside. Consequently, no sophisticated aquaculture systems using both waste heat and nutrients have been developed at this point, but it is probably only a matter of time before we will have extensive aquaculture using man's waste products.

Storage of Pollutants

Another method of controlling pollution, utilized for certain pollutants, is to store them at some distance from man's activities so that they are as inaccessible as possible to the major fraction of the population and pathways to man. Thus we essentially throw them away, but we thrown them away, in a place where no one can get to them and their effects cannot get to man Occasionally nuclear waste produ ts have been dumped in deep oceanic areas in the hope that when they do break out of their canisters, they will not find can easy pathway back to man since the deeper life forms are probably not in any food chain involving man. Perhaps not so well known is the fact that deep ocean disposal has been used for other materials such as overage ordiance and poision gases for which the military has not further use.

In the case of nuclear products, there is a very vociferous school of thought that believes storage facilities should allow waste retrieval if a technological break through is ever accomplished that would allow these nuclear waste products to be profitably utilized. Another school feels that they should be placed in an areas as completely inaccessible as possible to everyone. This latter school in tuitively seems the safest, but, on the other hand, most common storage places are just not the type. There is always a small probability of a pathway back in man being found. One suggestion for a nonretrivable storage place which holds some promise has been made by Issac Asimov. According to moder Geological theory the earth's crust is composed of a number of separate plates, all moving with respect to one another. In some places the plates are moving together and in others apart, following the motion of the mantle, the layer of material underneath the earth's crust. As a result of convection, the mantle tends to rise toward the earth's crust in certain areas, producing oceanic ridges such as the North Atlantic ridge. At these divergence areas, where the mantle material is brought up to the earth's crust, the motion becomes horizontal and the crustal plates are carried away from the ridges at a rate of a few centimeters per year. The convergent regions where the plates come together are where the mantle material is carried back down toward the centre of the earth. In direct contrast to the regions of divergence associated with ridges, the convergent areas are associated with oceanic trenches where crustal material is carried down and under the continental plates. These oceanic trench areas are very deep, often as deep as 10,000 meters, and at the same time are actively engaged in transporting material into the bowels of the earth.

Controlling Pollution by Zonec

Another method of controlling pollution is by specifying certain areas that can be utilized for effluent discharge and other areas that cannot. This method has been used on land as records have been kept. Although zoning of certain regions as industrial, commercial, or residential is a relatively recent innovation, there always was city dump. Now-a-days we are even starting to convert our city dumps into usuable areas, such as gulf courses or sky slopes by convering, planting, and landscaping as rapidly as possible. This is an exciting concept that is gaining in popularity as dumping areas become more and more scarce, but it will be some time before ocean dumping areas are reclaimed in the fashion.

Even though we are attempting to utilize our dumping areas for other purposes as rapidly as we can, the concept of zoning still pervades our society. Certain areas are set aside for certain types of use. Society is willing to accept a factory in a particular location where it is hidden, while at the same time people will not accept that factory as a next door neighbor. The same concept has been suggested for marine coastal areas. Certain regions would be reserved for industry, others for sewage treatment, while still others would be set aside for recreation. Some of these activities are such that they may be pursued in conjunction with one another, whereas others cannot. The idea is for every coastal area to try to obtain utilization of marine resources available. In order to accomplish this type of zoning most effectively, a great deal more knowledge is required than is presently available about the synergistic effects of various types of activities. One of the major advantage of optimum zoning is that it would allow maximum avoidance of undesirable synergistic effects.

The biggest stumbling block to coastal zoning probably is in overcoming entrenched interests in regions where the optimum activities are different from those presently underway: A socio-economic problem rather than a technological one, the Coastal Zone Management Act encourages coastal states to attempt to take the first step in planning for optimum utilization of the coastal areas. After plans are complete, the states are to implement them with the financial assistance of the federal Government.

The concept is an interesting one, because it essentially allows some pollution of certain areas while refusing to permit any pollution of other locales. This is somewhat different from the way pollution is presently controlled, where the effort is made to limit pollution in all areas to the minimum possible amount. With the zoning concept pollution would still be limited as much as possible, but it would be permissible to allow the water quality to degrade below the mean in some places, since in others it would be higher than the mean.

Controlling Pollution by Taxation

One last method of pollution control that has been suggested, although it has met with a great deal of resistance and antagonism, is taxation. As is well known, taxation can be utilized to encourage or discourage certain activities in addition to raising funds to support government programs. Pollution would be allowed, but it would be taxed at a rate proportional to the environmental insult. This general philosophy is followed at the present time by requiring the polluters pay fines roughly proportional to the amount of pollution, and in many cases industries will purposely pollute and pay the fine because it is apparently cheaper than making the necessary plant modification required for cleanup.

Obviously the system is not working if this is the case; the fines are too low.

Some economists suggest that a tax on pollution will simply be a license to pollute and will therefore encourage pollution rather than discourage it. Other economists, however, indicate that pollution taxes should be based on the severity of the pollution with some sort of graudated tax. A little pollution requires a little tax, a large pollution requires a large tax. An important aspect of this concept is that the words the true and total cost to society of these pollutants. Every time the common resource is utilized by an individual, this society for the right to use this common resource. This payment would be in the form of a tax set at a level determined by how much society economists believe that anyone utilizing the resource should pay for its degraded' then the individual degrading should pay for the degradation. This is an interesting concept that is being discussed in economic circles taxation certainly is a powerful tool for societal behavior modification that has worked many times. Generally speaking, taxation encourages particular activities and discourages other if the taxation amount is large enough to completely discourage undesirable activities.

From a management point of view there are a number of different directions that can be taken to control pollution, including both technological and socio-economic alternatives. So far society has tenced to aim more in the direction of the technological alternatives, but there appears to be definate swing toward other methods. In the year to come it appears that more and more emphasis will be placed on these non-technical methods especially as the tradeoffs, costs, and benefits become better understood.

The Forces Involved in Dispersing Pollutants

Once a pollutant has been introduced into the marine environment, it becomes a matter of no small interest to determine where this pollutant goes and how the concentration of the pollutant varies with time and location These process fall into two basic groups: advection and dilution, advection is the mechanism by which the pollutant is carried from one place to another, while dilution results when the pollutant is caused to reduce its concentration by some sort of spreading mechanism. Advection simply has to do with oceanic currents and will include three primary types of current since these are encountered most often in the oceanic regime.

Management of the Marine Environment

Up to this time we have been primarily concerned with the technical aspects of pollution. Space has been devoted to discussion of what pollution is, where it comes from, and where it goes in the marine environment. Now we must consider how to control this pollution so that the problems resulting from it are kept to a minimum. The previous sentence has a number of words in it which should probably be defined very carefully, but probably never will be. For example, the statement that pollution should be controlled so that the resulting problems be kept to a minimum may be intrepreted many different ways be many different people since a problem for one group is not necessarily a problem for clear-cut. Just as one man's trash is another man's treasure, one man's pollution is another man's enrichment, and this is not the only dichotomy that faces a conscientious marine manager. There are problems of jurisdiction involved in whether the responsibility for running the operation lies with the federal government, a local government, or some regulatory commission, and always there is the application of priorities supposedly set by society as a whole. The basic tool the manager has to work with is the law, however, and this is where we begin.

The Legal Background

The legal background for pollution control goes back to the Rivers and Harbors Act of 1899, recently interpreted so as to be used as a pollution control measure. This act set up responsiblities for protecting navigational and environmental aspects of all navigable waters to the U.S. Army Corps of Engineers. The Corps therefore has the responsibility not only of protecting navigable waters so they remain navigable but also protecting them against their loss as a viable vehicle for various other uses that society considers desirable.

An interesting aspect of this law and one reason it has become such a powerful tool in the hands of the environmental protectors is the redefinition of navigable waters. It turus out that the modern definition includes just about every stream going into a large river in the United States. Thus the Army Corps of Engineers was given the responsibility for protecting the environment 1899 and to all intents and purposes still retains this primary responsibility as far as brackish and salt water is concerned.

In 1934 the Fish and Wildlife Coordination Act was passed. This has since been amended many times, but essentially it involves the fact the U.S. Fish and Wildlife Service and The National Marine Fishers Services have the responsibility for determining the effect of any proposed project on fish and wildlife resources. They then report to the crops of Engineers which makes the final decision as to whether or not the proposed project is allowed.

In 1948 the Federal Water Pollution Control Act was passed and this also has been emended periodically. It requires the Corps of Engineers to apply environmental standards and criteria in approving the disposal of spoil in navigable waters. The most recent amendment of this act was the Federal Pollution Water Control Act of 1972. This was a complete rewrite of the 1948 law and it set out four basic requirements. In the first place, a national goal for the elimination of all pollution from America's waters by 1985 was proclaimed. This is the famous zero discharge goal. Note that this is not a mandate to have zero discharge by 1985, but as a national goal it is something to aim at and it is to be hoped that we will come as close as possible. Second, the Act of 1972 set as another goal the addition of secondary treatment to all municipal sewage treatment plants by 1977. This goal has not been met but there has been a strong effort in that direction. Third was the effort to encourage the use of new, more advanced treatment and disposal methods by 1983 so that some of the problems will be resolved by the use of advanced technology rather than by simply improving on present methods. And last, the act established an industrial cleanup program with restrictions becoming tighter with the passage of time. Each year the requirements involving effluent standards will be tightened so that these will be continuing cleanup of the nation's waters. This particular aspect of the bill was backed by stiff penalities including both fines and imprisonments.

This 1972 Act is the basic law under which most anti-pollution suits are brought. The Water Pollution Control Act of 1948 encouraged the creation of uniform laws to control pollution, supported research, or firms to cease practices leading to pollution, and established the Federal Water Pollution Control Advisory Board. This has been succeeded in recent years by the Council Environmental Quality.

The year 1965 saw the passage of the Water Quality Act. In this act states were given an opportunity to adopt and enforce federal water quality standards for interstate waters. The Clean Water Restoration Act of 1966 authorized massive federal participation in the construction of sewage treatment plants. About 3.5. billion dollars were allocated to be spent between 1967 and 1971.

The National Environmental Policy Act of 1969 provided prepartion of environmental impact statements when the U.S. Army Corps of Engineers determined it to be necessary. The Act also declared it to be national policy to encourage the production of enjoyable harmony between man and his environment.

The Water Quality Act of 1970 addressed oil pollution from vessels and offshore facilities, federal permits, sewage pollution from vessels and hazardous substance discharged into the nations's waters.

Also in 1970 recorgnization plan No. 3 was submitted to the Congress by the Chief Executive. This reorganization plan established the Environmental Protection Agency, setting up the organization and transferring responsibility for various activities from other agencies. Unfortunately, the executive order does not address the problems of the objective or the purpose of the Environmental Protection Agency (EPA) and this objective or purpose has been left to the Agency Adminis-trator to interpret for himself. This omission has resulted in a general grey area with EPA being as strong or as weak as the Administrator and Congress want it to be.

In 1972, in addition to the amendent to the Water Pollution Control Act, two other act of some import to the protection of the marine environment were passed. The first of these was the ocean Dumping Act of 1972. This act requires the Army Corps of Engineers to apply Environmental Protection Agency standards and criteria in approving ocean disposal of dredge spoil materials where transport passes through United States territorial waters. This is an interesting law because it controls the material that orginates in United States ports and not that material which is dumped in United States water. Consequently no matter where the material is dumped, as long as it orginates in a United States port, the Corps of Engineers has some control over it.

The other act passe in 1972 having important ramfications to the marine community was the Coastal Zone Management Act. This act gave the individual states primary responsibility for determining land and water uses to more effectively balance environmental protection and economic development objectives in the coastal zone. It delneated the coastal zone as including all navigable waters and defined them as all waters up to the mean high tide line, including we lands wholly or partially covered at high tide, whether privately or publicly owned. Under this act large amounts of money have been given to participating states, and all coastal and Great Lake states have so far indicated a desire to participate. Funds are initially for planning purposes aimed at developing a general zoning plan for the use of the coastal zone. Later funds will be available for the implementation of these plans.

In an attempt to get at specific causes of pollution, the Ports and Waterways Safety Act was passed in 1972 which addressed the problem of pollution from ships. This act allowed for ship design and construction regulation with respect to possible environmental damage and it applied to all

United States flag vessel as well as all foreign vessel entering United States waters carrying either oil or hazardous liquid cargo in bulk. Vessel design and operational standards for all these vessel in United States waters were finally promulated on 23 January 1977. In this manner the United States government is attempting to prevent as many large catastophies involving vessel carrying oil or harzardous materials as it possibly can by simply not allowing marginal vessel to navigate within the territorial limits of the United States.

Another fact of marine pollution having a source outside the continental area is involved with driliving for oil and gas offshore. The Outer Continental Shel Lands Act gave the responsibility of Granting leases for continental shelf drilling to the Department Interor. These leases require the leasees to reimburse the federal government for any oil spill cleanup cost and in addition they require the installation of bolwout prevent equipment on the wells themselves.

International Convenants

The foregoing is a brief list of the basic framework of federal laws which govern the discharge of waste products into our territorial waters. In addition there are a few international convenants under which the United States operates. The Intergovernmental Maritime Consultative Organization (IMCO) has sponsored three conventions resulting in a number of regulations. The first of these was the 1954 Oil pollution convention which was amended in 1962 and 1969. This convention places limitations on the rate of discharge, the oil content, and the distance from land for oily ballast discharge water from ships. The enforcement of this convention is left up to the flat state, that is the country where the ship is registered.

The second convention was the 1971 amendment to the Oil pollution Convention which branched out in different direction by addressing vessel design. Unfortunately this part of this amendment has not been rectified by any martime nation.

In 1973 a ship pollution convention was sponsored by IMCO, and this convention resulted in a set of regulations establishing standards for ship board sewage treatment equipment and also specified the requirement for segregate ballast tanks for new ships of specified sizes. It also specified methods for storing dirty oil ballast residue, oil discharge monitoring systems, and oily water oil extraction systems. Unfortunately this convention also has not been ratified by any martime nation. Consequently, behavior on the high seas is left strictly to the conscience of the individual ship's master.

At this time there are also no international agreements on ocean dumping or the environmental effects of seabed resource exploitation. There have been many attempts to draw up an International Law of the Sea agreement but as of this writing none has been successful

Jurisdictional Responsibility

One of the problems facing a marine resource manager is the problem of jurisdictional dispute. Who does have responsibility ? In the four general areas the responsibility is somewhat dispersed. The first of these areas is water drainage, capture, or use which is exclusively on a local level. Since this is primarily a problem of private rights which is usually involved with state of private ownership. This area does sometimes get involved as a pollution source so it is of concern to us. The third area of interest includes the bays and coastal waters which are controlled by a combination of state and federal regulations. Generally speaking, the state has control over resources and the federal government has control over navigational and environmental considerations, but there are many exceptions.

Most state laws are not quite as strigent as the federal environmental requirements so that the federal requirements must be obeyed. However, there are some state laws more strict than the federal and when this is the case, the state laws take precedence. The last areas is the region beyond the coastal region wherein the responsibility is somewhat loose. We have seen that there are no viable international agreements for the deep ocean, but in many cases the United States has acted unilaterally to protect its continuous waters. With the passage of the Ports and Waterways Safety Act and the Outer Continental Shelf Lands Act attempts have been made to protect against the effects of oil and hazardous material, corgo ships and offshore oil-wells.

Political Processes

Once the problem of jurisdiction is settled, there then appears the problem of political processes. The political process is such that technical standards will almost always yield to such things as hardship cases, emergency situations, or strong public sentiments. Consequently, any decision to be made where the environment is involved must have a public input or else the decision will probably not be effective. The manager must not only face an often emotional public, but also individual agencies, both state and federal, working at cross purposes. For example, the Environmental Protection Agency is primarily concerned with water quality, the U.S. Fish and Wildlife Service is primarily concerned with fish habitat improvement, while the Army Corps of Engineers has a primary concern in the areas of navigation improvement. These concerns must be balanced against common public needs such as high employment, protection of scenic environments, and housing demands, and very often these conflict very strongly so that at least one of the many groups must eventually compromise. This compromise, in the long run, must be based on some sort of a set of sodietal objectives. Society must somehow or other determine the most important things it wants from its marine resources.

The activities range from aesthetic enjoyment of the area to commercial shipping and waste disposal. Obviously waste disposal is not exactly the type of activity to enhance aesthetic enjoyment, nor is utilizing the coastal zone for military maneuvers encouraging to the maintenance of a reguge or a sanctuary. Some of the uses of the marine coastal area must be sacrificed in certain cases for other uses which society deems more important.

Somehow or other society must set priorities so, that the areas can be managed to obtain the ends that society wants from them. This is a very important point and one that is often completely ignored. In very few cases has society overtly set down priorities for the use of marine areas, and until priorities are specifically stated, marine area managers will be forced into making bad decisions. It is to be hoped that some of the planning being done under the Coastal Zone Management Act will involve priority setting, especially regarding the use of particular areas. If this is the only outcome of the coastal zone management act, it will indeed be a valuable contribution to the management of the activities of society in the marine coastal zone.

Costs, Risks, and Benefits

In order to set priorities in a rational manner, managers must by one means or another determine benefits, costs, and risks associated with any and all activities. Once these three parameters have been quantified, then cost/benefited rations may be determined and priorities may be set on the basis of these ratios. However, this is much easier said than done. All three of these parameters are usually quite qualitative and very difficult to quantity. Benefits, for example, are often what people perceive them to be and therefore are essentially a political evaluation rather than an exact calculation.

Costs can often be determined accurately in terms of the actual physical nature of the activity. Buildings, machinery, and labour can be quantified in terms of their cost. However, very often an attempt to control pollution or the effect of pollution on society results in costs that simply cannot easily be quantified.

Risks also are difficult to evaluate. How much is a life worth ? Does it make a difference if it is yours or someone else ? Thus we find that we must be satisfied with some approximation to these three parameters. Some methods for obtaining approximations to values for costs, risks, and benefits will be discussed below.

The cost versus pollution control curve, is an exponential curve wherein the initial costs of controlling pollution are relatively inexpensive, but the final 5 or 10% of pollution control may cost as much as the initial 90 to 95%. The benefit pollution control curve, on the other hand, is parbolic in shape. Here the benefits in the initial cleanup phase are quite large while the benefits accrued from the final stages are quite small. We might consider then some sort of a cost/benefit ratio, knowing these two functions.

The optimum cost benefit ration is determined on the basis of the incremental cost per incremental benefit. If, example, an additional dollar of environmental control will produce more than a dollar's worth of benefits, then it is more effective to spend additional money on control. If, however, additional control results in fewer dollars worth of benefit, then it appears that the control process has been carried too far. The optimal level of pollution control is not at point A where the cost of pollution control and benefits are the same, but is at point B, where the rate of increase of cost per unit pollution control is equal to the rate of increase of benefit per unit pollution control. At point B the slopes of the Curves are the same. We may then write

$$\frac{dc}{d(pc)} = \frac{db}{d(pc)}$$

From a cost benefit analysis then it appears that it is not desirable to completely clean up the environment since the benefits accured would not be worth the expenditure required. However, this is not the complete story. It is obvious that in certain cases even a small amount of pollutant is not acceptable because of the danger to health. Thus the risk too much be considered.

Each activity and each pollutant has an associated risk, some of these to the environment and some to man. It is difficult to quantify these but one method commonly used is to determine the number of fatalities per million hours of exposure for each person involved in the activity considered. This is expressed as a statistical probability. Table 7.1 is a listing of risks expressed in this manner for various common activities.

TABLE 7.1

Risk Table

Risk	*Death rate per million hours of exposure*
Voluntary	40.0
Rock climbing	6.6
Motorcycle	2.4
Scheduled airline	2.4
Smoking cigarettes	1.2
Death by disease	—
Including old age	1.0
Private auto	0.95
Sking	0.71
Railroad and bus	0.08
Involuntary	—
Electric power	0.002

Notice that the activities are divided into two groups, voluntary and involuntary activities. The voluntary activities are those which the individual can decide for himself whether or not he wishes to do. Notice that many of these activities have a probability very close to that of death by disease, including old age. Others, however, such as rock climbing, have an extremely high risk associated with them and therefore are only for the adventuresome.

Interestingly enough, the risk associated with the one involuntary activity listed, electric power, is less by about three orders of magnitude than most of the risks in the voluntary portion of the table Apparently then we are loath to let others do in to us what we happily do to ourselves. Pollution, of course, falls within this area of involuntary activities since any pollutant discharged to the marine environment is not directly controllable by any individual. Consequently we would expect that the risks associated with pollutants would be down in the area of that of electric power rather than up with that of railroad and bus travel.

In order to quantify priorities, it if necessary then to develop some sort of risk benefit ratio, which, in turn, requires quantification of benefits. One possibility of quantifying benefits is to simply assume that in the case of voluntary activities the amount of money spent on the activity by the average involved individual was proportional to its benefit, while in the case of involuntary activities, the contribution of the activity to the individual's annual income as porportional to its benefit. Here risk is plotted relative to the benefit for various kinds of voluntary and involuntary exposure.

From these graphs and some other works that has been done, a number of conclusions can be drawn. First, the public is apparently willing to accept voluntary risks roughly a thousand times greater than those involved with involuntary exposure. Second, the statistical risk of death from disease and old age appears to be a psychological yardstick for establishing the level of acceptability of other risks. Third, the acceptability of risks appear to be crudly proportional to the third power of the benefits, whether they be real or imagined. Fourth, the social acceptance of risks appears to be directly influenced by public awareness of the benefits of an activity as determined perhaps by advertising or the number of enhanced by increased public awareness.

A determination of the level of optimum pollution control and general management schemes involved with addressing the total pollution problem is not as easy one. We find that everything costs something. There is no such thing as a free lunch. For every cleanup process involved there is a cost. Sometimes this cost is minimal but other times the cost is extremely high. For example, it has been estimated that in order to meet the 1983 goals of the Federal Water Pollution Act or 1972 it would cost 350 billion dollars just to treast municipal sewage in an adequate manner. This includes the cost of controlling nonpoint sources along with sewage treatment plant updating. Whether or not the America public is willing to spend this much on this sort of program is at this time unclear, but the American public must be madea ware of the necessity of costs and trades of any cleanup program. If we are going to spend this amount of money for pollution cleanup then there will not be as much money available for other activities, and once again we must decide which to these activities, and once again we must decide which to these activities is more important to us. But the decision can only be made if we have as much data as possible in hand to allow as accurate as possible a determination of benefits, costs, and risk involved with each process.

The Future of the Marine Environment

In the previous pages we have seen that the oceanic volume is extremely large, while at the same time, that portion of the oceanic volume available for pollutant discharge is relatively small. Consequently, we hope to have demonstrated a need for some kind of marine pollution management since there is a very real problem associated with dumping wastes in the ocean. It has also been shown that an ever increasing population, distributed primarily around coastal areas, will inevitably increase the total amount of waste discharged to the oceans. This is coupled with the fact that technology is continually growing and its growth will be associated with an increasing amount of pollution per capita with the passage of time. It all boils down to the realization that the total volume of water available for waste dilution will remain relatively constant while the total amount of waste will probably increase as far into the future as can be foreseen at this time.

Management Requirements

Fortunately, however, in those nations which have reached a relatively high level of technology, there is an increasing awareness of the problem and a public requirement that planning and management proceed in order to utilize the marine resource in the best manner possible. In order to do this a number of requirements must be met.

In the first place the effects and pathways of all pollutants dumped into the ocean must be known. This is an extremely difficult task. Many of the patways are known but the effects are not. For other pollutants the effects are well known but the pathways back to man are still mysterious. This obviously will require a great deal of research, and even then there is no guarantee that all effects and pathways for all pollutant materials will ever be known.

Second, the average residence time for all materials discharged into the marine environment should be known. Here again we are faced with an almost impossible problem due to the tremendous amounts and number of different materials discharged into the oceanic environment.

There should also be a continuing monitoring of the environment if only to determine gross changes so some action may be taken before the situation gets out of hand.

Lastly, we must continually determine and redetermine what people consider to be important. The more and folk ways of society constantly change, altering values and priorities.

2. Setting Priorities

At this time managers have no clear understanding as to what people's priorities are, nor is there any real indication that the people themselves have any great insight into their needs and desires We do not know, for example, whether the major portion of the populace considers sport fishing or ocean dumping to be higher in priority with respect to usage of the marine environment. We do know what the small special interest groups have to say about this situation, but in terms of jobs lost or consumer goods price increases which would result from the discontinuance of ocean dumping. there is very little information. In order to determine society's needs and desires. the people must first be educated as to the costs, benefits, and risks associated with any environmental protection solution being considered. Obviously a much better choice of alternatives can be made if the advantages and disadvantages may very well be a utopian dream, but it certainly should be the goal of each manager to come as close to this as possible.

At the present time choices are made on the basis of limited knowledge since not all of the costs, risks, and benefits are available to the manager making a decision, every those that are available to the manager are usually not available to the pulbi at large so that the manager's decision can be evaluated. This situation must change if utter choice is to be avoided.

Once our cards are on the table where they may be seen by all interested parties, we may proceed by setting goals that are both popular and attainable. A goal such as "zero discharge by 1985" is not an attainable one and when such a goal is set and not met, very often the result is a certain cynicism regarding all future goals.

3 Goals, Guidelines, and Standards

At this point it may be desirable to define some words commonly used in the management of the marine environment. In particular there are four words needing clarification : goal, guideline, criterion, and standard. Although the definitions which follow may not necessarily agree with those in a standard dictionary, they follow the usage of most people involved in marine area management, standard : A plan established by governmental authority as a program for water pollution prevention and abatemeut.

Criterion : A scientific requirement on which a decision or judgement may be based concerning the suitability of water quality to support a designated use.

Guideline : An acceptable methodology for achieving any given standard.

Goal : The ultimate standard which all current standards may eventually approach.

4. Involving the Public

Thus goals must be set with two criteria in mind. One is the scientific requirement defined above, but there is also a personal requirement on the part of the public based on its sense of priority. The public will not support a particular criterion, even with substantiating scientific data, if it interferes markedly with the present lifestyle. Until the citizenry can be educated to the risks involved in not accepting scientifically based criteria, looser criteria must surface. But it is the duty of the manager not only to choose the acceptable criteria but also to attempt to educate so that more logieal criteria may receive public support.

Along with the choice of particular goals, standards, criteria, and guidelines for a particular time, it must be assumed that these are not permanent but may very well change with the passage of time. Both the environment and public attitudes must be constantly monitored to effectively meet the needs of a changing society. With a proper monitoring system, not only may the standards, criteria, and guidelines be change but also the goals may be update. In this manner the public is made a working part of the management process adding support to the process and consequently making it more effective. The coasta Zone Management Act was designed along these line and it hasl been in operation long enough for a major portion of coastal states to have prepared detailed plans on the optimum use of coastal areas. These plans are undergoing extensive public hearings and it is to be hoped that when they are finally adopted the public will actively support them. If this is indeed the case, it can be hoped that the effect will, at the very least, be to stop the increase in marine pollution and may be even reverse the trend by decreasing pollution. In any event, however, regulations set down to protect the environmental quality of the marine environment will be enforced with popular support.

IMPACTS ASSOCIATED WITH CLEANUP TECHNIQUES

1. Cleanup Effects on Marhes

The equipment used for several cleanup techniques considered here does not impact on the marsh itself. For example, mechanical and weir skimmer are deployed in tidal channels, and pools, not in the marsh proper. Vacuum skimming in itself produce no impact on the marsh, but it is frequently accompanied by substantial foot traffic. Foot and equipment traffic and considered secondary impacts and may, in themselves, produce substantial adverse effects The following sections are modified from Maiero et al. (1978).

2. Effects of Traffic

The most obvious type of disturbance caused by traffic in a marsh is physical breakage of plants In both grass-dominated and succulent-dominated marshed, physical damage effectively reduces the amount of photosynthetic tissue and may expose the interior of the plants to toxic franctions of the oil. Plants are likely to recover from one such event, but recurrent trampling may clear a parth that will persist for years. If the soil is soft, as it is in many marshes, roots and rhizomes may be broken and thereby accelerate erosive processes.

Foot traffic potentially accelerates erosion even where the substratum is firm and the rhizome may remains eesentially intact. Shorelines that consist of steep escapements are particularly vuluerable. Cleanup activities that entail foot traffic should be used in such regions only after other methodologies have been considered and rejected.

Sometimes it is necessary to transport heavy equipment to remote portions of marsh. The impacts of foot traffic described above apply even more strongly to vehicular traffic. Traffic on soft marsh soil may bury plant stems and leaves and reduce their productivity until they resprout or grow back above the soil surface. Further, traffic under these conditions is likely to bury oil. In the anaerobicsoils that characterize mangroves and marshes, residual oil may persit for years. If the buried oil is toxic, it may inhibit the growth of anything in the contaminated zone until it eventually dissipates.

3. Flushing

Low pressure flushing with sea water (from a nearby source and thus likely to be of a salinity to which the marsh is accustomed) may be beneficial if used with caution. Where vegetation cover is continuous and sediments relatively stable, low pressure flushing may be effective in removing substantial amounts of oil from vegetation. Drawbacks of the method are ;

- All oil is not removed from leaves and a sufficint amount may adhere to the waxy plant culticles to cause damage. This is especially true when the oil is fresh in which case it adsorbs onto leaves very strongly an penetrates them.
- Foot traffic required to deploy the flushing equipment may cause damage.
- Oil flushed to creeks, etc., will be available to re-oil the marsh or other areas unless properly collected or otherwise removed.

Where vegetation cover is incomplete where much bare mud is in evident, or where sediments are sort and muddy, sediment disturbance or erosion may produce additional damage to that of the oil. Wherever possible, sediment disturbance should be avoided.

High pressure flushing may cause some erosion, local rearrangement of the substrate, and physical damage to the plants. These forms of damage may be less severe than similar impacts caused by foot traffic, but this depends upon mode of deployment. High pressure flushing may cause oil to be driven into the substrate. If steam or heated water is used, marsh animals and plants in the spray pattern may be killed or stressed by thermal stock.

Sorbents : Sorbent pads, oil snares, and similar cleanup aids have two major drawbacks :

- They are usually used by a large group of personnel who heavily traffic the marsh and
- They must be recovered. Additionally, if cleanup teams are not trained in the use of these material, there is chance that oil may be mised with a shallow layer of the substrate in the course of recovery.

Because complete recovery of sorbent materials is seldom possible in a field cleanup exercise, remanants of sorbents may persist. Most remanants are merely unsightly, although some may ensure birds and animals. Large concetrnations of undergraded materials could block the light from an appreciable porti, n of the marsh surface and consequently reduce marsh productivity in that region. Biodegradable sorbents avoid many of these problems.

Oil sorbent materials (synthetic and biodegradable) should always be recovered from the marsh, those that are not collected are a potential source of recontamination and a hazard to marsh animals.

4. Cutting

Cutting of oiled plants is a cleanup technique that entails direct physical destruction of plant tissues. As such, it severely reduces the amount of photosynthetic tissue and may expose the interior of the plant to toxic substances in the oil. Moreover, cutting operations are likely to require a great deal of foot traffic and the attendant adverse effects.

Cutting is probably most beneficial with certain species of grasses and rushes that have been heavily contaminated with viscous oil and are not subject to natural cleaning. If the entire aerial portion of the plant is coated, the roots are likely to suffocate unless some passage way is opened to the interior of the plant. Cutting accomplishes this, provided that free oil that might replug the cut stem has been removed from the surrounding marsh. However, if oiled marsh plants are not throughly coated with oil air can still diffuse down the stem to the foots, so that cutting is unnecessary unless other threats are present.

Spartina marshes are very tolerant of occasional cutting, especially late in the growing season. Saltwort marshes are less tolerent.

Burning is sometimes an effective method of removing oil and cotaminated vegetation from a marsh without encouraging injurious foot traffic. Spartina marshes can withstand occasional burning. In fall and winter, they die back to a state of dormancy. During this period, the plants are dry and may support burning. In fact, fall burning of marshes used for agriculture is a commonly applied management tool. During the dieback period, burning can be achieved in spartina marshed without damaging the buried portions of the plants and can stimulate tneir regrowth. In all other seasons, however, not only in Spartina difficult to burn, but the growning portions, shoots, and buds are injured by burning. However, this damage does not necessarily permanently harm the marsh since the underground portions of the buried plants are likely to sprout and replace the destroyed portions soon after the burning. Saltwort marshed do not die back seasonally and the plants do not have large, protected underground systems; thus, burning is injurious at any time.

5. Soil Removal

Removal of soil entails elimination of marsh plant habitat and should be avoided. Nonetheless, if the substrate is heavily saturated with toxic oil and no predicted to recover naturally, this may be the only available cleanup technique. On soft areas of find mud, it may not be feasible at all.

6. Dispersant Chemicals

Dispersant chemicals have been applied to oil in salt marshes following spills and in a number of experimental situations. In many cases, these have caused additional damage to the oil alone, and in some cases can be demonstrated to enhance the penetration of oil into intertidal sediments. Recent evidence suggests that new generations of dispersant may cause little additional geological effects to oil along when used at appropriate concentrations. However, the value of using them in most cases if unclear particularly on extensive marshes where, following application, dispersed oil may enter creeks to affect other part of the marsh or intertidal systems. They may be of value in cleaning small and stable fringing marshed in combination with low pressure flushing, but, in general, dispersant use is not recommended for salt marshes. It should be borne in mind that spraying of near dispersants onto vegetation produces damage and correct dilution to manufacturer recommendations is vital.

Marsh cleaning methods do not appear to decrease damage done by oil and often increas in (Baker 1977). The need for cleaup should be carefully reviewed before any action is taken.

7. Cleanup Effects on Mangroves

Few publications are available that deal directly with the effects of oil spill cleanup on mangroves. The several observations of the effects cleanup on mangroves at the Florida Keys oil spill of 1975. So many authors summarize effects of cleanup of marine wetlands and include numerious general statements concerning mangroves.

The following summary is based on the publications and ther personal observations several scientists made during cleanup operations within oiled mangroves.

Recovery of Marshes from Oil Damage

Although a definition of recovery has been attempted, mainly to distinguish the process from that of restoration, the definition includes the terms structure and function. The majority of scientific literature on the effects of oil deal with changes in the structure of marshes relatively few deal with the function of marshes let alone the part oil damage may play. Hence, we may be able io determine the time at which a marsh returns to something approaching its original structure, but not necessary. Alternatively, a similar marsh funct on could be achieved with a different structure. This is a line of investigation that desrves further attention, but at present we can do little but recommend that marsh structure be used in the assessment of recovery.

In an earlier section, the rate of recovery of salt marshes has been shown to be considerably influenced by a large number of factors. Their precise action and interactions are often poorly known, which means that in practice each spill must be treated as unique and assessment of damage must be dealt with in each case on its own merits little more than generalization is possible from the scientific literature.

Recovery processes begin when oil toxicity is reduced or removed. In most cases, recovery starts irrespective of the activities of man, although cleanup or other action may influence the rate. Where oil damage is relatively light and littl- of the toxic material remains in the system recovery can be rapid, either by regrowth from rootstock or from seeds. Baker (1971 a and personal, communication) reports that single oilings in field experiments, although toxic to mary salt marsh species, may produce effects detectable only for one to three growing seasons. Where oiling is repeated or where damage is servere and toxic materials are retained in sediments, recovery may take much longer, and the effects of the spill may be detectable over decades. Where erosion of sediments takes place, recovery may not occur.

OIL SPILL PREVENTION AND CLEANUP IN THE VICINITY OF CORAL REEFS

1. Prespill Mapping

Prespill contingency planning is now an accepted part of prepartion for, and response to, oil spills. Vulnerability mapping has been used by several authors to identify those area of shoreline that may be particularly sensitive to oil spill damage and to help ensure that damage due to the use of inappropriate eleanup procedures is minimized. One frequently used vulnerability index was devised by using the assumption that coastal geomorphology frequently determines the types of econological communities found there. Information about points of access to a spill site is essential in the event that men and equipment must be deployed at shore notice. Therefore, accessibility mapping is an important adjoint to vulnerability mapping.

Coral reef vulnerability to oil spill damage will vary with reef type, zonation patterns, and tidal actions. For example, in a fringing reef, the seward facing reef creast is generally exposed to high wave strees; here oil will probably have a short residence time before being dispersed naturally. . In contrast, wave action is a lot less severe in the shallow reef flat that frequently supports seagrass beds. Here, a long oil residence time with a correspondingly high risk of oil damage is likely. Similarly, oil that strands on reefs with a limited tidal range will likely tend to persist for longer periods than that in areas with large tidal ranges.

Although vulnerability and accessibility mapping techniques are now well established, little evidence suggests that such techniques are being applied to reef ecosystems. Some reef areas are well mapped and information is readily available on the location of refineries, tanker terminals, oil platforms, and major tanker routes (*e.g* , International Union for Conservation of Nature and Natural Resources (1980). This information can be used to produce maps that help locate areas of high potential risk. Newly developed techniques for mapping large areas of coastline, such as low altitude video overflights seem particularly suitable for use in reef areas but have yet to be applied.

2. Cleanup and Treatment of Spilled Oil

The sensitivity of reef ecosystems and the likelihood of their being impacted by oil will depend upon a variety of factors, including the quantity and type of oil and the degree of weathering. The likelihood of econological impact will also very according to whether the reef is an emergent, shallow submergent, or a deep water type. The field and laboratory studies reviewes indicate that the likelihood of damage is increased if the oil is incorporated into the water column of if it comes into direct contact with the coral surface. This, therefore, places the margent or shallow submergent section of a reef as areas of high potential sensitivity. It also indicates that any cleanup of treatment attempt should endeavour not to enhance the transport of oil into the water column or into the permanently subermerged sections of a reef.

Careful consideration should be given to the treatment of oil in the vicinity of a reef as situation may develop where the cleanup or recovery attempt may be more damaging then the oil alone. Baker (1970) has pointed out that merely the shipping activity associated with the cleanup attempt may be damaging due to sediment resuspension by propellers and anchor drag breaking up corals.

Although practical experiences of oil cleanup in the vicinity of coral reefs are lacking, mechanized techniques for containment and recovery of oil using booms and skimers are acceptable as they do not cause oil to sink or become incorporated into the water column. Any restriction on use of these techniques in coral areas is likely to be brough about not by the risk of ecological damage but by other environmental considerations such as high current speed, servere wave action, or shallow water depth that make their deployment impossible.

At present, only few data are available on the impact of dispersants and dispersed oil on corals. Most information that is available has been derived from laboratory studies. Laboratory studies have also been carried out on biota associated with reefs. Both categories of study noted damage by dispersed oil, but the applicability of these in vitro data to a field situation is questionable. Similarly, these studies used early generation dispersants which of themselves, where toxic to the corals. Using dispersants currently available, indicated that concentrations of 20 to 50 ppm dispersed oil in a 24-hour exposure produced temporary stress reactionsi n corals. Few deleterious effects from 24-hour exposures at 1 to 5 ppm were observed.

An oil removal technique that cannot be recommended for use in coral areas is the application of particulate sinking agents. These materials absorb oil and because they have a density higher than that of sea water, sink with the oil attached. Deleterious effects could be expected from the sunken oil coming into direct contact with the corals.

Several methods currently in the developmental stage appear to be potentially suitable for use in coral areas and other marine environments likely to be sensitive to oil. Among these are agents that have been developed that, when added to oil, gel in a semisolid from that can then be recovered. Research is also being carried out to develop nutrients that accelerate the bacterial biodegradation of oil.

Several studies have shown that corals are seemingly uneffected by a layer of oil floating on the water surface. Therefore, where unsuitable hydrographic conditions or problems of access preclude the use of mechnical containment and recovery techniques, it it probably best, given our present knowledge, to leave the oil alone to weather naturally.

Measures of Damage at the Species Level

Structural changes occur on a reef when a species or combination of species that are dominant components of a system are replaced by other species are eliminated from the system. If the replacement of elimination of a species is significant, then community, or functional level changes can become evident.

Changes in species richness, coral cover, and species diversity are potential criteria for the assessment of catastrophic structural damage to corals and any subsequent recover. Loya (1972) has modified the Shannon-Weaver diversity measure for use with corals as well as any encrusting assemblage. Grigg and Maragos (1974) used these parameters to describe recolonization by hermatypes on lava flows, as did Sheppard (1980) when assessing the impact of harbor construction on corals. Porter et al. (1981) used species richness, coral cover, and relative abundance to assess structural recovery of hermatypic corals following hurricane damage.

In a recent paper, pearson (1981) argued that measures of diversity, percentage cover, and similarity taken individually do not provide useful measures of either damage os recovery. He suggested that measures of damage and recovery should totally incorporate measures of percentage cover, mean colony-height, surface-index, species diversity, and similarity indices. In addition, because reefs are dynamic systems that can undergo change due to numerious environmental factors, any observed structural changes should be evaluated in terms of the structural characteristics of neighbouring reef systems.

Measures of Damage at the Communiiy Level

The structural diversity of reef ecosystems is paralleled by their function a complexity. When attempting to assess damage and recovery of coral reefs in functional terms, a useful line of investigation may be the development of indices that provide a measure of total reef functions or malunction.

One major functional characteristic of reef ecosystems is their high rate of primary production that may be 10 to 100 times greater than that of the phytoplankton in surrounding waters (Lewis 1981). Much of this reef primary production is attributable to benthic alage. A principal determinant of this high rate of productivity in nutrient poor areas is the retention and recycling of nutrients within the reef. This feature may be a useful means of determining the status of total reef function. For example, Pilson and Betzer (1973) found that, although concentrations of phosphates in water passing over a reaf were low, there was no difference in the upstream and downstrem levels, thereby indicating that a reef recycling mechanism was present. Evidence of phosphate recycling has been found by Pomeroy et al. (1974). There is also evidence of ammonium and nitrate recycling mechanisms. An increase in nutrient loss suggestive of a breakdown in nutrient recycling mechanisms may be a potential indicator of a total reef malfunction. Further evidence for the steady state nature of a reef ecosystem is provided by the ratio of gross production to community respiration (P/R) that frequently approaches unity (Lewis 1981). Again, any large be change in P/R ration could be indicative of reef malfunction.

1 Coral Reef Recovery

Our ability to measure recovery in a coral reef system hinges on the success of a program to define or measure than is damage. Endean (1977) said that complete recovery "involves the return of those species typically associated with corals and forming part of the coral reef community in the particular geographical region concerned and the reestablishment of the complex relationships normally existing among the species," While this definition is theoretically correct, from a practical sense in terms of measuring recovery. it is probably too broad. Coral reefs are among the most complex marine ecosystems in terms of communities of structure and ecological function. Monitoring all aspects of reef biology in an attempt to confirm a recovery or to define a stage of recovery is not feasible. There are, however, aspects of reef structure and function that could logically be used as indicators of a level of recovery. Specifically, a coral reef has patterns of species composition, abundadce, dominance, reproduction, recruitment, growth, and mortality among the hormatypic organisms. A gauge of recovery may be generated by comparing qualitative observations and quantitative measurments of these patterns on the recovering reef with those presumed to be characteristic of the chosen model of a fully recovered reef at the site in question.

This methodology, however, requires the assumption that recovery of the coral organisms will eventually result in the recovery of the entire reef community.

Few reefs in the world have been subjected to quantitative ecological assessments. The means that it is unlikely that any site-specific information will be available for comprative purposes. However, reef morphology and biotic community structure are typically similar over a definable range of variation within the area or region. Therefore, there is likely to be a basis upon which to roughly estimate the former structure and condition of nearby unimpacted reefs existing under similar conditions of natural environment, along with the remains of the impacted reef. If it is possible to infer pre-impacted structure from regional patterns, there is at least a structural and functional model for a recovered reef at the locality in question.

The measurement of recovery is complicated by the fact that recovery on coral reefs tends to be a long-term process Endean (1977) found that the recovery period is correlated with the extent of the damages inflicted on the hard coral cover. Small scale localized destruction from natural events generally requires less than 10 years for recovery provided that major sectors of the community remain virtually intact and the area is conductive to coral growth. Heavy destruction requires 10 to 20 years for full recovery, while especially severe impacts may require several decades for complete recovery. If a chronic source of pollution is present in the area of the damaged reef, recovery may be further prolonged or may not occur at all (*e.g.*, see Rinkevich and Loya (1977).

Cleanup

What cleanup measures are appropriate and what are their relative effectiveness are critical questions regarding oil spills in tundra and taiga. Whenever possible, hydrocarbon spills should be avoided or their effects mitigated. Several measures can be employed to help accomplish this. All above ground fuel storage containers should be contained within a pit or depression lined with a hydrocarbons in previous layer. Oil pipelines should be designed to withstand weathering, corrosion, and limited displacements such as those due to earthquakes. Finally, whenever possible, oil pipelines should be routed to avoid sensitive ecological stress such as populations of endangered species. Unfortunately, containment or evoidance is not always possible, so cleanup measures for the various soil and vegetation types must be considered.

Once a spill has occurred, the choice of cleanup strategies will depend upon the type of oil spilled, the nature of the spill t e amount of oil, the season of the spill, and the location of the spill. Site aspect, vegetation, and soil types are critically important factors. In addition, the presence of permafrost in most areas of tundra and much of the taiga will preclude the use of many cleanup methods routinely used in warmer climates or nonpermafrost areas (Brown et al. 1969 Greena et al 1975).

For example, in permafrost areas with a high ice content, any surface disturbance, such as removal of the oil-soaked organic soil surface horizon, tillage, or vehicle movement. will induce thermal degradation of the permafrost and subsidence (thermokarst), which will increase rather than decrease total environmental damage of the site (Brown et al. 1969 Chapin and Shaver 1981 Mackay and Mohtadi 1975). Under such conditions, passive (or no active) cleanup should be considered (Johnson et al. 1980 a,b). Passive measures may also be the best means of facilitating natural recovery in cases of small spills of crude oil or contained or limited spills of industrial oils with high proportions of light fractions, much of which will be readily lost by volatilization (Johnson et al. 1980, b; McGill 1977). However, recent work by Linkins and Fetcher (1983) has shown that residual oil in the Oe Ol horizon of tussock tundra soils may alter reproductive and biomass allocation patterns of Betula nana and Eriphorium vaginatum such that their successful reestablishment in oil-contaminated soils is questionable.

When active cleanup measures are necessary, there is heavy reliance on site access for transporting equipment and manpower to the spill. In remove locations, this can involve considerable cost as well as be environmentally damaging unless it can be accomplished with the appropriate equipment, especially during the persnow or thawed soil times of the year or snow preseason. Generally, the choice of which active cleanup techniques are used depends upon the time of year when cleanup must occur. In winter periods when the ground is frozen or snow covered both access and cleanup are facilitated. The dormant stage of the plants and low winter temperatures that aid in cooling and congealing crude oil so that its spread is limited both contribute to minimizing damage (Johnson et al. 1980 a, b; Hutchinson and Freedman 1975, 1978). Snow also acts as an absorbent and cushion protecting surrounding vegetation from oil exposure as well as vehicle damage. Generally, the oil-contaminated snow can be mechanically scraped off the site, removed, and placed in properly contained areas such as was done at the February 1978 Steele Creek spill along TAPS.

Burning the spilled hydrocarbon may also be used as a cleanup measure either before or after mechanical removal. Combustion may be difficult to initiate and generally will be incomplete. However, burning can help to remove the more toxic light fractions of the oil if done soon after the spill occurs (McKendrick and Mitchell 1978). Small spills may be difficult to ignite if not immediately burned (McKendrick and Mitchell 1978 a, b), but large spills seem to burn readily even several months later (Johnson et al. 1980 a, b). This may be due to a large proportion of the light fractions being rapped within the soil in large spills as surface weathering produces as extensive asphalitic cover. Burning is relatively inexpensive, but may leave a tarry residue on the surface that can inhibit microbial decomposition of the oil and vegetative recovery (McGill 1977; McKendrick and Mitchell 1978 a).

Finally, following any winter cleanup procedure, appropriate measures should be taken to ensure against, remobilization of the oil during snow melt. Such measures as absorbent booms, straw, or in nonpermafrost and thaw stable permafrost areas, containment ditches or dikes may be used. The hydrocarbon will then be intercepted or contained to facilitate removal.

The choice of active cleanup measures during the summer or snowfree period will depend upon the phenological stage of the plant, the soil moisture content, depth of the soil water table, and ice content of the permafrost as previously discussed. Mechanical removal of oil contaminated soil should be considered only at times when potential damage to plants is great from prolonged extensive contact with the hydrocarbon, the ice content of the permafrost if low, and there is relatively easy access to the spill site. Also, the volume of the spill should be such that natural recovery is unlikely and there is high potential for extensive contamination of adjacent areas through contained movement or later remobilization.

If removal of the contaminated soil is not possible, burial can be considered. However, burial should be done only in thermally stable, frozen material since subterranean remobilization can occur and cause contamination of adjacent areas (Linkins, personal communication at Galbraith Lake, Alasks).

Oil may also be removed by floating the oil and vacuming it off the surface of the water. This was used successfully at the TAPS value 7 spill in July 1977, ready access to the site as well as availability of a large volume of water, a wet site, and feasibility of containment. However, in some cases, oil may continue to appear on the surface of the water for a year of more after the spill as it is displaced from the surface organic horizon.

Finally, manual cleanup with minimal soil disturbance should be considered in permafrost areas. Absorbents such as straw or commercial materials can remove much of the oil present on the ground surface. Although costly and very time-consuming, this method will minimize any physical disturbance and decrease the chance of thermal degradation of the spill and adjacent sites.

The extensive reliance on reseeding with non-native species and long-term fertilization, whereas a relatively easy but expensive means of revegetation, does not guarantee optimal long-term revegetation or restoration (webber and Ives 1978). Observations of natural restoration on a 1949 disturbance (Lawson et al. 1978) and on a 1970 disturbance (Deneke et al. 1975) at Barrow, Alaska (Linkins 1980 a, b) suggest that it may be preferable to let some hydrocarbon disturbances recover naturally through reinvasion by native plants in lies of reseeding with exotic plants. Recent work discussed by Shaver et al. (1983) that shows that the shallow organic soil horizons can serve as a major seed bank for revegetation suggests that preservation of the upper organic soil horizons may also be preferable if possible to maximize potential for native plant reestablishment. Their discussion also points out the possible deterrents of fartilization on delaying restoration of the natural vegetation.

Penetration of the hydrocarbons into the soil plant rooting zone as previously discussed will influence the choice of revegetation/restoration techniques. On wet sites where there is limited penetration of the hydrocarbon into the soil rooting zone, natural recovery by the native vegetation may be sufficient if cleanup activities adequately remove the surface hydrocarbon contamination. On drier sites, however where the hydrocarbon will rapidly penetrate the soil rooting zones, killing the majority of the vegetation, it may be necessary to institute extensive soil cleanup, rapid revegetation efforts. This will be especially true if site stability (othermokarst, slope erosion, etc.) is a problem. Regardless of the cleanup, revegetation/restoration activities it should be reiterated that care should be taken to preserve of site integrity. Slower spill site revegetation/restoration (Linkins and Fetcher 1983; Shaver et al 1983) should always be preferable to risking both on and off site degradation (Johnson et al. 1980 a, b).

Hydrocarbons spills in the Arctic and subarctic cause both short-and long-term effects on the soils microbial populations, vegetation, and wildlife. Although a number of descriptive studies on the effects of hydrocarbon spills have been conducted, these have generally focused on short-term effects. Furthermore, there has been very limited development in our understanding of the important mechanisms of the direct toxic effects of oil and the effects of altered soil characteristics on organisms. When our ignorance in these areas is compounded by our limited knowledge of the in site rates and nature of hydrocarbon degradation in cold soils, it makes it very difficult to estimate effectively the duration of the influence of hydrocarbon in the soil. Likewise, it is very difficult to predict which cleanup, revegetation techniques will be most successful in alleviating hydrocarbons related deterrents to microbial population and vegetation growth.

Development of better methods for restoring Arctic and subarctic hydrocarbon spills requires a commitment to long-term research efforts focusing on integrated cleanup, revegetation/restoration research. Research should focus on the development of integrated postspill functionally based ecosystem efforts to determine and evaluate the relative importance of factors limiting site restoration. These studies should be connected on new sites that have been throughly described and on existing spills sites where adequate documentation exists as to the specific cleanup and revegetation activities that were employed. Efforts should also focus on natural hydrocarbon seep areas and long-term unaided spill sites where native vegetation exists. Integrated research efforts directed toward these goals as well as toward associated off site cleanup and revegetation disturbances should then begin to provide the information necessary to formulate effective revegetation/restoration programs in Arctic and subarctic areas. Unfortunately, until research is initiated, there will be limited advancement in more effective, less costly revegetation/restoration practices.

Bibliography

Atlas and R. Bartha, 1972, Degradation and mineralisation of petroleum in sea water, Bio-tech., Bio-engg., 14 : 297-318.

Baker, J.M., 1970, The effects of oil on plants , Environ., pollut, 1 : 27-44.

Baker, J.M., 1977, The effects of single spillage. The Ecological effects of oil pollution symposium, Washington, D.C. Pp. 128.

Biman Basu, 1991, Gulf spill : No threat to India, Science Reporter, March, 1991.

Brown et al, 1969, The effects of disturbance on permafrost terrain, Hanover. N.H : U.S.A. Army CRREL Special Report 138.

Chapin and Shaver, 1981, Changes in soil properties and vegitation following disturbances of Alaskan Arctic tundra, J. Appl. Eco. 18 : 605-617.

Chemical Products Finder, 1988, The journal of materials and equipment for the process industries, vol. 7(4) Pp. 61.

Chemistry and Industry, 1990, Marine Environment, Secrets of the sea, Second April, Pp. 205.

Cormack, D., 1983, Response to oil and chemical Marine pollution Applied science publishers.

Cox. G. V. et al., 1979, Oil spill studies : Strategies and Techniques J. Environ. Path., Toxicol. 3 : 3, Pp. 148.

Denckc et al., 1975, Biological aspects of terrestrial oil spills, Hanover, N.H. : U. S. Army CRREL research report, Pp. 346.

Endean, 1977, Pollution of coral reefs, fifth FAO/SIDA workshop on aquatic pollution, suppl., Pp. 343-369.

Exxon Corporation, 980, The offshore search for oil and gas, Exxon background series, 4th edition, Pp. 20.

Freed Man, 1978, Physical and biological effects of experimental crude oil spills on low Arctic tundra in the vicinity of tuktosktuk N.W.T. Canada, Can. J. Bot. 54 : 2219-2230.

Friede, J.P. et al. 1972, Assessment of bio-degredation potential for controlling oil spills on the high seas. Department of transportation, U>S> coast guard project report, 4110, 1/3, 12, Pp. 130.

George Camougis, 1981, Environmental Biology for Engineers, Mc-Graw Hill publishers, New York, Pp. 49-58.

Green et al., 1975, Cleanup after terrestrial oil spill in the Arctic. Arctic, 28 : 140-142.

Grigg, R.W. and J.E. Maragos, 1974, Recolonisation of hermotypic corals on submerged lava flows in Hawali, Ecology, 55(2) : 387-395.

Gunlach, E.R. and M O. Hayes, 1978, Vulnerability of coastal environments to oil spill impacts Mar. Tech. Soc. J. 12 (4) : 18-27.

Gutrick and Rosenberg, 1977,O il tankers and pollution, Ann. Rev. Microbiol. 31 : 379-396.

Hassan Jawaid Khan, 1991, The oil spill, Science Reporter, Pp. 9-11.

H.J.K., 1991, Gulf oil slick making history, Science reporter, March, 1991.

Indian Institute of Ecology and Environment, 1990, occational manograph numbers—26, 54.

Jerrome Williams, 1979, Introduction to marine pollution control, John willey and sons, New York.

John Cairus and Buikema, 1984, Restoration of habitats impacted by oil spills, Butter worth publishers, London.

Johnson et al., 1980 a, The fate and effects of crude oil spilled on subartic permatrust terrain interrior Alasca. Washington, DC : USEPA, EPA - 600/3-3/400.

Johnson et al., 1980 b, The fate of the crude oil spilled on subartic permatrust terrain in interrior Alasca. Washington, D C. USEPA/EPA 600/80-89.

Keith, H.L., 1982, Energy and environmental chemistry, volume-I, Ann Arbor science, England.

Lawson et al., 1978, Tundra disturbances and recovery following the exploratory drilling, Fish Greek, Nortuers Alasca. Hanover. N H : U. S. Army report, Pp. 18-28.

Lewis, J.B., 1971, Effects of crude oil and spill dispersant on coral reefs. Mar. Pollut. Bull. 2 : 59-62.

Lewis, J.B., Coral reef Ecosystems in analysis of marine ecosystems, A.R. Longshurst, ed. London, Acadamic press, Pp. 127-158.

Linkins, 1980 a, Impacts of crude oil on selected components of the below ground tundra ecosystems, Alaskan projects symposium, (Washington, D.C.), Department of Energy, Pp. 54.

Linkins, 1980 b, Impac's of crude oil on selected components of the below ground tundra ecosystems, Department of energy, Pp. 128.

Linkins and Fetcher, 1983, Effects of surface applied Prudhose Bay crude oil on vegitation and soil process in tussock tundra. Fourth International conference proceedings, Pp. 723-728.

Loya. Y., 1972, Community structure and species diversity of herrmatypic corals at Eilot, Red Sea, Mar. Biol. 13 : 100-123.

Loya. Y., 1977, Recolonisation of red sea corals affected by natural catastropes and man made perturbations, Ecology, 52(2) : 278 289.

Mackay and Mohtadi, 1975, The area affected by oil spills on land, Can. J. Chem. Eng. 53 : 140-143.

Mc Gill, 1977, Soil restoration following oil spills a review, J. Can. Pet. 2 : 60-67.

Mc Kendrickk and Mitchell, 1978, Effects of burning crude oil spilled in to six habitats types in Alaska. Arctic. 31 : 277 295.

Nair, P.K.G., 1990, Principle of Environmental biology, Himalaya publishers house.

Nebel, J.B., 1981, Environmental Science, Prentice-Hill inc.,

Nelson and Smity, 1973, Oil pollution and marine ecology, Plenum press, New York.

Ottway, 1971, The comparative toxicity of crude oils, The ecological effects of oil pollution on lethal communities. Institute of petroleum, London, Pp. 172-180.

Pearson, R.G., 1981, Recovery and recolonisation of corals reefs, Mar. Eco. Prog. ser. 4 : 105-122.

Perry, J.J. and C.E. Gerneglia, 1973, Studies on the degredation of petroleum by flamentous fungi. In the microbial degradation of oil pollutions, D.G. Ahearn and S.P. Meyers eds., Lousiana state University. centre for wetland resources, sea grant publications, Pp. 89-94.

Pilson and Betzer, 1981, Phosphorous flux across a coral reefs. Ecology 54 : 581-588.

Pomeroy et al., 1974, Tracer studies of the exchange of phosphorous between reef water and organisms on the wind ward reef of Eniwetok Atoll. Proceedings of the second International coral reef symposium, Pp. 87-96.

Porter et al., 1981, Population trends among Jamaican reef corals, Nature 294 : 249-250.

Ray, J.P., 1980, The effects of petroleum hydro carbons on corals in petroleum and the marine environment. Proceedings of the petromer 80, (London, Graham and Trotman Ltd.)

Rice, S.P., 1976, Toxicity of cook inlet crude oil and No. 2 fuel oil to several Alaskan marine fishes and invertibrates in symposium on sources, effects and sinks of Hydrocarbons in the aquatic Environment. Washington, D. C. American Institute of Biological sciences, Pp. 394-406.

Science Reporter, 1991, Source-oil spill intelligent report, ISSNOO 36-8512, March, 1991.

Shaver et al., 1983, Revegitation of Arctic distributed sites by native tundra plants in permafrast. Fourth International conference, Washington, D.C. Pp. 1133-1138.

Sheppard, C.R.C., 1980, Coral reef fauna of deigo Garcial Largoon following harbour constructions, Mar. Pollut. Bull. 11 : 227-230.

Straaughan, D., 1979, The importance of sampling tragedy in ecological damage assesment. In the Ecological damage conference, Arlington, VA : society of petroleum industry biologists, Pp. 3-27.

The Hindu, 1991, The marine secrets, Daily News, March 6, 1991.

Ben Barber, 1991, The environment as weapon, The Hindu, Daily News, March 10, 1991.

The Young World, 1991, Oil crisis, The Hindu, Daily News paper, Second February, 1991.

The Young World, 1991, The fate of Petroleum products, The Hindu, Daily News, April 20, 1991.

Thorhaug, 1980, A recovery of restored major plant communities in the United States, High to low altitude, desert to marine, in recovery process in damages.

Weber and Ivis, 1978, Damages and recovery of tundra vegitation, Environ. Conserv. 5 ; 171-182.